DRESS AND IDENTITY IN AMERICA
The Baby Boom Years 1946–1964

Dress and Fashion Research

Series Editor: **Joanne B. Eicher,** *Regents' Professor, University of Minnesota, USA*

Advisory Board:

Vandana Bhandari, *National Institute of Fashion Technology, India*
Steeve Buckridge, *Grand Valley State University, USA*
Hazel Clark, *Parsons, The New School of Design, New York, USA*
Peter McNeil, *University of Technology, Sydney, Australia*
Toby Slade, *University of Technology Sydney, Australia*
Bobbie Sumberg, *International Museum of Folk Art, Santa Fe, USA*
Emma Tarlo, *Goldsmiths, University of London, UK*
Lou Taylor, *University of Brighton, UK*
Karen Tranberg Hansen, *Northwestern University, USA*
Feng Zhao, *The Silk Museum, Hangzhou, China*

The bold *Dress and Fashion Research* series is an outlet for high-quality, in-depth scholarly research on previously overlooked topics and new approaches. Showcasing challenging and courageous work on fashion and dress, each book in this interdiciplinary series focusses on a specific theme or area of the world that has been hitherto under-researched, instigating new debates and bringing new information and analysis to the fore. Dedicated to publishing the best research from leading scholars and innovative rising stars, the works will be grounded in fashion studies, history, anthropology, sociology, and gender studies.

ISSN: 2053-3926

Previously published in the Series

Angela M. Jansen, *Moroccan Fashion*
Angela M. Jansen and Jennifer Craik, (eds), *Modern Fashion Traditions*
Heike Jenss, *Fashioning Memory*
Paul Jobling, *Advertising Menswear*
Maria Mackinney-Valentin, *Fashioning Identity*
Magdalena Crăciun, *Islam, Faith, and Fashion*
Kate Strasdin, *Inside the Royal Wardrobe*
Daniel Delis Hill, *Peacock Revolution*
Elizabeth Kutesko, *Fashioning Brazil*
Annette Lynch and Katalin Medvedev (eds), *Fashion, Agency, and Empowerment*
Alessandra Lopez y Royo, *Contemporary Indonesian Fashion*

DRESS AND IDENTITY IN AMERICA
THE BABY BOOM YEARS
1946–1964

DANIEL DELIS HILL

Author 1955 Author 1962

BLOOMSBURY VISUAL ARTS
LONDON • NEW YORK • OXFORD • NEW DELHI • SYDNEY

BLOOMSBURY VISUAL ARTS
Bloomsbury Publishing Plc, 50 Bedford Square, London, WC1B 3DP, UK
Bloomsbury Publishing Inc, 1385 Broadway, New York, NY 10018, USA
Bloomsbury Publishing Ireland, 29 Earlsfort Terrace, Dublin 2, D02 AY28, Ireland

BLOOMSBURY, BLOOMSBURY VISUAL ARTS and the Diana logo are trademarks of
Bloomsbury Publishing Plc

First published in Great Britain 2024
Paperback edition published 2025

Copyright © Daniel Delis Hill, 2024

Daniel Delis Hill has asserted his right under the Copyright, Designs and Patents Act, 1988,
to be identified as Author of this work.

Cover design: Untitled
Cover image: Detail of a Bell Telephone ad, 1959 (public domain).
Enhanced and modified by Daniel Delis Hill.

All rights reserved. No part of this publication may be: i) reproduced or transmitted in
any form, electronic or mechanical, including photocopying, recording or by means
of any information storage or retrieval system without prior permission in writing
from the publishers; or ii) used or reproduced in any way for the training, development
or operation of artificial intelligence (AI) technologies, including generative AI technologies.
The rights holders expressly reserve this publication from the text and data mining
exception as per Article 4(3) of the Digital Single Market Directive (EU) 2019/790.

Bloomsbury Publishing Plc does not have any control over, or responsibility for,
any third-party websites referred to or in this book. All internet addresses given
in this book were correct at the time of going to press. The author and publisher
regret any inconvenience caused if addresses have changed or sites have
ceased to exist, but can accept no responsibility for any such changes.

A catalogue record for this book is available from the British Library.

A catalog record for this book is available from the Library of Congress.

ISBN: HB: 978-1-3503-7391-4
PB: 978-1-3503-7395-2
ePDF: 978-1-3503-7392-1
eBook: 978-1-3503-7393-8

Typeset by Deanta Global Publishing Services, Chennai, India

For product safety related questions contact productsafety@bloomsbury.com.

To find out more about our authors and books visit www.bloomsbury.com and
sign up for our newsletters.

CONTENTS

Preface viii

1 The Man in the Gray Flannel Suit: Growing Up 1
Sociocultural legacies from his childhood 1
American manhood during the Second World War 6
Civilian dress and identity during the Second World War 11
Conclusion 13

2 The Man in the Gray Flannel Suit: The Postwar Years 17
Masculine identity in transition 17
The GI Bill of Rights 20
Postwar marriage 22
Masculine identity in suburbia 26
Fatherhood in the baby boom era 35
TV dads of the 1950s 39
Conclusion 45

3 The Man in the Gray Flannel Suit: Crisis in Masculinity 47
The feminization of American manhood 47
Conformity and Cold War masculine identity 50
The stress of success 52
Noncomformist Beats, beatniks, and bikers 54
Playboys 58
"Lavender Lads" 63
Conclusion 68

4 Men's Dress from Ivy League to Continental to Mod 71

Ivy League style 71
Continental suits 73
Accessories 75
Sportswear 78
The dichotomy of desexualized dress and erotic masculine styles 86
The British Invasion: From the London Line to Mod 88
Conclusion 92

5 Ethnic Men's Identity and Dress 95

The zoot suit 95
The social significance and cultural meaning of the zoot suit 100
The zoot suit riots 103
Soul style in the 1960s 105
Conclusion 107

6 Women of the Baby Boom Era: Lessons of Youth 109

Feminine role models and expectations 109
American women during World War II 112
Sociocultural changes for women during World War II 120
Conclusion 123

7 Women's Identities in the Baby Boom Years 125

Marriage reunions at the end of the war 125
Postwar newlyweds 127
Postwar marriage: Not happily ever after 130
Postwar suburban wives 134
Motherhood in the baby boom era 141
TV wives and mothers of the baby boom era 146
Working women of the baby boom era 148
Feminism in the baby boom era 151
Conclusion 154

8 Women's Fashions of the Baby Boom Era 157

The New Look 157
Mod and the miniskirt 168
Women's accessories of the baby boom years 171
Decade of "miracle fabrics" 177
Conclusion 180

9 Baby Boom Children 181

An era of children 181
Gender role socialization 182
A new consumer demographic 190
Children's dress 196
Standardization of children's sizes and textile regulations 203
Children's body modifications 205
Conclusion 207

Notes 211
Bibliography 232
Index 239

PREFACE

The baby boom era in America is usually defined as the years 1946–1964, during which a higher-than-average birthrate added more than 70 million babies to the population.[1] It was a period of sociopolitical conservatism, a backlash to the economic and cultural disruptions of the Great Depression and World War II. Politically, the nation shifted right significantly, electing a Republican president and Congress in 1952 after 20 years of Democratic progressivism. This rightward swing ushered in conservative extremism that manifested in McCarthyism, the establishment of the John Birch Society, a revitalized Ku Klux Klan, reinforced Jim Crow laws and policies, the purging of gays from government and the military, and a red scare from the Korean War and global communist expansion. The patron saint of postwar conservatism, William F. Buckley, summed up the goal of the right in the era when he wrote as the mission statement for the founding of the *National Review* in 1955: "A conservative is someone who stands athwart history, yelling Stop, at a time when no one is inclined to do so, or to have much patience with those who so urge it."[2] This regressive conservatism was embraced by much of American society and persisted well into the 1960s. Looking back at those postwar years, Betty Friedan wrote in 1963,

> We found excuses for not facing the problems we once had the courage to face. The American spirit fell into a strange sleep; men as well as women, scared liberals, disillusioned radicals, conservatives bewildered and frustrated by change—the whole nation stopped growing up. All of us went back into the warm brightness of home, the way it was when we were children.[3]

That introverted emphasis on the home redefined the identities of men, women, and children in the postwar years. For the 10 million men who demobilized from military service after the Second World War, their transition from soldier to civilian focused on a return to normalcy, to find a new identity that would allow them to put the war behind them and get on with life. The first four chapters explore the emergence of the forms of that identity, the corresponding dress, and how both impacted the broader ideas of masculinity from the late 1940s though the mid-1960s. For millions of veterans, the GI Bill guided them toward marriage and the role of family breadwinner by offering guaranteed loans for homes and businesses as well as opportunities for advanced education and vocational training. In their role as family breadwinners, postwar American men readily found jobs in the booming economy and moved their wives and baby boom children into one of the new suburban communities that began to sprawl across the American landscape. There they settled into comfortable conformity and rivaled the Joneses next door in a race of consumption and materialistic indulgence. From their new ranch houses, they commuted six days a week to corporate offices in the city and joined the herds of other suburbanites in their quest for upward mobility.

With each of the new postwar masculine identities—husband, father, family head, suburbanite, corporate man—new styles of dress complemented each. The corporate breadwinner was the iconic man in the gray flannel suit, dressed in the masculine uniform of the era—the shapeless, straight-hanging Ivy League suit. Yet, in his leisure time as suburbanite homeowner and family man, his dress of colorful casual sportswear allowed some degree of personal style and expression.

In Chapter 5, the identity and dress of nonwhite men of the era is examined. In the years immediately before the beginning of the baby boom, many African American and Latino men expressed their pride of self through the zoot suit and the urban masculine performance that went with the style. Similarly, as the civil rights movement achieved legislative goals in the mid-1960s, Black men were inspired to claim their African heritage as a new identity, which they demonstrated with the Afro hairstyle, and African styled clothing such as the dashiki.

Women of the postwar years were especially impacted by the regressive and repressive sociocultural shifts in America. Chapters 6–8 look at how millions of women who had donned pants and had worked in defense factories and service sectors during the Second World War now were told to stay home and focus on being a wife and mother. Postwar women were not expected to pursue higher education, and especially were not encouraged to work outside of the home, let alone become career women. The whole of American society—the masses, government, religious institutions, medical and social science, popular culture—seemed to concur that a woman's place was in the home.

For millions of white, middle-class women, the traditional identity of homemaker was enhanced by the additional cachet of suburbanite. In their new ranch houses, in a new community development, many suburban women delighted in excelling in their expected roles as housewives and mothers. For them, the American dream was caring for a husband and children, and spending their days managing their homes with modern labor-saving appliances and conveniences. Their identities as American suburbanite woman, wife, and mother were additionally reinforced by their dress. At home, they dressed in an endless variety of comfortable, casual sportswear, and for women's club and

PTA meetings, they wore ready-to-wear versions of the cinched, ultrafeminine New Look fashions from Paris.

For many other women, though, the roles of suburban wife and mother were not sufficiently fulfilling. What came to be variously called the "woman problem" or "suburban syndrome" in the 1950s was a pervasive feeling of discontent and uneasiness among many American women.[4] Their traditional roles of wife and mother seemed limiting. They felt isolated in suburbia and bored by unending and uninteresting housework. Richard Gordon called this life of "drudgery" in "disturbia" a "split-level trap,"[5] from which there was no way out short of the unthinkable—divorce and child abandonment.

In Chapter 9, the children of the postwar era are collectively represented by two groups: those born in the late 1930s and early 1940s, who were school-aged and teenagers through the 1950s, and the baby boomers born between 1946 and 1964, who grew up to become the youthquake generation of the 1960s. Together, these millions of children became a new consumer demographic in the affluent postwar economic boom. Through various media, especially television, this youth market was directly targeted by makers of soft drinks, snack foods, toys and games, movies, comic books, rock and roll music, and clothing.

Yet, in the regressive conservativism of the era, children were subjected to strict gender role socialization by parents, teachers, religious leaders, and pop culture ranging from comic books to television programming. Boys in particular were inculcated with sociocultural standards of masculine behavior to guide them toward a proper manhood. Competitive sports, tool use, machine maintenance and repair, and healthful outdoor activities were vital training for America's future Cold War soldiers, husbands, and fathers. Boys were restricted in the toys they played with, the clothes they wore, even the colors of their environment, ever avoiding anything that might remotely threaten feminization. A weak sissy was not to be tolerated.

Girls, though, were less limited, at least until their teen years. The tomboy schoolgirl in jeans and a boy's sweatshirt who played ball with her brothers and boy classmates was indulged since she was expected to outgrow the phase. She could play with toy trucks and cap pistols where a boy was forbidden to touch a doll after toddler age. Even so, girls underwent rigorous gender role socialization too. Girls were given toy kitchen and home appliances, cookware and tea sets, play beauty kits, Barbies, and baby dolls to prepare them for their future roles as homemakers and mothers. Pink for girls and blue for boys became the norm. Academics were less important for girls than the development of their skills in cooking, sewing, interior decorating, and similar feminine activities they learned at home with Mom or at school in sex-segregated classes like home economics.

Children's dress reinforced the gender identities of boys and girls. Most children's clothing after the toddler age was basically scaled-down versions of adult styles. Boys wore the same boxy, loose Ivy League suit or casual sportswear of their dads. Girls dressed in miniature versions of New Look dresses. Jeans were for all ages, just gendered by the way cuffs were turned: rolled once or twice at the ankles for boys, and rolled to the knees for girls. Some fashion fads were youth specific, such as poodle skirts and Scottie saddle oxfords for girls, and buckle-back strap slacks, chukka boots, and ripple sole shoes for boys.

Much of the period research material available on the baby boom era centers on white, middle-class suburban families. The overwhelming evidence of materials of the time from social scientists, psychiatrists and sociologists, journalists, government propaganda and policies, consumer surveys, movies, television programming, books, advertising, and other realms of popular culture demonstrates that the white, middle-class man in the gray flannel suit, the suburban housewife, and the consumption-driven teenager were the ideal. "In effect the [postwar] generation made a pact. The wives agreed to marry earlier and have more children than their mothers, at whatever expense to themselves. The husbands agreed to get ahead and take good care of them. This agreement was kept."[6] And even though these *identities* were not universal across America, whether through institutionalized exclusion, racial animus, socioeconomic inequalities, or religious and political biases, the *dress* of most Americans largely was universal. The men's Ivy League suit, the woman's New Look fashions, and the teen's dungarees and saddle oxfords were worn by all ethnicities and sociocultural groups.

1
THE MAN IN THE GRAY FLANNEL SUIT: GROWING UP

Sociocultural legacies from his childhood

The American men who fought in World War II and returned afterwards to become suburban husbands, fathers, and conformist career men of the 1950s had their views and understanding of manhood shaped as children and teens in the Depression era. Their (white) male identities developed in the 1930s from the role models of their fathers, who had been the doughboys of the First World War, and their grandfathers, who came of age in the late Victorian period.

    The identities of husband, father, and breadwinner were norms expected of every American man in the 1930s, as it had been for generations before. Key to a man's success in these roles was his ability to earn a living sufficiently to provide for a family. Despite the loss of jobs, wage cuts, reduced hours, and the constant threat of unemployment in the 1930s, the cornerstone of male identity in the Depression years was work. As sociologists Robert and Helen Lynd noted in *Middletown in Transition,* a study of middle America's culture and society in the mid-1930s, "The long arm of the job" determined "who one is, whom one knows, how one lives, what one aspires to be . . . Men get the living, i.e., earn the money to buy the living for the family; they pay for the children's education and the family's leisure, as well as for food, clothing, and shelter."[1] Children of the middle and working classes of the Depression years were inculcated with this unequivocal message of proper manhood from their parents, teachers, and religious leaders. Schools were oriented around the Victorian concepts of separate spheres—one set of guiding principles for boys, and a different set for girls. Community "patterns of customary acceptance," as demonstrated with

Lynds' research, were cohesive, regular, and repetitive. "The things a man is and does have remained fairly clearly and comfortably fixed," concluded the Lynds.[2]

In addition to the role models and guidance of parents, teachers, and community leaders, an array of fictionalized manly characters in popular culture of the 1930s exhibited defining qualities and traditional traits of American masculinity. Movies featured hypermasculine protagonists ranging from adventurers, detectives, and cowboys played by actors such as James Cagney, Humphrey Bogart, Gary Cooper, and Clark Gable, to athletic heroes like Tarzan, portrayed by Olympic champion Johnny Weissmuller, and Flash Gordon, also played by an Olympic champion, Buster Crabbe. This idea of the manly man—strong, dutiful, and selfless—was also perpetuated in radio programs of the time, such as *The Lone Ranger, The Green Hornet,* and *The Shadow,* which instilled in boys the ideas of physical and moral strength, and a selfless duty. Comic strips and the first comic books were additional sources of masculine identities for Depression-era boys. Good-guy heroes such as Dick Tracy, Superman, and Batman were introduced in the 1930s, presenting strong men who fought the good battle against crime and injustice. In the first comic book that introduced Superman in 1938, he was described as a "champion of the oppressed"[3]—a comforting notion during the uncertainties of the Great Depression.

Surprisingly, sports for boys were not much of a consideration for Middletown in the 1930s. The Lynds did not even mention the topic in the chapter "Training the Young," and it was only briefly discussed as a spectator's activity in the chapter "Spending Leisure."[4] Certainly boys of the 1930s enthusiastically participated in sports of all kinds, but this lack of emphasis on sports as a developmental tool for boys was a significant departure from a generation earlier. Their grandfathers had been proselytized as boys on several fronts—parents, teachers, civic leaders, mass media—with messages of the importance of sports for achieving a proper masculine identity and countering the threat of feminization.

During the late nineteenth century, American society had become obsessed with a fear of the feminization of boys. Increasingly, breadwinner fathers left farms and rural communities to work in urban factories and offices, usually for ten to twelve hours a day, six days a week. The absent fathers meant boys were mostly in the care of women all day—mothers and elder sisters in the home, women schoolteachers and neighbors, and other female caregivers. In addition, middle-class homes of the Second Industrial Revolution were filled with modern conveniences—labor-saving appliances, manufactured prepared foods, efficient furnaces and indoor plumbing, and abundant ready-made clothing. Competitive athletics were advocated as a counter to the emasculating influences of women and modernity. Athletics taught boys manly virtues such as "coolness, steadiness of nerve, quickness of apprehension, endurance . . . and above all, courage . . . Team contests demanded a strength, vigor, and physical assertiveness that undermined the ease and debility of modern affluence."[5] Schools established team sports for boys such as baseball adopted from the American National League established in 1876 and intercollegiate football organized in 1873. New team sports were invented at the end of the nineteenth century to teach boys the manly values—basketball in 1891 and volleyball in 1895; the Olympics were revived from ancient times in 1896.

Equally important for what a man should be was what he should not be. The Lynds documented a number of those views and conventions. One of the core beliefs of Middletown's middle class was, "in being, when in doubt, like other people."[6] This idea of sociocultural conformity was strongly impressed upon American boys of the 1930s and would remain integral to their adult notions of manhood in the 1950s.

The Victorian fear of the feminization of boys also remained a powerful concern for Depression-era parents. Not only was the threat of feminization debilitating for boys—making them weak, subordinate, and effeminate—but also strong influences from women, they thought, could make boys into homosexuals as adults. Late nineteenth-century medical science introduced the concept of homosexuality as a mental disorder, which remained a potent worry for American parents, teachers, and religious leaders of the twentieth century. "We are prone to distrust and hate those whom we regard as uncommon," observed a Middletown newspaper editorial. "Deviant members" of the community "who were too radical, too unconventional, too artistic, too little imbued with community loyalties, too different in any respect to be happy in and accepted by Middletowns have been thrown off to the Chicagos, the Clevelands, the New Yorks."[7] In the 1950s, homosexuality would be at the top of the list for what not to abide in the American male—a condition that was considered a mental disorder by medical science, criminal by law, sinful by religious dogma, and a national security threat equal to communism by McCarthyite witch-hunters.

The masculine dress identity of the Depression-era man was the drape cut suit, also called a blade cut for the way it fitted over the shoulder blades, or the London cut, since it originated with Savile Row tailor Frederick Scholte. As an apprentice in the 1910s, Scholte worked for the tailors who dressed the Royal Household Guards and came to admire the masculine silhouette of the athletic V-shape fit of the young guards' jackets and coats. When he set up his own shop after the First World War, he developed a new cut of the men's jacket with gentle horizontal drapes in the back that narrowed across the shoulder blades without padding. In the front, the fabric descended from the shoulders in discreet ripples rather than a smooth, shaped construction over stiff, layered interfacings. "Correct drape causes wrinkles, but they are quite legitimate and entirely graceful," advised a men's wear journalist in 1928.[8] Lapels were rolled rather than lying flat, which provided the illusion of a broad, muscular chest. The upper sleeves were generous to allow a wide range of motion, and the armholes were cut high and small to prevent the collar from gaping at the neck when the arms were lifted. The waist was slightly raised and slimly tapered, and the skirt was trim over the hips. By the beginning of the 1930s, the athletic drape cut silhouette had been adopted in America by both tailors and ready-to-wear makers. (Figure 1.1.) The style would be the distinct masculine dress identity through the 1930s and into the early 1940s when wartime restrictions on fabrics and other materials would impact most men's and women's apparel.

The trousers for the drape cut suit were also a style departure from the previous trends in men's suits. During the 1910s, men's suit jackets had been trim and fitted, and trousers were snugly cut with what was jokingly called a

Figure 1.1 From the late 1920s into the early 1940s, American men's suits were based on the English drape cut, an athletic silhouette with broad shoulders, tapered waist, and muscular sleeves and trouser legs. Men's single and double-breasted suits by Oliver E. Woods, 1936.

sausage casing fit at about 15 to 16 1/2 inches in circumference at the cuff. For Scholte's new suit silhouette, the trouser legs were a more capacious 22 inches at the cuff, and pleats were preferred since, as a fashion editorial noted, they "give a great deal of comfort and make it easier to use the pockets without drawing the trousers out of shape."[9] Pleats were usually in pairs at each hip, with the front leg crease descending from the innermost tuck. Inverted pleats that faced inward became especially popular in the 1930s.

One of the controversial advances in men's wear of the 1930s was the addition of zippers to fly front closures, replacing the centuries-old button style. Versions of hookless closures had been developed since the mid-nineteenth century, but in 1923, a slide closure made with interlocking brass teeth was introduced by the rubber manufacturer B.F. Goodrich for their galoshes. Named the "zipper" by a company executive, the slide closure was initially used for utilitarian items such as shoes, purses, tobacco pouches, and luggage, but by the second half of the 1920s, it was applied to outerwear and children's playwear. Gradually through the 1930s, the zipper was added to other garments, notably the fly front of men's trousers. Tailors resisted the device, and many men were wary of the location of interlocking metal teeth. But in 1934, the Prince of Wales began to have his trousers custom-made with a zipper fly closure by a New York tailor, and quickly, US ready-to-wear makers adopted the new trouser construction for the mass market.

Despite the social conservatism of the Depression era, one of the new dress identities of the 1930s that American men widely adopted was sexual exhibitionism. Popular culture was abundant with depictions of nearly nude athletic men, ranging from ads for Charles Atlas body building regimens to movies of former Olympic athletes portraying Tarzan. This exhibitionism took two paths in American men's wear, one public and one private.

The public form was swimwear, sexualized styles of which had been emerging since the late nineteenth century. In addition to bared arms and legs, the formfitting knit swimsuits were especially clinging and revealing when wet. During the 1920s, the standard set of swim shirt and trunks or singlet style of swimsuit was gradually diminished by shortened trunks and crab back styling that reduced tops to a bib with straps around the torso. As suntans became increasingly popular in the late twenties, men began to turn down the tops to expose more skin to the sun. In response to the trend, during the early 1930s, swimwear makers produced singlet swimsuits with removable tops attached to the trunks at the waist with a zipper.

Two radical developments of men's swimwear designs in 1932 furthered men's erotic near-nude exhibitionism. First was the appearance of a shirtless brief cut swimsuit on the beaches of the Riviera. The fashion press called the abbreviated style the "pearl diver's model"[10] because it was similar to skimpy swimsuits worn by Pacific island divers who worked the oyster beds. By the mid-1930s, the shirtless brief style swimsuits were common on beaches and poolsides across America. In 1936, mass-market retailers such as Sears included the swim brief in their seasonal wish book catalogs. The second development in men's swimwear that emphasized an erotic exhibitionism was the introduction of a new type of two-way stretch knit made from an elasticized yarn called Lastex. Earlier types of knit fabrics were formfitting, but Lastex fabrics molded the body like a coat of wax.

Inspired by the popularity of the new brief cut swimsuits, in 1934, an executive at the Coopers knitting mills of Kenosha, Wisconsin, developed a new form of men's cotton knit underwear modeled after the swim brief but with an elastic waistband. Because the brief cut underwear reminded company executives of athletic jockstraps, the style was branded Jockey. For men of the Depression era, Jockey briefs—and similar versions produced by competitors—were a private form of sexualized clothing. "Jockeys are snug and brief, molded to your muscles," avowed the copy in a 1936 ad for Coopers' "masculinized undergarments."[11] The formfitting underwear brief was an instant success and changed the way men thought about underwear and their bodies.

The physical identity conveyed by men's wear of the 1930s was muscularity and brawn. The boys and teens of the 1930s grew up wearing the styles of their dads: shaped suits, sport coats, and outerwear that projected broad shoulders and chest and a trim waist. Trousers were fuller than in the 1910s and early 1920s, but still emphasized narrow hips and strong thighs. Even if men were not the "physical marvel" that Superman was declared to be in his first comic book,[12] the drape cut suit helped make him look it.

Yet, by the 1950s, the dress identity of the American man was distinctly different from that of his boyhood in the Depression era. A transition in men's wear that developed through the 1940s evolved into something very different—a masculine dress identity reflective of the era of the Cold War, McCarthyism, and a socially conservative backlash to the war years.

American manhood during the Second World War

In September 1939, Germany invaded Poland, and Europe erupted into the Second World War. In Asia, imperial Japan, already at war with China since 1931, began a conquest of other regional territories in 1941 for the resources and raw materials needed for their war machine. In December 1941, Japan attacked the US fleet at Pearl Harbor, Hawaii, and Germany and Italy declared war on the United States, violently wrenching America from its isolationism into the global conflict.

In anticipation of war, President Franklin Roosevelt had signed the Selective Training and Service Act in September 1940, requiring men between ages 21 and

45 to register for the military. It was America's first peacetime draft. At that time, the entire US armed forces had just over one million men. By December 1941, the war in Europe had been going on for more than two years, yet America's military had barely doubled its manpower. But within a year of the attack on Pearl Harbor, by November 1942, 6,773,809 men were serving; and by October 1943, the US armed forces were at 10,425,916 men.[13]

The boys and teens of the Depression era came of age in the 1940s. Journalist Tom Brokaw wrote of those boys who became young men during the war and served in the military as "The Greatest Generation":

> They answered the call to help save the world from the two most powerful and ruthless military machines ever assembled, instruments of conquest in the hands of fascist maniacs. They faced great odds and a late start, but they did not protest. At a time in their lives when their days and nights should have been filled with innocent adventure, love, and the lessons of the workaday world, they were fighting, often hand to hand in the most primitive conditions possible, across the bloodied landscape of France, Belgium, Italy, Austria. They fought their way up a necklace of South Pacific islands few had ever heard of before . . . They were in the air every day, in skies filled with terror, and they went to sea on hostile waters far removed from the shores of their homeland.[14]

And all Americans keenly understood the courage and sacrifice of their young men so far from home. They were anxious for their sons, brothers, husbands, and, later when the draft was expanded, fathers, who were in harm's way, but they were also very proud of them.

The young, vigorous serviceman of the war years replaced the patriarchal breadwinner worker of the Depression era as the American masculine ideal. "The Second World War provided a crucial opportunity for men to demonstrate characteristics such as strength, bravery, and usefulness that had been called into question during the 1930s."[15] Whether they had voluntarily enlisted or been drafted, the hero servicemen were protecting the nation, their homes, and their families. As *Time* magazine noted in 1942, "The heroism of the soldiers of democracy is . . . a record that glows like an endless string of pearls. For they have made World War II a time of gallantry, sacrifice, incredible toughness; of comradeship among all fighters for freedom."[16]

The significant masculine dress identity of the war years was the military uniform. Servicemen were required to be in uniform at all times, even when on furlough. The uniform was evidence of American manhood at its finest—proof that the man had measured up and met the test. The man in uniform was a celebrated icon in popular culture from movies to mass-market advertising. (Figure 1.2.) Among the Hollywood stars who famously donned a uniform and went to fight for America were Jimmy Stewart (Air Force), Clark Gable (Air Force),

1942

1942

1944

1944

Figure 1.2 (this page and facing page) The military uniform projected the masculine identity of the American hero who had measured up to the challenges of manhood in wartime.

1944

Kirk Douglas (Navy), and Henry Fonda (Navy), to name a few. American movies of the war years that portrayed the sacrifice and valor of American soldiers included *Standby for Action* (Robert Taylor, 1942), *To the Shores of Tripoli* (Randolph Scott, 1942), *Air Force* (John Garfield, 1943), *December 7th* (Walter Huston, 1943), *A Guy Named Joe* (Spencer Tracy, 1943), *Sahara* (Humphrey Bogart, 1943), and *The Fighting Seabees* (John Wayne, 1944).

Opposite of the war heroes, though, were the 4-F men. The US Selective Service appointed local boards of civilian volunteers to interview and examine men for qualifications to serve in the military. A final decision was made at induction centers by medical examining staff. The director of the Selective Service in conjunction with the Surgeon General's Office issued a "list of defects" in 1940 as a guide for disqualifying recruits (or sometimes classifying them for limited service).[17] In addition, in October 1943, every Selective Service board was assigned a medical field agent with the authority to investigate the background of each registrant, including education, work history, personal medical records, and even hobbies. All were compiled by the military into a profile to determine acceptance and the best assignment for the registrant.[18]

Men who were determined as unfit for military service were issued a 4-F classification. In the movie *It's a Wonderful Life* (1946), the Jimmy Stewart character is classified 4-F because he is deaf in one ear. The townsfolk know this fact and are understanding and sympathetic. But for most 4-F men, especially in large towns and cities, a 4-F classification was a social stigma that haunted the bearer his entire life. Besides the obvious physical conditions such as a lost limb, obesity, or blindness, a broad assortment of other concealed physical conditions was cause for a 4-F status, such as hernia, surgical removal of certain organs, poorly healed bone fractures, or dental deficiencies, and diseases like tuberculosis, arthritis, diabetes, and syphilis, among others. Between November 1940 and the end of the war in August 1945, 6.4 million men, or 35.8 percent of registrants, were rejected for active service.[19]

A 4-F status also included mental and personality disorders. The largest number of disqualifications for service between 1942 and 1945 was due to "mental illness," nearly two million men or more than 30 percent of registrants.[20] Examiners especially watched for indications of homosexuality, which was classified as a mental disorder until 1973, when the American Psychiatric Association removed it from their diagnostic manual on mental disorders. Not only were homosexuals vilified as defective men who would make poor soldiers, but also psychiatrists of the era thought that openly homosexual men might spread their perversion to other men, thus affecting troop morale. Social and political views, too, could get registrants branded as 4-F. For instance, if African Americans replied negatively to questions about segregation and Jim Crow laws, they were often rejected with a 4-F status as mentally deficient.[21] Even illiteracy was viewed as a mental deficiency, for which many men were disqualified, particularly among poor Southern whites and disadvantaged African Americans from rural communities. Intelligence tests that indicated a registrant may have difficulty with rapid learning or following instructions disqualified still other men. And men were rejected on grounds of moral integrity that included criminal records such as murder, rape, or kidnapping, and sexual perversion that usually meant homosexuality.

Although recruitment center physicians had been instructed to "exercise care in labeling a registrant with a diagnostic term which might in some way be injurious to him,"[22] a 4-F rating was a difficult stigma for most men. Unless a physical condition was obvious, young men not in uniform were commonly asked by family, friends, neighbors, and even strangers on the street why they had not enlisted. Servicemen and civilians alike viewed the 4-F-ers as either defective rejects or slackers. The social opprobrium against 4-F men was compounded when, in 1943, the US military began drafting married men and fathers.

Even those who were inducted but were classified for support roles felt some degree of shame for not participating in combat. In the movie *Mona Lisa Smile* (2003), the male instructor of Italian at Wellesley College in 1953 was thought to have acquired his language expertise in the Italian campaign, but instead had spent the war in a military language center on Long Island. When confronted, he simply replied that people assumed he had been in combat and he just never corrected them.

To distinguish honorably discharged soldiers from those often disparaged as "4-F draft-dodging bastards,"[23] veterans in civilian clothes were provided with tiny gold-plated pins of eagles to wear in public, which helped reduce tension and public contempt for men not in uniform. The 1945 ad shown in Figure 1.3 features an illustration of the pin and a depiction of an honorably discharged father explaining to his son that the "simple gilt button . . . says a world of things":

> It says a service well done for our country . . . for freedom and humanity the whole world over. It says that America, every American, is proud of the wearer . . . be it your dad, or any one of the 13,000,000 men and women who, like him, served in the armed forces. It says that America will not forget their service—but will strive to make sure their service was not in vain.[24]

More importantly, a 4-F identity could especially hinder a man's employment or career advancement, especially since Selective Service records were available to employers in the 1940s and 1950s. It was common practice after the war and well into the 1960s for employers to ask what a male applicant did during the war, with preference points granted to veterans. Into the 1990s, the World War II records of political figures such as President H.W. Bush and presidential candidate Bob Dole were included in campaign materials and mentioned in news reports.

Civilian dress and identity during the Second World War

When America entered the Second World War, the design of American men's clothing was significantly impacted by materials shortages and rationing. Within the early weeks of the war, restrictions were put in place to conserve wool for

Figure 1.3 Honorably discharged veterans of the Second World War were presented with a gold-plated eagle pin in recognition of their duty and service to the nation.

uniforms and blankets, silk for parachutes, leather for boots, and metal for armaments and munitions. In January 1942, the US War Production Board (WPB) issued Order M-73, a series of sweeping regulations for the manufacture and sale of men's, women's, and children's clothing. These "style simplification" orders were later rolled into the broader, more detailed WPB L-85 series of General Limitation Orders in April 1942.[25]

The athletic silhouette of the men's drape cut suit jacket, with its rolled lapels, broad shoulders, and trim, tapered waist, continued into the early 1940s. But following the implementation of L-85 regulations, many elements of construction and details were reduced in size or eliminated altogether. As *Men's Wear* reported in February 1942, styles of the new wartime "economy suit" shown at the recent annual convention of the Merchant Tailors and Designers Association were much trimmer and narrower than a year earlier. Jacket skirts were shortened, lapels narrowed, inner facings reduced, and pocket flaps and patch pockets eliminated. Some jackets were without lapels, and others completely collarless. Trousers were without pleats and cuffs; leg widths were reduced from 22 inches to 18 1/2 inches at the hem. The new suits used 2 5/8 yards of fabric compared with the typical 3 1/2 yards.[26] The muscular, athletic drape cut suit jacket now resembled more the slim, boyish styling of World War I suits. "Extremely wide shoulders and excessive drape are hardly in accordance with the spirit of the WPB conservation regulations," advised *Esquire* in 1942, "nor do they conform to the present standard of good taste in dress."[27] Similarly, style simplification rules were instituted for other woolen men's wear, including prohibitions of "tucks, bellows, gussets, yokes, belted backs and vents of suit coats."[28] Where previously most tailored and ready-to-wear suits came with two pairs of trousers, the second pair was prohibited by WPB sales regulations, as was the vest that came with three-piece suits. By the fall of 1943, though, some restrictions were relaxed as wool fabrics were successfully stockpiled through conservation and improved trans-atlantic shipping that had increased imports from Britain. Allowed once again were trouser cuffs and pleats, and jacket pocket flaps and patch pockets, particularly with suits made from reprocessed wool or wool/rayon and wool/cotton blends. Lengths of non-wool suit jackets were permitted a half-inch more at the skirt, and the limits to trouser inseams were rescinded. (Figure 1.4.)

Conclusion

The masculine identities of postwar American men had been shaped through their childhood gender role socialization in the 1930s. They had learned from their fathers and grandfathers the traditions of manhood rooted in the Victorian notion of separate spheres—one set of traits and guiding principles for men and a different set for women.

In the Depression era, fictional characters in American popular culture also provided boys with reinforcing messages of traditional masculinity. Movies of the 1930s were filled with hypermasculine role models such as adventurers, detectives, and cowboys whose moral strength and selfless duty defined them. Radio program storylines similarly featured men who were strong, dutiful, and

Figure 1.4 Beginning in early 1942, the production of all apparel made in the United States was subject to government regulations. To conserve fabric, men's suits were redesigned with a shortened jacket skirt, narrowed lapels, reduced inner facings, and the elimination of details such as patch pockets. Trousers were trimmer and without pleats and cuffs. Suits from Sears, 1943.

stoic. And comic books presented heroes who fought the good fight against crime and injustice.

The dress identity of Depression-era men reflected the idea of the strong, vigorous male. The drape cut suit that had been developed in London in the late 1920s became the standard silhouette for men's wear throughout the 1930s. The athletic contours of the suit jacket featured a V-shape cut from broad shoulders to a trim, youthful waist. Jacket sleeves tapered from a rolled shoulder seam to the wrist, suggesting strong biceps and triceps. The trousers became fuller and were modernized with the addition of zippered flies and multiple pleats.

The drape cut suit remained the prevalent men's style through the mid-1940s. Due to materials shortages and rationing, some minor changes to details were required by governmental L-85 restrictions. But the most significant masculine dress identity of the Second World War years was the military uniform—proof that the man had met the test and measured up. Regardless of their roles in the war, servicemen in uniform were viewed as heroes and were celebrated in popular culture from movies to advertising.

2

THE MAN IN THE GRAY FLANNEL SUIT: THE POSTWAR YEARS

Masculine identity in transition

When the Second World War concluded with the surrender of Japan in August 1945, the American military moved quickly to demobilize its massive, global armed forces. In the first year after the war, between August 1945 and August 1946, over 6 million men were deployed back to civilian life, and a million more the following year.[1] These men came home with hopes for a return to normalcy, to put the war years behind them and get on with life.

Government propaganda, popular culture, and especially advertisers celebrated the returning war heroes. There were countless images of men still in their discharge uniforms being welcomed home, having home-cooked meals at a cozy kitchen table, and embracing moms, girlfriends, wives, and children. (Figure 2.1.) But, for many veterans, the readjustment to civilian life was difficult and took time. In October 1945, Lieutenant Frederick Robin wrote for the *Ladies' Home Journal* about what civilian friends and relatives should expect "when your soldier comes home." The first consideration was that for the overwhelming majority of returning veterans, the war had "meant drudgery, not heroics." A very few endured "forward foxholes, house-to-house fighting or combat missions. For most men, it meant handling supplies, checking reports, driving vehicles, drilling recruits, building roads, repairing equipment, working in offices and a host of other necessary functions." Instead of horrible memories of war, the returning soldier likely felt guilty, and perhaps a bit "cheated out of a great experience." The guilt, though, was especially powerful and haunting, advised the lieutenant. Many veterans felt they had not done enough—if stationed at home, he should

Figure 2.1 Depictions of a veteran's happy homecoming in the months after the war was a popular theme in advertising. In reality, though, for many ex-servicemen the readjustment from soldier to civilian was difficult and took time. Ads from December 1945.

have been overseas; if in the rear echelon, he should have been in the front lines. If wounded and sent home, he felt guilty leaving those who remained. After a fierce battle, he felt guilty to have survived while friends and comrades died. Once home again, "No matter how proud he may be of his participation in the war or of his decorations, the soldier's conscience within him says, 'You've come back while others, braver and more deserving, have died.'"[2]

Through the war, the veteran's masculine identity had been that of a soldier, a member of a "society of fighting men." He had found a home in the military, and "had belonged to this special world whether he liked the Army or not." The visible representation of his manhood had been a uniform of the American Armed Forces. In that uniform, he had been part of a historic, noble mission to save the world. Now, back home and officially separated from the service, he was only allowed to wear that uniform for 30 more days during "readjustment." The lieutenant suggested to the *Journal's* readers to "have patience and understanding" of the returning veteran. And, "Don't belittle him if his adventures were not very martial, or urge him, if he did not know combat, to recount his battle experience before an audience of your friends." But especially, "do not begrudge him the minutes when you feel him by your side and yet apart from you, for then he is back in the war with his comrades beside him and it is good for his soul."[3]

Similarly, a month after the war ended, the War Information Administration ran a full-page ad in several newspapers and mass-market magazines asking the public, "How do you look to a Hero?" The ad answers the question with examples of five types of insensitive citizens metaphorically depicted with animal heads. The lion wants to loudly brag to every veteran about how much he did for the war with his Victory Garden and the war bonds he bought. The fox is the type of person who prospered during the war years and boasts of his successes to the veteran. The ad warned that "veterans who saw land traded for lives don't enjoy this kind of talk." The thick-skinned rhinoceros does not believe in the "fancy-pants stuff about vets needing rest before they go back to work." His view is to "holler at 'em . . . What's wrong with you, Soldier? Get up! Get to work! Be a man!" As the rhino saw it, "a few hours in a foxhole" would do a young man good. The ferret insists on details of the soldier's experience—"the gorier the better." The ad reminded the public that "doctors may spend months helping a soldier forget some particularly bad battle experience," but the ferret "can bring it all back in minutes." The crocodile is a "morale wrecker." Her tears flow at the sight of a wounded soldier, and "her sympathy flows over him like carbolic acid" by turning "her high-powered spotlight on a veteran's disability." Most Americans, though—the "Star-spangled Citizens"—saw the returned veteran as "an abler, more capable citizen than the boy who went away . . . They weep no tears, ask no questions, listen when a veteran wants to talk." The ad concludes with a depiction of the gold eagle service pin and a reminder that "the man or woman who wears this button has been honorably discharged from our armed forces."[4]

Hollywood also contributed to the public's awareness of the returning veteran. The transition of the American veteran from soldier to civilian was one of the core themes of the 1946 movie *The Best Years of Our Lives*. Based on the novella *Glory for Me* by MacKinlay Kantor, the movie presents the lives of three veterans returning to their Midwestern home town after the war: a bombardier captain who worked at a soda fountain before the war and cannot find a better job afterwards; a middle-aged Army sergeant who returns to his wife, two teenage children, and his bank management job but becomes discontented with both family and work; and a former high school jock who lost both hands from an explosion during the war. (The latter was portrayed by an actual veteran who had lost both hands and functioned with prosthesis hooks.) Most veterans who saw the movie understood the title to mean the time they had served in the war was their best years, now behind them. As the *Hollywood Quarterly* reported of the movie in 1947, "Truth is evident in every sequence. There is immense patience for detail and emotional texture, especially in the homecoming scenes."[5] The film was a box-office success and won seven Academy Awards, including Best Picture for 1946.

As with the three protagonists in *The Best Years of Our Lives,* the first priority of readjustment for veterans—after the homecoming reunions—was to get a job. The young men who returned to civilian life after the war were ever mindful of the hardships and privations of their childhoods during the Great Depression. They were keenly aware of what steady employment meant to a man's identity and his family's security. As in the movie, postwar veterans stepping back into their roles as civilians found an America that was vastly different from the dismal, uncertain days of the 1930s. The war had brought an end to the decade-long economic depression with plenty of well-paying civilian jobs. Unemployment dropped from 17.2 percent in 1939 to 1.2 percent in 1944.[6] Despite ready cash in the wallets of wartime American workers, there was less to buy as factories converted from manufacturing consumer goods to producing planes, tanks, munitions, and other wartime needs. In addition, conservation and restrictions of materials and manufactured goods were implemented as soon as the war began, such as the L-85 regulations for clothing previously discussed. Strict rationing of foodstuffs and basic commodities such as tires and gasoline were in effect through the war years. With the end of the war, though, Americans were more than ready to splurge, to buy new instead of make do, to indulge in the latest fashions, to forget meatless Mondays and wheatless Wednesdays, and to travel just for fun.

Although the sharp decline in US government spending caused a brief postwar recession at the end of 1945, factories quickly retooled and shifted manufacturing from wartime production back to consumer goods. After the shortages, privations, and sacrifices of the war years, Americans went on a spending spree, setting off an economic boom that continued through the 1960s.

The GI Bill of Rights

Despite millions of veterans demobilized from military service during the first two years after the war, the unemployment rate only increased to 3.9 percent in 1947.[7] The reemployment provisions of the Selective Service Act of 1940 ensured that men honorably discharged from service were to be "restored to such position or a position of like seniority, status, and pay."[8] That meant men who had been too old to be drafted or were classified 4-F could be fired to permit veterans to have their old jobs back. Women especially gave up or lost jobs to make way for veterans. As discussed in Chapter 7, many women who went to work outside the home as a patriotic duty during the war quit their jobs to resume their roles as wives and homemakers. But many other women who wanted to continue working were laid off because companies revived "marriage bars" against retaining and hiring married women and women with small children.[9] The discriminatory policies that resurfaced in the postwar years were implemented to prevent women from competing for jobs viewed as men's work—jobs needed by men who were expected to be family breadwinners. These revived policies also reinforced the postwar social shift toward women's roles in American society, a regressive social consensus that women should focus their time and energy on providing a proper home for their husbands and children. And young single women, whether employed or not, should focus with equal vigor on getting married and starting a family.

To help the transition of America's veterans back into civilian life, in 1944, Congress enacted the Servicemen's Readjustment Act or GI Bill of Rights as it was more commonly known, to reward veterans with special financial benefits. The three major types of benefits offered to veterans were a year of unemployment compensation of about $20 a week; up to four years of government-paid college or vocational training; and loans guaranteed by the Veterans' Administration for financing a home, farm, or business.[10] By 1955, of the nearly 16 million World War II veterans, over 8.3 million of them (about 52 percent) had received unemployment compensation, almost 7.8 million (just under 50 percent) got education benefits, and 4 million (25 percent) received VA-guaranteed loans to buy a home or business.[11] Not only was the GI Bill a significant readjustment aid to veterans, but it also helped stimulate the postwar economy, improved the nation's level of education, and provided better housing for millions of families.

The educational benefits of the GI Bill were especially generous. Depending upon the veteran's length of service, he could receive up to 48 months of VA-paid tuition, fees, books, and a monthly stipend. At the end of the war, only about 47.4 percent of Americans had completed high school; by 1950, that had climbed to 57.4 percent. College graduates were 5.4 percent of the population in 1940 and 7.1 percent in 1950.[12]

Higher education in America became democratized in the postwar years. In many colleges, white Protestants attended classes with Catholics, Jews, and Blacks for the first time in their lives. The sons of poor Depression-era laborers proved as capable and smart as their privileged middle- and upper-class classmates. Married adults, many with children, shared classrooms with teenage high school graduates and often set the grade curve high. Some women's colleges became coeducational, admitting married students and those with children for the first time.

But not all of the 7.8 million veterans who signed up for educational benefits of the GI Bill went for a high school diploma or college degree. While in the service, many soldiers with too little education were taught reading improvement and technical skills ranging from electronics and communications to auto mechanics and machine operations. Once home, these veterans still participated in the GI Bill education program through vocational training, often on the job, to further hone their skills. Many thousands of other veterans preferred to return to farms and were able to get GI Bill loans for farm machinery and equipment, infrastructure, and livestock. In addition, many veterans opted for on-the-farm training in advanced agricultural methods, business maintenance, and improved living conditions such as rural electrification and indoor plumbing.

The education provisions of the GI Bill were a huge success. Many veterans became the first in their families to earn a high school diploma or college degree. The US census estimated in 1950 that the average annual income for men with a high school diploma was $3784 and with a college degree, $6179.[13] (Without a diploma, the average annual income for a man was $2829.) The GI Bill had enabled millions of veterans to aspire to the middle class. In a corporate or local business arena of the 1950s, education was as much of a masculine identity as a job title or type of work. In a fraternity of similar alumni, the man in the gray flannel suit might be introduced to coworkers as a Harvard Man or Princeton Man or from whatever other private or state college he had attended. Among the favorite forms of men's jewelry in the 1950s were school insignia rings, tie clips, and cuff links. These eye-catching accessories were testimonies of a man's achievement and his membership in a special alumni club.

Postwar marriage

The GI Bill also encouraged marriage with its VA-guaranteed loans for the purchase of homes and businesses. In 1946, US marriage rates jumped to 16.4 percent of the population, a significant leap from the Depression-era low of 7.9 percent. More than 2.2 million couples were wed the first year after the war.[14] The median age for a man's first marriage dropped from 24.3 at the start of the war in 1940 to 22.7 in 1949.[15] Youthful marriage in the postwar years was encouraged by national sentiment, peer pressure, government propaganda, popular culture, and especially advertisers who saw in a young married couple a lengthy lifetime of consumers. Marriage experts, psychologists, and physicians suggested that marrying young, even in their late teens, could have a maturing and stabilizing effect on the emotional development of young people.[16] Although for some young couples, financial conditions required continued support from parents, perhaps even living with parents initially, for many other young couples, getting married and setting up their own homes was the break from dependence on their parents that they especially wanted. Moreover, youthful marriages often forced young people to leap rapidly from childhood to adult roles of husband and wife, and many times right into parenthood in a short span of time. For those who could cope, the responsibilities of being married (and parenthood) at such a young age demanded an equally rapid adaptation to finding their footing as mature grown-ups; for those who could not cope, there was disappointment, heartbreak, and, increasingly in the baby boom era, divorce. Romantic notions and naive expectations of what marriage should be, especially as idealized television programs of family life became more prevalent in popular culture, had to be set aside as young couples grew into their roles as husbands and wives.

Among the challenges of postwar young couples was the education factor. The GI Bill encouraged young men to finish high school or attend college, which millions of veterans took advantage of. But in juggling classes, study time, sometimes part-time jobs, and setting up housekeeping, young married men struggled to cope with the pressures, and their wives too often felt neglected. Most young women who married while in school dropped out to focus their time and attention on their husbands and likely their babies. But with financial worries and perhaps cramped living conditions such as makeshift dorms or one-room garage apartments with the in-laws, the glow of the honeymoon wore off fast.

Part of the transition period in the early years of a marriage included learning to get along with each other. Dating and periods of engagement were not enough to prepare young couples for the intimacy of married life. Living with and getting to know a wife was far more complex for the young husband than his boyhood experiences with his mom and sisters prepared him for.

Compromise was necessary, but was not always a two-way street. Adjustments for new wives, discussed more in Chapter 7, were usually significantly greater than for young husbands, often leading to unmet expectations and depressing disappointments. Young women unhappily found they had to leave behind their schoolgirl social circles and perhaps even family support if a distant relocation was required by the husband. Sometimes a young wife had to give up higher education goals or drop out of school early. And a career was highly unlikely for a young married woman. Even if she had a solid job and career prospects, she most often had to abandon those when she got married.

Most women brought to their marriage preconceived ideas of the roles they and their husbands were to perform. With their Depression-era mothers as role models, newlywed women of the 1950s often saw their path solely as a traditional housewife and mother. Popular culture, especially television programs and mass-market magazines such as *Good Housekeeping, Ladies' Home*

Journal, and *Woman's Day,* reinforced these conventional notions of the wife's role and duty. Among the earliest points of contention in young marriages often were decisions on the division of labor. Men of the era saw their roles largely as breadwinners and authoritarian heads of the household. Their chief responsibility was to go to work and earn an income to support the family. Even when at home, men considered their designated tasks largely to be other than homemaking or childcare, such as lawn mowing, auto maintenance, and perhaps some exterior and interior house repairs. "Helping" the wife with "her" work may include occasionally cooking on an outdoor grill or taking the family to a restaurant on a Saturday night. And if the wife did not fulfill adequately what the husband considered to be her homemaking responsibilities, there could be friction as he tried to reform and reshape her into his concept of the proper wife.

For middle-class white suburban families, that concept of the proper wife also precluded her working outside the home, a view with which most women of the time agreed. In the postwar years, the young adults who had grown up during the 1930s negatively viewed the role reversals of their parents during the Depression when their fathers were unemployed and their mothers were forced to go to work outside the home. Similarly, conventional gender roles were further eroded during the war years when military mobility displaced millions of young men from traditional environments, and millions of women went to work outside the home as a patriotic call to the nation's labor shortage needs. "As young adults, these experiences prepared them to embrace traditional gender roles and early marriage and to place a high value on children as a family resource in the 1950s."[17] In a backlash to the socioeconomic and cultural disruptions of the Depression and the war, the traditional separate spheres of gender roles became as accepted during the baby boom years as they had been for their Victorian grandparents and even more so than with their Depression-era parents.

For many young couples of the postwar years, though, the adjustments and compromises of marriage were sometimes an unbearable strain. Some couples sought to preserve and improve their marriages through counseling from social workers, physicians, psychiatrists, and other practitioners in the burgeoning "family therapy" field of the 1950s.[18] If there were children, the fear of the impact of divorce on their children kept many unhappy couples together despite their misery. These baby boom parents had grown up in the 1930s with the understanding that a "broken home" was a significant factor in juvenile delinquency.[19] Others suffered an unhappy marriage year after year because they believed their vows for better or worse were permanent, "till death do us part." And some were codependent types who would rather have a miserable marriage than be alone. Probably the most prevalent consideration against divorce, though, was economic. Not only was the financial cost of lawyers and court fees significant, but also the division of assets could be complex and take years to resolve. Men who controlled the family finances could hide assets or provide incomplete records. In addition, for men, there might also be costs for alimony and child support. For women, collecting payments for either, especially if the ex-husband moved out of state, might never be realized.

For couples who could no longer endure the misery, the only option was divorce. In America, an increase in divorce rates climbed from a low in the 1930s of 1.3 percent to a high of 4.3 percent in 1946. Although the Depression-era parents of the 1950s man had taught their children that divorce was "bad" and "undesirable," a social ill to "be checked as much as possible,"[20] the divorce rate through the 1950s remained in the 2.1–2.6 percent range.[21] In 1951, *Ladies' Home Journal* complained, "Divorce is so commonplace today that some persons take it for granted as a solution to domestic difficulties; if trouble arises in marriage, they can exchange it for another."[22] But through the 1950s, divorce was made even more emotionally taxing by a complicated guilt/innocence process. "Existing divorce laws made the spouses into opponents who engaged in a battle over who was guilty and who was innocent," often leaving the ex-spouses with an "unfortunate legacy of indignity, hostility, bitterness and aggression."[23] The typical grounds for divorce at the time included adultery, physical or mental cruelty, willful desertion, habitual drunkenness, imprisonment, sexual or mental incapacity, or bigamy. To grant a divorce, courts had to find one of the parties guilty of one of the bases of marital conduct, some of which could also lead to other legal complications ranging from criminal prosecution to mental institutionalization. Although "no-fault" divorce that removed a guilt/innocence conclusion from the legal process was proposed in the 1950s by law organizations such as NAWL (National Association of Women Lawyers), the first no-fault divorce law was not enacted until 1969.

For many couples considering divorce, television provided some sobering insights with reality programs such as *Divorce Court* (1957–1962) and *Divorce Hearing* (1958–1962). Each episode of *Divorce Hearing* began with the disclaimer from the host, marriage counselor Paul B. Popenoe, that it was "an inquiry program" that examined the real-life "complaints and problems of couples who have filed for divorce in the sincere hope that a better understanding of the causes and consequences of divorce may impress upon you the importance of saving your marriage."[24] For *Divorce Court,* actual cases were adapted to reenactments by actors performed before actor Voltaire Perkins as the judge. In these and similar courtroom dramas of the era, TV audiences saw and heard the personal tragedies and traumas of marriage dissolution.

To most women, a divorce represented failure and humiliation, as discussed more in Chapter 7. Similarly, many divorced men felt adrift and soon remarried. But for other divorced men, instead of a feeling of embarrassment and failure, they felt liberated. Without the need to be a breadwinner, some men escaped unhappy jobs and even changed careers to something perhaps with less income but greater interest and fulfillment than just a paycheck. Others adopted the idea of the single playboy, a masculine identity of the 1950s that especially became trendy with the launch of *Playboy* magazine in 1953. Rather than thinking of a second marriage, these divorcés began following the tenets of *Playboy* editorials and set up a bachelor pad, focused on themselves, traveled, and pursued serial dating without emotional investment or commitment.

Masculine identity in suburbia

The economic slump of the Depression years and shortages of labor and building materials during the war had caused a severe housing shortage across America. Even during the first couple of years after the war, materials remained in short supply, and housing developers had to compete with commercial builders that were renovating factories, stores, and warehouses. Many returning veterans and their families initially had to live in temporary arrangements such as spare rooms with parents, boarding houses, and makeshift dorms on college campuses.

The home loan provisions of the GI Bill "encouraged developers, under governmental supervision to build, bankers to lend and veterans to buy."[25] In the 1954 ad for National Homes shown in Figure 2.2, a large cartoon thought-balloon over the head of the man reminds house shoppers that for veterans in many areas, no down payment was required. Home ownership was a cornerstone of the postwar American dream of economic success and upward social mobility. From the late 1940s through the 1950s, the American landscape was transformed as thousands of acres of farmland were divided into grids of paved roads, fronted by small lots on which were built mass-produced single-family houses. One of the first of these planned community subdivisions was Levittown, New York, built on Long Island between 1947 and 1951. The subdivision was named for the builders, Abe Levitt and his two sons, who also built similar Levittowns in Pennsylvania, New Jersey, and Puerto Rico. Soon after completion, the Long Island community had an estimated population of 70,000.[26]

The planned community offered families an escape from urban problems that included slums, densely crowded streets, insufficient parking, abandoned buildings and vacant lots, scattered shops, and dangerous, noisy traffic. Instead, everything in the self-contained suburbs was new. There was no "wrong side of the tracks" and every street was a "good neighborhood." Roads were clean and well paved without heavy traffic and dangerous intersections; grassy playground areas were set aside for the children; adjacent new schools and churches were built; and one-stop shopping centers provided supermarkets, a variety of specialty shops, and plenty of off-street parking. In addition, through the 1950s and 1960s, the expanding interstate highway system helped make suburban sprawl sustainable with fast, easy commutes to nearby city jobs.

Figure 2.2 For many veterans after the war, the GI Bill encouraged marriage, family life, and home ownership in one of the new suburban developments by providing guaranteed mortgage and business loans. Ad, 1954.

Residents of these suburban communities had been "screened," meaning the "selection of people by fixed criteria," according to *Harper's* magazine in 1953.[27] In the early postwar years as suburbs began to expand across the country, about 90 percent of the new homeowners were newly married veterans who took advantage of the generous provisions of the GI Bill to acquire a new house. All the houses were in a similar price range, usually $7,000 to $12,000, and looked similar in size, style, and landscaping. (Figure 2.3.) Most of the men held jobs with similar income levels of about $4,000 to $7,000 annually. "The status of the family in the community is determined probably more by the level of job he holds than by any other single factor," concluded sociologists Talcott Parsons and Robert Bales in 1955, "and the income he earns is usually the most important basis of the family's standard of living and hence 'style of life.' "[28] The homogeneity of these suburban subdivisions was largely white, Anglo-Saxon, Protestant, and middle income. "As a result, there are no poor, no Negroes; and as communities, they contain the best educated people in America."[29]

In the scary world of the 1950s—the Cold War, the spread of communism, the threat of nuclear annihilation, McCarthyism, civil rights activism, labor unrest—suburban enclaves were a "bastion of defense against a threatening, unstable world." The US doctrine of containment during the Cold War "encouraged postwar couples to turn their sights homeward. . . and shaped the family style."[30] A home is "both the symbol and the source of enduring values," observed *Ladies' Home Journal* in 1951. "It is the basis of individual security; for a happy home fosters that deep sense of 'belongingness' which is man's best preparation for withstanding the pressures of modern life."[31] Within the defined boundaries of suburban developments, homeowners could count on the shared values and standards of behavior of their neighbors.

One of the key values suburbanites shared with their neighbors in the postwar years was materialism. After the deprivations of the Depression and the rationing and shortages of the war years, Americans made up for lost time in a frenzy of consumerism. The consumer-driven American economy soared through the 1950s and 1960s. Yet, spending was not on luxury goods and personal extravagance but instead was on the home and family. These purchases were what historian Elaine Tyler May calls "virtuous consumerism," the acquisition and accumulation of commodities that "promised to reinforce home life and uphold traditional gender roles."[32] The mid-century home in the United States was designed with sufficient wiring, electrical outlets, plumbing, phone lines, and plenty of space for the types of appliances and consumer goods that a modern American family would need. The Levittown houses even came furnished with state-of-the-art kitchen appliances, a washing machine, and a built-in television. Everything had to be new. "Taste levels are high," reported *Harper's* in 1953. Wives collected ideas from mass-market home magazines to use as guides for interior decorating, and selected "early American or modern" furniture and accessories as social "approval insurance."[33]

The builders' models of the suburban Cape Cod or ranch-style house were functional and basic. Almost as soon as couples and families moved in, they undertook remodeling projects to customize and improve those standardized structures. Attics were finished, concrete patios were installed, and carports were converted to enclosed garages. Finishing touches such as awnings, decorative window shutters, or a front door painted in a contrasting color could set a house apart from those of the neighbors. Curb appeal involved labor-intensive gardening projects—planting flowerbeds, shrubs, and saplings to break the monotony of

Figure 2.3 From the end of the Second World War through the 1950s, suburban sprawl blanketed the countryside surrounding cities across America. By the thousands, moderately priced ranch-style houses lined newly paved roads in largely white, middle-class communities. Levittown, PA, 1959.

the newly bulldozed landscape. Consumption for the suburbanite now included collections of power tools, gardening implements, and building supplies.

Hence, the masculine identity of the successful suburbanite male was expressed in his pride and bragging rights for the size and look of his home, landscaping, car, and homeowner possessions such as a power mower, backyard patio, outdoor furniture, barbeque grill, perhaps a pool. As *Harper's* noted, "the pressure to keep up with the Jones" was a driving force in suburbia, and "these young couples, anxious for 'success,' look for material signs of it."[34] In fact, to be without a new car or a television might even seem suspicious to neighbors. "The nonpossession of an item becomes an almost unsocial act — an unspoken aspersion of the others' judgment or taste," suggested journalist William H. Whyte in 1956.[35]

Leisure-time possessions were also a hallmark of the successful suburbanite male. His set of golf clubs and tennis rackets (and membership in the country club to use them) and his specialized sportswear for each of these leisure pursuits were as much symbols of his success as an upwardly mobile suburbanite as was his car or house. The status of white middle-class suburbanites was the masculine identity that millions of postwar American men achieved, proudly, and millions more aspired to.

The success of the suburbanite male was further enhanced and reinforced by the possessions of his children. Most postwar suburban parents wanted to ensure their children had a better and happier childhood than they had experienced as children in the Depression era. The telltale proof of suburbanite parental indulgence included bicycles and pedal cars on the front sidewalk; skates, balls, and other toys scattered about on the lawn; basketball hoops over the garage door; and volleyball nets and jungle gyms in the backyard. Where before the war, children and teens were invisible, or at best, to be seen and not heard, during the 1950s, middle-class youth became a mass-market phenomenon through their collective power as consumers. Advertisers spent millions of dollars directly targeting children and teens through comic books, food packaging, in-store point-of-sale displays, and especially through television. For suburban parents, the clothes their children wore, their toys, their memberships in organizations like the Boy Scouts and Girl Scouts, music lessons and recitals, and trips to private summer camps were all reflections on the upwardly mobile, successful suburbanite.

Television programming of the 1950s especially encouraged the aspiration for suburban living. Family sitcoms, discussed more in the next section, presented an idealized life in the suburbs. The fictional Nelsons of the *Adventures of Ozzie and Harriet*, the Stones of *The Donna Reed Show*, the Cleavers of *Leave It to Beaver*, and the Andersons of *Father Knows Best* lived the American dream in their modern, well-accoutered suburban homes. Each week, millions of Americans visited with these TV families in their neat, clean, and orderly homes filled with an abundance of consumer goods. Even the urbanite New Yorkers, Lucy and Ricky Ricardo, in TV's most popular comedy *I Love Lucy* submitted to the siren call of suburbia and left the city for the country. After six years of episodes (1951–1957) centered in a cramped, three-room apartment in New York, the Ricardos, too, realized the American dream and moved into a spacious, two-story suburban house in Connecticut.

However, despite being the American dream, homeownership in suburbia had drawbacks that social scientists and journalists began to examine even in the early 1950s. In 1956, journalist John C. Keats wrote in *The Crack in the Picture Window,* "Today's housing developments . . . destroy established cities and trade patterns, pose dangerous problems for the areas they invade, and actually drive mad myriads of housewives shut up in them."[36] The term "white flight" became widely known in the postwar years, as white families left city apartments and row houses for single-family houses with grassy yards in the suburbs, and the vacuum created by their departure from inner cities was increasingly filled by immigrants and families of color. These new arrivals in suburbia were ever mindful of their upward social mobility, suggested William H. Whyte, and "the influx of Negroes into the houses they left behind, is a specter they do not for a moment forget."[37] Moreover, the urban neighborhood economies of small retailers, grocers, restaurants, and service providers were disrupted by the changing inner-city demographics as businesses closed or relocated to suburban shopping centers. And the madness of housewives Keats suggested was not far from the truth in many cases, as stay-at-home wives left old friends and family in the city to settle into isolation in the monotonous suburbs.

To combat the sameness of builders' standard model ranch houses in suburban developments, many women immediately went to work with interior decorating, and their husbands launched into home projects to customize their castle. Yet, these improvement projects were usually subtle, or what Whyte called "inconspicuous consumption."[38] Choosing a different paint color for the front door meant selecting a shade of beige or brown, not opting for something too unique (nor outside the guidelines of the homeowners' association). The fake shutters selected for flanking the front picture window were identical to those throughout the neighborhood, prepainted by the manufacturer in a limited choice of black, white, or hunter green. The patio awning may have a straight or crenulated edge but was made of a multicolor-striped canvas similar to everyone else's. Perhaps the homeowners imagined they were putting their personal touches on these cookie-cutter houses, but in fact their "mimetic rivalry" with their neighbors was actually conforming to the "undifferentiation" of the community.[39] John C. Keats observed that suburbanites agreed they were "constantly being badgered to look around us and make sure we're doing and saying and thinking what the mass of our neighbors will accept."[40] In the conformist suburbia of the 1950s, too much individuality was suspicious and unacceptable. Instead, the similarities of the home improvements actually reinforced what *Harper's* called a "super-conformity" of suburbia.[41]

The social pressure to "be one up on the folks next door"[42] with home improvements, the latest model car, and acquisitions of the newest and best of everything for the middle-income family resulted in spending beyond their means for some suburbanites. The competitive worry that "they'll miss what the Joneses are enjoying"[43] pushed those envious suburbanites into "digging themselves deeper and deeper into debt out of a desperate fear of failing to keep up with crowd."[44] They, in turn, became the benchmark by which other neighbors may have felt the need to keep up with, and who then also fell into an equally burdensome debt. "The word 'success' is on everyone's lips and 'successful people' are those who advance economically," reported *Harper's* in 1953[45]—or at least appear to succeed at achieving affluence. Homeowner consumption was spurred on and on not only by competition with the Joneses but also by the "good life" depicted in television programming, enticing messages from mass advertising, and easy installment credit plans from merchants and manufacturers. When finally a financial crisis was reached, the upwardly mobile suburbanites found themselves instead slipping downward.

One of the most significant drawbacks of the new postwar suburban developments was its lack of population diversity. As noted previously, couples and families who wished to move into one of the new suburban developments were "screened" by the builders, realtors, and mortgage lenders. Suburbanization not only segregated American society through socioeconomic class but even more so by race.

For white, Anglo-Saxon, Protestant veterans in the postwar years, the path toward achieving the American dream of homeownership was usually green-lit and expedited every step of the way. For nonwhites, though, the first obstacle was house hunting. Even in the north, realtors were limited in where Black buyers could be shown properties for sale. Subdivisions such as the Levittowns of New York, New Jersey, and Pennsylvania had whites-only covenants written into purchase applications and homeowners' association policies. As *Harper's* reported in 1953, "No other question arouses so much heat, guilt, and dissention as racial discrimination against Negroes, a pattern the residents did not create but which they now sustain . . . Levittown is now the largest community in America that has no Negro population."[46] Bill Levitt was typical of postwar builders when he told the press in 1949,

> Levittown has been and is now progressing as a private enterprise job, and it is entirely in the discretion and judgment of Levitt & Sons as to whom it will sell or rent . . . It was not a matter of prejudice, but one of business . . . I have come to know that if we sell one house to a Negro family, then ninety to ninety-five percent of our white customers will not buy into this community.[47]

But Bill Levitt's private enterprise would not have been possible without substantial help from the government. The great majority of the white homebuyers in his subdivisions relied on easy mortgage loans with no down payments guaranteed by US government agencies. In addition, federally funded interstate highway systems made possible expanding suburbs and exurbs, and homeowner breadwinners relied on these expressways to commute to jobs in distant cities. Equally important, state and county governments offered special tax incentives to builders, as well as contributing to the community through infrastructure projects such as paved roads, water and sewer systems, and electrical utility poles and connections, often funded by bonds paid from taxpayer coffers.

Typical of the discrimination against Blacks by all-white suburban communities was a closing scene of the 1959 play *A Raisin in the Sun,* made into a movie starring Sidney Poitier in 1961. In the storyline, the Black Younger family lives in a small, run-down Chicago apartment, but when the matriarch receives a $10,000 insurance check from the death of her husband, she puts a down payment on a house in an all-white neighborhood. She is not making a stand against segregation but rather assesses that the same house would cost more in a Black neighborhood. When the homeowners of the all-white subdivision discover a Black family is about to move in, they pool resources to buy the house, including a profit on the deal for the Youngers, and send a representative to make the offer. Although the Youngers ultimately keep the house, it is not a happy-ending story, "since the family members are only moving into another situation where they will be unhappy victims of prejudice."[48] Even worse is the potential danger they will now face from segregationist violence, suggested when a neighbor in the tenement mentions a current newspaper report of a Black family being bombed out of their home in a white neighborhood.

Acquiring a mortgage was the next roadblock for nonwhites. The Federal Housing Administration (FHA) was one of the alphabet agencies of the New Deal established in 1934. Its purpose was to insure mortgage lenders against losses in case of default by the borrower. Among the underwriting guidelines of the FHA was a policy called redlining, which steered private mortgage lenders away from minority neighborhoods often outlined in red on their reference maps, a common practice until the passage of the Fair Housing Act in 1968. Similarly, for white veterans of the Second World War and the Korean War, the housing provisions of the GI Bill were instrumental in helping them buy into the suburban developments. These ex-servicemen were entitled to loans guaranteed by the Veterans Administration. But for nonwhite veterans, the promises of the GI Bill too often were unrealized. Local banks, even in the north, regularly refused to grant mortgages to African Americans based solely on race, even if the applicant had a good job and was a low financial risk candidate. "By allowing local control in administering the GI Bill, the federal government acquiesced to racist practices at the local level that resulted in the discriminatory implementation of this legislation, and African American veterans were denied access to the benefits and services that white veterans received."[49] Racial segregation was enforced by government mortgage loan policies.

In addition to segregationist covenants in purchase applications, deeds, and mortgage documents, another layer of legal racial discrimination came from homeowners' associations. To protect the value of a homeowner's property and that of their neighbors, strict policies were implemented regulating house maintenance and improvements, yards, new construction, pets, and car parking to name a few. Homeowners' associations had the legal right to attach liens to property if the homeowner failed to resolve a violation of community standards for which the association had to step in and remedy. Written policies of homeowners' associations also reinforced racial exclusions as a matter of protecting property values for all members. "Racial identity and racial difference assumed a material dimension imposed onto the geography of the city by the emerging real estate industry through the use and enforcement of racial restrictive covenants and the creation of exclusionary homeowner associations."[50] These restrictive covenants were regarded by prospective home buyers as an incentive for joining a suburban community. The all-white identity of the residents was an expected social value as well as an economic protection of the value of the property.

By the late 1950s, doubts and questions of idyllic suburban living became so well-known and documented in the media and books that Hollywood found a fresh topic for a movie. In 1957, the film *No Down Payment* "provided a fairly accurate . . . potpourri of social ills" and an "honest sketch" of life in a postwar suburban development in southern California. The "suburban woes" ranged from the typical financial difficulties of homeowners that impeded upward social mobility to a surge of racial discrimination, here against a Japanese-American family that tried to move into the community.[51]

Two new social grievances of suburbanites that *Harper's* identified in its 1953 reports were regarding children and dogs. Certainly, the spacious, green landscape, playgrounds, and safety and security of a suburban neighborhood had a special appeal to parents with school-age children, particularly when compared to the dangers of crowded, traffic-filled streets of a city. For the same reasons, newly married couples were attracted to suburbia in large part as the best place to begin a family. But as *Harper's* reported, because suburban children are "out-of-doors most of the time and less dependent on adults than children in traditional [urban] communities . . . they are the primary cause of tension and irritation" among neighbors. The issue, continued the magazine, was "a result of unconscious neglect, a major blind spot expressed in the attitude that children can just be 'turned loose'" to run around the neighborhood unsupervised. With plenty of nearby children of their own age and an abundance of toys and games to share, they could happily run and play in noisy gangs for hours daily. These joyous outdoor excursions for the children could then become friction between neighbors, who may complain that "children are not taught to respect other peoples' property . . . Common offenses: walking through gardens, flower beds, into others' homes; carrying off toys and tools."[52] As William H. Whyte discovered in his research of the suburbs, an additional complaint about suburbanite children was "their freshness"; that is, the "kids here call everybody by their first names." But then, "though not many [parents] think their own children lack discipline, they are very sure that everybody else's children do." And, when it came to disciplining their children, "parents are somewhat unreasonable about this; whatever their faults, harsh parental discipline is not one of them." To compound the problem, children did not receive discipline from teachers either since parents could "not fairly ask the schools to do what they won't."[53]

Similarly, dogs were a new point of contention for suburbanite neighbors. With all the builders' thorough and cohesive planning of the ranch houses and the developments to build them in, "nobody thought about dogs," observed *Harper's* magazine. Because most of the new homeowners in these parceled subdivisions had previously lived in cramped city apartments, a suburban yard seemed to invite the addition of a dog, especially if there were children. But usually, these ex-city dwellers knew nothing about training and disciplining dogs, and the pets were simply turned loose in the yard. Without a fence, the dogs would roam in packs, "wrecking gardens and flower beds, and raising general hell." If the owners tried to chain their dogs up in the yard, the animals would "howl and bark until no one can stand it." If the dog were kept inside, it would charge out the door at the first opportunity to bite mailmen and deliverymen. (Thirteen mailmen were reportedly bitten in one community during a single summer.) In one instance, a Chicago suburb tried to ban dogs that resulted in "the bitterest, hottest, meanest, most tearful fight in that community's history." To most Americans, "our conception of private property includes the right to own a dog even though he may be the damnedest nuisance in the world," concluded *Harper's*.[54]

Fatherhood in the baby boom era

With the surge of marriages in America following the war came an inevitable baby boom. The postwar US birthrate spiked from 20.4 births per 1,000 population in 1945 to 24.1 in 1946 and peaked in 1947 at 26.6. From 1954 through 1964, the annual birthrate topped 4 million each year, but then began to decline in 1965. More than 70 million babies were born in America during the 1946–1964 baby boom.[55]

The rugged individualism that defined masculinity in the nineteenth century no longer applied to the mid-twentieth century. For most modern American men to achieve their goal of financial security and the "good life," they largely had to surrender their autonomy. They had to conform and "play well with others" in a factory, corporate, or business arena where they were subordinate to a hierarchy of management. But in the home and as a father, the postwar American male was the authority, and his dependent wife and children were subordinates. He was the indisputable head of their household.

For baby boom dads, fatherhood was a departure from that of their fathers and grandfathers. Prior to the 1940s, fatherhood was primarily a duty, a parental teaching task to ensure their sons grew up to be proper men. (Daughters were the responsibility of mothers, aunts, and elder sisters.) Before the war, depictions in popular culture of father and son activities centered on nineteenth-century notions of separate spheres and gender role socialization. Fishing and hunting were manly ventures that put food on the family table. Sports were mock warrior training and exercise for developing strong bodies. Using tools and operating machinery were necessary for a secure, safe, and functioning home, and perhaps a job. These activities for boys were teaching methods regarded as effective means of countering the feminization influences of mothers and women teachers with whom boys spent so much time. A momma's boy or sissy was intolerable and could be an indication of an abnormal son, who might develop into one of those "perverts and dupes of the communists" that McCarthyites had railed against.[56]

Equally important to a father in the gender role socialization of his son was preparing him to earn a living and become a breadwinner family man. Since the late nineteenth century, the urbanization and industrialization of America increasingly created class-based socioeconomic divisions. Men migrating to cities from rural farms or by immigration from the Old World usually submitted their labor to mechanized factory tasks, services, or manual labor for hourly wages. These were the working-class men, whose masculine identity was often expressed by an emphasis on physical ability on the job, and public demonstrations of manliness off the job, such as drinking in bars, gathering in pool halls, rough labor union protests and activities, and similar social bonding. For other men, industrialization created opportunities in cities for salaried office administration and management work as well as jobs requiring education-based training such as accounting, engineering, or the sciences. Also, men with exceptional interpersonal skills could succeed in sales and make a good income through bonuses and commissions. These men formed the middle classes. Working-class fathers had to find ways within their sphere to prepare their sons for the industrialized workplace, often by introducing them to an entry-level, low-wage job in the same place they worked. Middle-class fathers, though, had to plan for a more extended education of their sons that would enable them to choose their own career paths. "Middle-class men . . . measured their manhood through their ability to ensure the son's upward social mobility, and thereby preserve their families' often tenuous middle-class status."[57]

In the 1950s, though, technology presented new challenges for gender role socialization that prewar fathers did not have to face. Schools were more sophisticated, and high school graduation was expected. Television provided a barrage of information that often outpaced a father's education and experience. Instead of taking a son to a ballpark, a wide assortment of sports was available on TV from the convenience of the living room. As boys transitioned to their teen years, they developed interests that fathers often had no experience with, such as rock and roll music or building model rockets that could launch from the backyard. These interests could be either learning experiences for the baby boom dad or, more likely, generation gaps that were ignored.

Still, fatherhood could add great joy and fulfillment to a man's life. "For men who were frustrated at work, for women who were bored at home, and both who were dissatisfied with the unfulfilled promise of sexual excitement, children might fill that void."[58] Popular culture and especially advertising of the 1950s often depicted the delight a father enjoyed with both sons and daughters, playing games, sharing hobbies, and going on family vacations. Father's Day became a holiday of greater significance in the postwar years than when it was first introduced in 1910. (Figure 2.4.) This joy, though, was with school-age children,

1952

1955

1957

1961

Figure 2.4 In the postwar era, fatherhood was redefined from what it was with earlier generations. Baby boom era dads not only were role models for the gender socialization of their children but also enjoyed nurturing and spending playtime with their offspring.

as depicted in the ads shown here, "when they're more like real people."[59] Teenagers preferred being with their friends and enjoying as much independence from parental chaperoning as possible. And infant and toddler care was seldom attempted by dads, despite encouragement from parenting manuals, such as Dr. Benjamin Spock's *The Common Sense Book of Baby and Child Care.* In the 1957 revised edition, Spock acknowledges that many fathers "think the care of babies and children is the mother's job entirely." But "the time for him to begin being a real father is right at the start." For Spock, though, that did not necessarily "mean that the father has to give just as many bottles or change just as many diapers as the mother." Yet, he should consider helping out with bottles and diapers maybe on Sundays or sometimes at 2 a.m. "when the mother is still pretty tired."[60]

Another popular childcare guide of the 1950s was *The Gesell Institute's Child Behavior.* The Connecticut-based Gesell Institute was founded in 1950 and named for former Yale professor and pediatrician Dr. Arnold Gesell, whose decades of research in child development were the institution's guiding principles. For baby boom era fathers, the 1955 edition of the handbook noted that "unlike the authoritarian Life-with-Father fathers of an earlier generation" (a reference to the 1947 movie of that title), some postwar dads could be "almost as handy with a bottle or diaper pin or burp cloth as are mothers." Still other fathers, though, "just don't have the knack of handling young babies" particularly when confronting a "messy diaper." The handbook is careful not to "fit all fathers into one mold" but suggested that each should find his own footing in fatherhood "according to the dictates of his own personality." The authors advised fathers that their children would have different relationships with them depending on their age. Babies and toddlers may not take to their fathers well and cry when approached by Dad. After all, Dad is away at work all day and it is Mom whom the infant sees most waking hours. As preschoolers, children acknowledge that Dad is the "ultimate authority" and "his word is often law . . . Father's firmness, but also . . . his understanding are both essential ingredients for a stable family life." By the time children are in their early elementary school years, they begin to experience independence away from parents in a classroom or with friends on the playground. Dads (and moms) are forewarned that at this age, children may explore deviance with a "no" when told to do something. Dads may "make things worse" by "bringing vigorous physical punishment to bear" on the child. Instead, suggests Gesell's guide, "a patient and even moderately inventive father" can help with the "worst trouble areas." Perhaps Dad might take charge of some of the child's routines, such as dressing for school or getting ready for bed, and thus "contribute a very great deal to the harmony of the household." By the time children are age eight or nine, the relationship with Mom "overshadows any other personal relationship," and a "father may feel a trifle left out." Perhaps he "is actually fortunate" in this regard, since children are "less demanding of him," and he can pretty much "go his own way." By the age of ten, though, "children are now quite old enough to be interesting to those fathers who may not have enjoyed them too much earlier . . . Ten is one of the happiest ages from the point of view of the father-child relationship. You don't even have to be an exceptionally superior or expert father for things to succeed now." Fathers are cautioned, though, not to make the mistake of waiting for the child to be a little older than nine or ten to enjoy spending time with him, because "if you do wait, you may find that now he himself does not have time for you."[61]

Particularly challenging to dads of the baby boom era was a father/daughter relationship. He found little specific help from parenting guides and magazines on the topic. The drawings of school-age children in Spock's manual depict boys playing sidewalk "step on a crack," slouching at the dinner table as bad manners, and in a rough-and-tumble backyard football game. Girls are depicted in the section on jealousy and the new baby, the invalid, and as an adolescent dancing awkwardly with her immature male peer classmate. For the father "as a companion" to a son, Spock offers several points of gender role socialization, especially for Dad to be a role model that a boy can "copy, to pattern himself after." But for girls, it is the "little things he can do, like complimenting her on her dress, or hair-do, or the cookies she's made." A daughter will not "pattern herself after him, but she gains confidence in herself as a girl and a woman from feeling his approval."[62] By tradition, though, a daughter became a cause of worry for fathers when she became a teenager. "A father, somewhat remote before, may become greatly concerned as his daughter approaches dating age and takes her first steps toward independence. He wants his son to stand on his own feet, but in his anxiety for his daughter, he deprives her of opportunities to develop maturity."[63] Spock provided some basic information about "puberty development in girls,"[64] but these facts of life would have been difficult for the great majority of 1950s dads to discuss with their daughters, let alone for the daughters to hear from their dads. And for the "psychological changes" that a teenage daughter might be going through, the best advice Spock offered dads of 1957 was to expect "tension" between father and daughter. The reason "why a daughter may be surprisingly antagonistic to her father at times" may be because of a "rush of strong feelings" toward her dad, but she "realizes subconsciously that this is not right." To compensate, she "covers up positive feelings with negative ones."[65]

TV dads of the 1950s

One of the most significant contributors to the idealized concept of American fatherhood in the 1950s was television. As soon as the war ended, electronics manufacturers retooled factories and resumed production of consumer goods, including television sets. (Figure 2.5.) The census reported that about 8,000

Figure 2.5 The number of American households with television sets rapidly grew from just over 8,000 in 1946 to more than 50 million by 1964. Product-sponsored programs and commercials reached a mass consumer market, encouraging the materialism and consumption that fueled the postwar economic boom. Ad, 1954.

households nationwide owned TVs in 1946, receiving programs from only 30 urban-based stations broadcasting limited programming just a few hours a day. By the last year of the postwar baby boom in 1964, the number of stations had increased to 582, broadcasting 18 hours a day, 7 days a week to 51 million households with TV sets.[66]

Television programs of the 1950s depicted white, middle-class fathers who were more than simply the family breadwinner and disciplinarian. Programs like *Father Knows Best* (1954–1960), *The Adventures of Ozzie and Harriet* (1952–1966), *Leave It to Beaver* (1957–1963), and *The Donna Reed Show* (1958–1966) presented family melodramas with "an emphasis upon the father as the validation for successful narrative resolution . . . Television dads are wise and funny, well-educated and nurturing, loving and demanding, omnipotent and omnipresent."[67] (Figure 2.6.) In addition, TV fathers were genuinely interested in what their children did at school and at play, what hobbies and pastimes they pursued, and what they might be feeling at any situation. TV fathers were usually at ease talking to their children about personal matters and often offered sage advice that helped solve concerns and issues. In fact, patriarchal fatherhood in these fictionalized households was the predominant masculine identity, even more so than that of breadwinner. Audiences never saw these men at their workplaces—only coming or going to work—and in some cases, never even knew what the father did for a living. These representations of what it meant to be a father had an audience of millions of viewers compared to only thousands that magazines and childcare guides might reach.

The presentation of the nurturing father in TV programs of the 1950s was the result of decisions by programming executives in collaboration with advertisers. TV programs followed the earlier radio programming models where a sponsor's control over production and content was almost absolute through the 1950s, ranging from script approval to set designs and product or logo placement in scenes and on the sets of live game shows and newscasts. Many sponsors even had their product names in the title of the program such as the *Colgate Comedy Hour* and the *Texaco Star Theater*. "How best to sell products was the primary concern."[68] Only after the quiz show scandals of 1958–1959 were networks able to gain full control of programming and establish the magazine revenue formula of selling to multiple advertisers per program.[69] Since the ideal target consumer group was the suburban nuclear family, programs were produced with the goal of presenting the white, middle-class family life that the sponsors and producers thought Americans would most like to emulate. "Television families were compelled both to ignore sexuality, bodily functions, and socially controversial or progressive attitudes and to promote morality, consumerism and patriotism."[70] Programs and advertisers also largely disregarded families of color, immigrant families, and poor inner-city and rural families. Despite the antiseptic, unrealistic dialogue and the orderly, well-scrubbed suburban homes depicted in family drama programs, millions of Americans viewed the weekly dynamics of these TV families with some degree of aspirational envy.

The film industry faced different methods and objectives than television broadcasting in the postwar years. Structural factors significantly impacted the viewing experience that seemed especially favorable to movies—big screen vs. small screen, color vs. black and white, high-fidelity sound vs. monophonic audio, less censored content vs. highly regulated content, an evening out at a theater vs. another night at home. Of special significance for movie studios was the 1952

Figure 2.6 Television programs of the baby boom era depicted the American dream invariably as white, middle-class families with a traditional breadwinner father, homemaker mother, and well-behaved children in their orderly, scrubbed suburban homes. Top, the Anderson family from *Father Knows Best* (1954–1960); bottom, the Cleaver family from *Leave It to Beaver* (1957–1963).

US Supreme Court decision in *Burstyn v Wilson*, which asserted that films were protected as free speech under the First Amendment to the Constitution, thus initiating the decline of the Hays Code of motion picture censorship.[71] Throughout the 1950s, movies gradually began to present more controversial themes that television could not even hint at, such as infidelity, divorce, drug and alcohol abuse, violent crime, teen pregnancy, abortion, prostitution, homosexuality, and politics. Nudity and profanity in films, presented with discretion and restraint, were increasingly common despite the protests of self-appointed watchdog and "decency" groups.

Yet, because of its mass reach, television supplanted movies as America's preferred entertainment medium. Television family programs were episodic in a continuing series, which allowed viewers an ongoing interest in the characters and storylines, whereas a movie was a complete entity that wrapped up in a couple of hours. Often family schedules included time set aside for certain days of the week and certain times of the day or evening for watching specific television programs. In some suburban communities, "the impact of TV is so concentrated that it literally affects everyone's life," reported *Harper's* in 1953. "Organizations dare not hold meetings at hours when popular shows are on. In addition, it tends to bind people together, giving the whole community a common experience."[72] Parents were comfortably certain that TV family melodramas would be nonthreatening and noncontroversial; and even without parental supervision, such programs were safe for children to watch. For movies, though, from the late 1920s into the 2000s, film producers and theaters continually struggled to develop and revise ratings and labels to guide moviegoers, particularly parents, about content.

Hollywood studios of the 1950s yielded the family hour to television broadcasting and instead primarily focused on the youth market and adult demographics. The father characters in movies were depicted very differently from television versions. TV dads seldom worked late and were usually home in time for dinner with the family each night. In the half-hour length of the program, TV dads dominated as the authoritative parent, joining in family celebrations or solving dilemmas. He distributed praise or guilt, arbitrated the children's disputes, and set the example for good moral behavior. His fatherly lectures or advice to the children carried a greater weight and commanded more respect than those from their mom. The title *Father Knows Best* said it all.

In family melodrama movies of the era, though, fathers were clearly the head of the family and necessary to the familial success but often were flawed and needing reform as a parent. In the course of the film's storyline, fathers had to learn lessons of parenting techniques that TV dads possessed inherently and demonstrated effortlessly. Movie fathers were usually the negative side of the positive presentation of TV dads. In films, the father often had failed as a parent and consequently created a family crisis. In her book *Living Room Lectures: The*

Fifties Family in Film and Television, Nina C. Leibman classifies 1950s movie storylines of father/child confrontation and resolution:

- "Materialism versus Love": The father's "substitution of material items or wealth for time and the expression of love." *Cat on a Hot Tin Roof* (1958), *The Long Hot Summer* (1958), *Hatful of Rain* (1957).

- "The Son as the Prize": The sons are viewed as mirrors of the fathers' successes and are pushed by the movie dads "toward some sort of goal, ignoring their sons' need for unconditional love." *Giant* (1955), *Peyton Place* (1957), *Splendor in the Grass* (1961).

- "The Father as Negative Moral Influence": The father is derelict as a role model because he is neglectful, self-absorbed, evil, weak, or overly macho. The resolution of the family crisis comes through a re-education of the father in which he comes to "recognize his moral responsibilities" as a parent. *Rebel Without a Cause* (1956), *A Summer Place* (1959), *All Fall Down* (1962).

- "Father is Too Strict": The fathers are depicted as unreasonably harsh or unresponsive to their children's needs. Confrontations that articulate the problem are not enough; instead, reconciliation requires a disaster and intervention by a third party. *East of Eden* (1955), *Tea and Sympathy* (1956), *The Young Stranger* (1957).

- "Father Needs a Wife": An unmarried father faces a parent/child crisis and decides to "remarry and reconstruct a secure nuclear family for his child." *Houseboat* (1958), *The Courtship of Eddie's Father* (1963), *The Parent Trap* (1961).[73]

Television presented to fathers of the baby boom years idealized representations of fatherhood—the patient, nurturing dad who regularly spent time with his children, listened to them attentively, cared about them as individuals, and provided wisdom and stability in their lives. For movie fathers who did not measure up to the same standards as TV dads, films depicted the consequences of failed parenting and offered narratives of familial restitution and reconciliation. But in reality, suggests sociologist Michael Kimmel, postwar American dads were hindered by an "institutional inflexibility" that prevented them from becoming the kind of fathers represented in TV family programs. In many corporate structures, men who left work early to attend school plays and recitals or little league games were viewed by bosses and coworkers as "less committed to their careers" and might find themselves "placed on a 'daddy track' from which there will be no advancement."[74] This institutional inflexibility was evident in the "combination of an unyielding workplace and an ideology of masculinity that promotes robotic stoicism over nurturing, competition over patience, aggression over justice." These characteristics of postwar masculine identity "contradict most with the qualities needed to be a good parent: patience, nurturing, emotional resilience."[75] For some fathers of the baby boom era, the role of nurturing dad was a rewarding masculine identity worth pursuing. For most, though, the role of family patriarch and breadwinner sufficiently defined them.

Conclusion

The years just after World War II were a period of adjustment for more than 16 million American veterans who returned to a much different country, hometown, and family than they left as new recruits. The military uniform that had defined their masculine identity during the war years now had to be packed away in trunks or closets. The civilian clothes they had left behind with mothers or wives no longer fit and were clearly out of style. The new postwar silhouettes of men's suit jackets and trousers and the new fabrics, textile prints, and color palettes of sportswear and accessories they found in department stores and mail-order catalogs were a distinct departure from what they had worn before the war.

More important than the new dress identities of postwar men were the new sociocultural identities of modern American manhood. The ex-soldier had to make the transition to civilian life quickly, and for some men, the adjustment was difficult. He was no longer the hero warrior in uniform, admired and celebrated for his self-sacrifice and duty. To help with the transition back to civilian life, the US government provided special services and benefits for the veteran through the GI Bill of Rights. He was allotted up to a year of unemployment compensation; up to four years of education benefits; and loans guaranteed by the Veterans' Administration for financing a home, farm, or business.

For most young veterans, one of their first goals was to get a job. As factories retooled and businesses expanded in the postwar years, America enjoyed a robust economic boom that would last for the following two decades. Although after the war, women initially faced layoffs and some companies implemented "marriage bars" to make way for returning veterans, the labor market grew quickly and jobs were soon plentiful.

With encouragement from government propaganda and with incentives for homeownership through VA home loan guarantees, millions of veterans also quickly got married and started a family. Popular culture, especially television programs and mass-market magazines, presented postwar couples with conventional ideals of the man as breadwinner husband and father and the wife as homemaker and mother. The traditional separate spheres of gender roles became as accepted for newlyweds from the late 1940s into the 1960s as they had been for their Depression-era parents and Victorian grandparents.

Along with the surge in marriages came a baby boom. Between 1946 and 1964, the US birthrate remained above 20 per 1,000 population before beginning a decline in 1965. Young fathers of the 1950s faced child-rearing challenges that their Depression-era fathers could not have imagined. Childcare guides advised baby boom fathers to go beyond the conventional gender role socialization of children and to enjoy playing games and sharing hobbies with their offspring. Television programs presented nurturing fathers who listened to their children and cared about what they felt and thought, often providing them with sage guidance and advice.

For millions of white middle-class couples in the postwar years, the road to the American dream of economic success and upward social mobility led to a home in one of the many new subdivisions that began to sprawl outward across the landscape surrounding cities. There, the breadwinner husband and father expanded his role to include that of the suburbanite. His masculine identity was expressed in his pride and bragging rights for the size and look of his home, landscaping, car, and homeowner possessions such as a power mower and backyard barbeque grill. His success as a suburbanite was further reinforced by his leisure-time accoutrements, ranging from his golf clubs to his specialty sportswear. Even the possessions of his children reflected on his success in achieving the American dream. Working hard and spending lavishly to keep up with, or outpace, the Joneses next door in acquisitions and home improvements defined his manhood.

3
THE MAN IN THE GRAY FLANNEL SUIT: CRISIS IN MASCULINITY

The feminization of American manhood

The masculine identities of the postwar American male discussed in the previous chapters—conformist breadwinner, nuclear family patriarch, nurturing father, suburbanite consumer—did not develop suddenly and fully mature immediately following the Second World War. The qualities that hallmarked the gender role orthodoxy of American manhood in this era had evolved through 150 years of significant social, economic, and political change. Beginning with the cataclysmic upheavals of the American and French Revolutions in the late eighteenth century, new ideas of masculinity emerged where patriarchal authority and socioeconomic power were no longer derived from a hereditary class system but rather were achieved by individualism, self-determination, and hard work. Through most of the nineteenth century, the masculine identity of the self-made man defined American manhood. But in the late 1800s, the socioeconomic changes wrought during the Second Industrial Revolution dramatically reshaped and redefined masculine identities in less than a generation.

Increasingly during the last quarter of the nineteenth century, men left farms and rural villages to work for wages in the burgeoning factories, service sectors, and offices in cities. The individualism and self-reliance that had defined the masculine identity of their fathers and grandfathers were replaced by subservience to a structured business or factory system. Instead of exercising autonomy and control of their time and labor, men became economically dependent on a company or business for a paycheck. This dependency was viewed by social critics of the time as a humiliating emasculation of the American male. Dependency was a feminine trait—wives, unmarried daughters and sisters-in-law, and children of a household were dependents.

The income-generating head of household also became a consumer, regarded as another feminine trait. In the early decades of the 1800s, consumption was largely woman's domain. The acquiring and purchasing of goods and services for the home, hearth, and family were within the feminine sphere. During this time, consumption was the precarious line that certain types of men might cross into effeminacy, notably the dandy. The mid-Victorian dandy was commonly regarded as effeminate not because he was perceived as exhibiting feminine characteristics later associated with the homosexual but because he was a flagrant consumer. The dandy's attention to current fashions and accessories and his keen interest in the tailoring and fit of clothes were viewed as an encroachment upon woman's domain. By the late nineteenth century, though, men who worked in cities ten to twelve hours a day, six days a week, looked to their homes and families as a refuge from the stress and stifling tedium of their jobs. Social history scholars consider this development as the emergence of "masculine domesticity" where "middle-class articulations of manhood became differentiated into two aspects—domesticity and breadwinning—that were both oppositional and mutually dependent."[1] The home, previously the exclusive domain of women for which men were simply permitted to pay the bills and occupy, now became a private space where men were free of the rigors and financial pressures of the public space of the workplace. In the mass-production and mass-merchandising world of the late nineteenth century, the home was filled with a wide variety of manufactured consumer products, many specifically selected by and for the man of the house.

In the post-World War II years, with the increase in homeownership in the rapidly expanding suburbs, domesticity became an even greater challenge to the American male's masculine identity than it had been for his grandfather. "The roles of male and female are increasingly merged in the American household," asserted *Esquire* in 1958; the suburbanite male is "changing diapers, washing dishes, cooking meals, and performing a whole series of what once were considered female duties."[2] (Figure 3.1.) Similarly, in 1954, *Life* magazine observed that the "new American domesticated male" actually enjoyed shopping for the home and "cannot resist a new can opener, iron, mixer, or screwdriver." In addition, when buying furniture for his suburban ranch house, "he is a tester, label reader and comparative shopper." He might even advise his wife on interior decorating since he works in modern city offices and "is more receptive to mobiles and functional furnishings than she is likely to be."[3] Not only was "performing" some household chores helpful to the wife and enhanced family cohesion, it was a counter to his

Figure 3.1 For many suburbanite men of the 1950s, enjoyment of homeownership also included "performing a whole series of what were once considered female duties," as *Esquire* magazine observed in 1958. A popular image in ads of the 1950s represented Dad in an apron preparing to feed the kids. Post ad, 1957; 7-Up ad, 1959.

workday stress of commuting, the tedium of corporate jobs, and so much time away from home and the family.

Yet, critics of the new masculine domesticity still regarded shopping for the home, backyard barbeques, comfortable armchairs in front of TVs, and similar homebound pursuits of the suburbanite male as feminizing. *Playboy* magazine was especially disparaging with editorials such as "The Womanization of America, An Embattled Male Takes a Look at What Was Once a Man's World" and "The Abdicating Male, and How the Gray Flannel Mind Exploits Him through His Women." For *Playboy*, this "deadly distaff of encroachment of what started as feminization . . . matured into wanton womanization."[4] And for those men who were "not skilled with home repairs or handy with tools"—in other words, unmasculine—he might even have to resort to calling a service repairman rather than tackling manly tasks himself. Such an option only added more stress and anxiety as the homeowner "fretted over the long wait before the craftsman could tackle the job and then fretted over the bill."[5] This weakening of the postwar American male through feminization or womanization caused a "loss of a sense of identity," concluded *Esquire,* which was "obviously a fundamental step in the decay of masculinity."[6] But for most suburbanite men, their domesticity did not undermine their ideas of manhood. Instead, fully enjoying their homes and families was very much a part of their masculine identity as homeowners, husbands, and fathers.

Conformity and Cold War masculine identity

One of the stereotypical masculine conditions of the postwar white suburban male was that of a conformist. From his "ticky-tacky" ranch house in suburbia to his drab gray flannel suit at work, American middle-class men appeared to embrace conformity en masse. This pervasive conformity was even more of a contributing factor to the era's sense of a crisis in masculinity than the feminizing influences of consumption and home life.

Throughout the 1950s, social scientists, economists, and journalists examined the causes of men's conformity and published their findings in critical assessments. In 1956, journalist William H. Whyte wrote of the men in the gray flannel suits as "the ones of our middle class who have left home, spiritually as well as physically, to the take the vows of organization life."[7] It was collectivism—a "belongingness"—rather than individualism that was thought to be the best course in postwar America to achieve the good life. The conformist masculine identity of the era seemed to close the book on the idea of self-reliant, independent men that had begun to erode in the late nineteenth century when they increasingly left their farms and rural way of life to work in city factories and offices. "An idea of individualism which denies the obligation of man to others is manifestly impossible in a society such as ours," continued Whyte. "The man of the future . . . is not the individualist but the man who works through others for others."[8] Likewise, for *Esquire* in 1958, this "cult of the group" was a significant factor in the "crisis of American masculinity" specifically because "we work and think and live and even dream in larger and larger units. . . not as an individual but as a member of a group."[9] And similarly, another observer of the mass conformity of the era was sociologist David Riesman, who suggested in his 1953 book *The Lonely Crowd* that the "other-directedness" of postwar men stemmed from an increased orientation to peer groups with their focus on consumption versus the "inner directness" of the earlier individualist man and his culture of production.[10] The conformist man's other-directedness, to Riesman, resulted in a masculine identity based on how men around him lived—their consumption of goods and services, and their work ethics, leisure pursuits, even their politics. By conforming to how others lived, the white middle-class suburban male could gain acceptance and approval but only by compromising autonomy.

Modern scholars have suggested that another cause for this pervasive white middle-class conformity of the 1950s was the US doctrine of containment of communism during the Cold War. Because Whyte, Riesman, and others who wrote of the American male's crisis of masculinity in the 1950s were contemporary to the emergence of the Cold War, they did not recognize the correlation between the suburbanite's containment in his modern subdivision and the era's national defense policies. Government propaganda, news reports and editorials, the Korean War, the McCarthy hearings, movies, and TV programming inundated Americans with a unified message that communism was the ultimate threat to peace, prosperity, and the American way of life. Containment of this threat, therefore, was worth the investment of blood and treasure by the United States. For the middle-class American man, the uncertainties of the Cold War heightened his insecurities and paranoia. Likewise, other social forces of the time outside of his white middle-class suburbia added to his anxieties: Black civil rights activism, anti-nuke peace advocacy, increasing numbers of married women in the workplace, and the much-publicized nonconformity of the Beats, beatniks, and other perceived sociocultural subversives. A remedy for the uncertainties generated in the Cold War era was his self-containment within his suburban home as head of his family far from the cities, which were assuredly targets of Soviet nuclear missiles. As Elaine Tyler May notes, "the home represented a source of meaning and security in a world run amok . . . The family seemed to be the one place where people could control their destinies and perhaps even shape the future . . . They may not have found the perfect contentment they hoped to realize in their comfortable suburban homes, but they had the best opportunity to pursue its promise."[11] Within the walls of his ranch-style house, the conformist American male's masculine identity was not in doubt or questioned where he was breadwinner, father, and head of household. The Cold War "provided a pronounced cultural emphasis on conventional domesticity as a pillar of American life."[12]

The stress of success

Once the postwar white middle-class male had achieved the American dream of a good job, marriage, children, and a suburban home, the pressure increased exponentially to continually improve his upward mobility. That meant moving to a larger house, getting a newer car and a second car for the wife, adding home improvements and better landscaping to one-up the Joneses next door, and upgrading the gray flannel suits from ready-to-wear to custom-made. It all required a bigger paycheck, regular salary raises, and annual cash bonuses. As Richard Gordon assessed in *The Split-Level Trap,* the suburbanite male of the 1950s "runs an endless race . . . His primary purpose in life is to get ahead . . . Success is defined as upward movement. Failure is defined not as poverty, not as losing one's shirt, but as lack of movement."[13]

William H. Whyte's analysis of the organization man suggested that the white-collar breadwinner could best get ahead in the postwar corporate world when "the manly virtues of individuality, autonomy, and entrepreneurship . . . were suppressed in favor of genial groupmindedness, consistency, and affable compliance."[14] Conforming to the culture of a company was expected of employees by the corporation, and for most white-collar men was understood as a job requirement. After all, since the majority of these men had gone from regimented schools as youths to the regimented military during the war, conformity to an organization system was a natural progression of life. Their Depression-era Middletown schools had taught them "the perpetuation of traditional ways of thought and behavior, the passing on of the cultural tradition, and, if need be, the securing of conformity by coercion." Middletown school children had learned from their parents, teachers, and community leaders that "hard work is the key to success" and that "one should try to get ahead of one's fellows."[15] Hence, upwardly mobile organization men of the 1950s knew that success could only be achieved by climbing the rungs of the corporate ladder, and those promotions were only possible through compliance with the corporate culture and exceptional job performance that the bosses would take note of. That upward climb often demanded working at the office late into the night and taking additional work home evenings and weekends. But a 60- or 70-hour workweek not only raised his stress levels but also cut into time he might prefer to spend with his wife and children, or pursue recreation or a hobby. This could lead to further stress from marital conflicts and children with behavioral problems.

Part of the drive for success, and another added stress, was fear on a variety of personal fronts. As Richard Gordon suggested in 1960, the suburban American male was "driven not only by the desire for success, but also by the fear of failure . . . to stand still while one's competitors forge ahead, to watch one's friends move away to bigger houses and more gracious living, . . . to see reproach in the eyes of one's wife and children."[16] Whyte similarly observed that the organization man worried that failing economically "does not threaten merely to rob a family of some luxuries; it threatens to take them away from a style of life. Suburbia does not condone shabby gentility."[17] The solution to the threat of failure was greater success at work, rung by rung up the corporate ladder. The American male "measures his own worth by the distance which he has progressed from his point of departure rather than by the position he occupies; he esteems high current income more than the possession of long accumulated wealth," assessed historian David Potter in 1954. "He is keenly aware of class distinctions and class levels, which are powerful realities in America . . . Mobility and change are natural products of his quest for success."[18] In 1960, Paul Newman portrayed investment broker David Eaton, one of these driven organization men, in the movie *From the Terrace*. At the end of the movie, Eaton is promoted to full partner in the firm, while he is still "on the sunny side of forty," as the chairman tells him at a board meeting. "You have dedicated yourself to your work with a devotion that might serve as an example to all young men who might aspire to success. You've sacrificed your own pleasures and pastimes for it . . . You have sat at your desk until 3 or 4 o'clock in the morning for it." In response, Eaton replies, "Like all well-brought-up American males, I have always been aware of the fact that nothing is more important in life than the attaining of wealth and high position. And I can honestly say that I have never allowed anything to sway me from my goal of achieving it." This assertion from Eaton receives nods of approval from the other partners in the boardroom. In a surprising conclusion, though, he speaks of the majority of American men whom these partners regard as "abject failures." "They take their place alongside the millions of mediocrities who value a house full of kids, a host of friends, photograph albums filled with trivial memories of all the truly important considerations of this world." (He then resigns and leaves his status-obsessed wife for his mistress and other "truly important considerations," becoming one of the "abject failures" he once disdained.)

These stresses of the constant need to excel in job performance coupled with conformity at the cost of individualism often resulted in anxieties, depression, and sometimes serious health issues. Throughout the 1950s, a new watchword in men's health was "stress." In 1956, Austrian physician and researcher Hans Seyle published *The Stress of Life,* in which he suggested that in its most extreme forms "psychological stress" could be a root cause for a variety of chronic illnesses and even actually lead to "sudden death."[19] White-collar organization men were warned that stress could contribute to the development of hypertension, heart disease, cancer, diabetes, or ulcers; psychological stress-related ailments might include depression, irritability, anger, sexual dysfunction, or more serious mental disorders. Key to stress management, suggested doctors and magazine articles, was to simplify one's life—to work less, take time off, and spend leisure time with the family. Since slowing the pace was not a realistic option for the ambitious, upwardly mobile breadwinner, the addition of health concerns only intensified his stress levels. Some men sought help with psychiatrists, even medication, which only seemed to be a further feminization of their manhood, not to mention an additional expense. Others exacerbated health risks through too much smoking and drinking as a way to deal with stress.

Noncomformist Beats, beatniks, and bikers

"Must you conform?" asked psychiatrist Robert M. Lindner in the title of his 1956 book. In postwar America, Lindner argued, "the rebel-nature of the individual is . . . twisted into the distortions of neurosis by pressures to conform." From birth, the American male is inculcated with the message "you must adjust." In school, children are not given the "tools of thought" but instead are "socialized, . . . regimented and made to conform." And the postwar college graduate is "a caricature of conformism" whose "opinions, attitudes, tastes and behavior are ultraconservative." Even so, continues Lindner, inherent in humans is an "instinct of rebellion," from which we can "change the environments and circumstances comprising the medium of both individual and social life . . . As a dimension of man, rebellion actually defines him."[20]

For some young people of the 1950s, rebellion was a hallmark of their lifestyle, philosophy, and work. The Beats especially were young nonconformist writers and intellectuals who gathered in the bohemian sections of New York and the West Coast to share ideas, debate politics, critique each other's work, collaborate on projects, and experience an America far removed from the white middle-class constructs of suburbia and corporations. The term "Beats" was adopted as an expression of their feelings of being beaten down, used, and marginalized by a "square" conformist society. Writers such as Jack Kerouac, Allen Ginsberg, Neal Cassady, and William S. Burroughs took their work to the gritty real world of coffee shops, jazz bars, loft parties, and art galleries where they read and performed to counterculture audiences of disaffected youths, petty criminals, street hustlers, drug addicts, and other downtrodden social outcasts. Through their poetry, writing, and lifestyles, the Beats "voiced a disaffiliation with the American mainstream, its conservative values and measures of success. In opposition to the materialism and prevailing standards that defined happiness as securing a place for oneself with the higher echelons of corporate America, the

Beats promoted a turning inward."[21] The Beats were not sociopolitical activists or protesters and never published manifestos or organized into a movement, but instead used their public appearances and writings to prod and offend status quo conformists. More than just opposing middle-class conventionality and materialism, and what they experienced as oppression and disapproval of their life ways by Main Street America, the Beats' vision was more about a personal, spiritual exploration of the well-worn paths of life through music, particularly jazz, uninhibited sex, and recreational drugs. They saw themselves as mystics seeking "spiritual regeneration through sensual experiences."[22]

As *Esquire* assessed in 1958, "Everywhere the Beat Generation seems occupied with the feverish production of answers—some of them frightening, some of them foolish—to a single question: how are we to live?"[23] The Beats achieved national notoriety in the late 1950s from the publication of two books by Beat writers. In 1956, the San Francisco publisher of Allen Ginsberg's poem *Howl* was arrested and charged with obscenity because the work contained profanity and references to homosexuality. The following year, a California court ruled that the book was not obscene and reaffirmed First Amendment protection for the freedom of expression in the arts. Mass-market magazines such as *Time* and *Life* featured reports on the trial, and suddenly, the literary works of the Beats were thrust before a national audience. The second book, and arguably the defining work of the Beats, was Jack Kerouac's *On the Road,* written in 1951 but not published until 1957. The book is a novel based on Kerouac's road trips with friends across America in 1947–1950 looking for adventure, life experiences, and "kicks." It became an instant bestseller and an inspiration to many of the young postwar generation who rejected the conformist conventions and repressive norms of conservative American society.

At the end of the 1950s, these young people who were influenced by the ideas of the Beats came to be labeled in mass media and pop culture as beatniks. The term was introduced by a San Francisco journalist soon after the Soviet Union successfully launched the first space satellite named Sputnik in 1957. The Slavic suffix "-nik" quickly became applied to a variety of other adjectives and names during the Cold War era, especially for subversive types who were thought to be affiliated with communism, such as "peaceniks" for antiwar demonstrators, "nogoodniks" for wastrels or scoundrels, and "chickniks"[24] for young urban women who dressed in beatnik styles of snug black pants or leotards, black oversized sweaters, black pencil skirts, leopard print accessories, and dark sunglasses. The beatniks were stereotyped in popular culture as young people who expressed their rebellion against the conformity and materialism of their middle-class parents by living in voluntary poverty with few possessions in inner-city slums. Much to the chagrin of the Beats, most Americans and journalists conflated the Beats and beatniks. "The Beats were serious, dedicated writers," but the beatniks were "considered more of a benign, adolescent fad."[25] In popular culture, the scary threat of the subversive, possibly communist-affiliated beatniks was replaced instead with a caricature of an idle, shabby young man playing bongos or reading poetry aloud in a smoky cafe. The comedic character of the beatnik was a subject of cartoonists ranging from animated cartoons such as Mr. Magoo to comic strips in *Mad* magazine, and culminated in the high school beatnik, Maynard G. Krebs, played by Bob Denver on the TV series *The Many Loves of Dobie Gillis* (1959–1963). (Figure 3.2.)

The linking of the Beats and the beatniks in the minds of most Americans was understandable, considering some of the common denominators the two subcultures shared. Both groups preferred jazz music to rock and roll, experimented

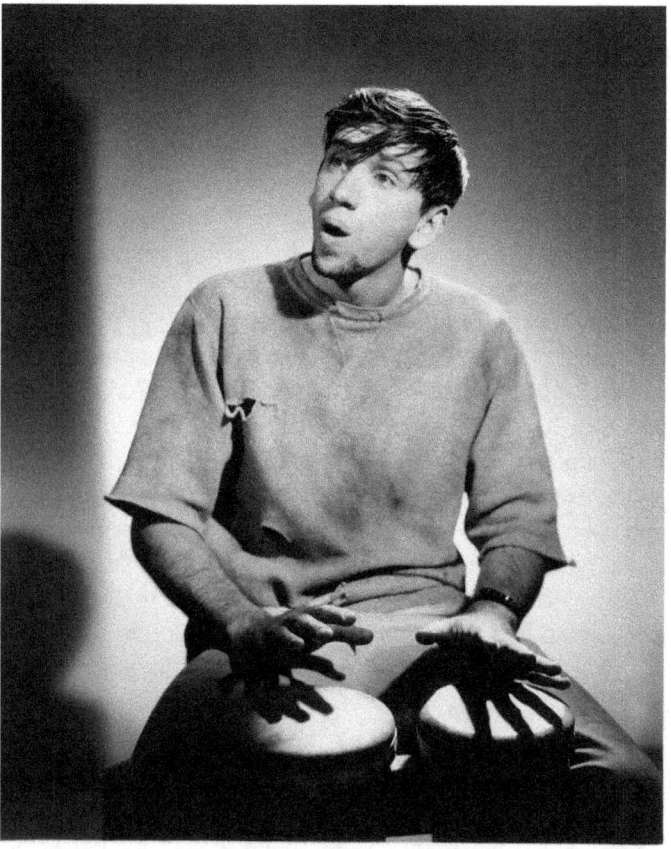

Figure 3.2 In the early 1950s, the most notable nonconformists were a group of young, urban writers and intellectuals called the Beats, whose lifestyles and writings rejected the materialism and conventions of American society. At the end of the decade, a counterculture of some like-minded rebellious youth came to be known as the beatniks. High school beatnik, Maynard G. Krebs, played by Bob Denver on the TV sitcom *The Many Loves of Dobie Gillis* (1959–1963).

with narcotics, and were careless about their appearance in public. The prevalent outward masculine identity of both groups was a comfortable casualness that exhibited a sharp contrast with the conformist organization man's gray flannel suit or his neatly pressed and coordinated weekend sportswear. The clothes of Beats and beatniks indicated no special thought given to fit, color coordination, modernity of style, or even recent laundering. Their well-worn beltless jeans and khakis, frayed plaid flannel shirts or faded chambray work shirts, knit pullovers in summer, and ratty sweaters in winter were worn in a negligent combination. The Beats were usually shod in dirty tennis shoes or scuffed, unpolished loafers; the beatniks often preferred sandals. Men of both groups also sometimes went unshaven for days or grew scruffy goatees to express a defiant contempt for men's conformist grooming standards of the 1950s.

For some beatniks, though, their masculine identity was a tribal uniform based on styles worn by Paris bohemians and West Bank artists. These costumed American wannabes dressed in all black accented with European touches such as berets and red neckerchiefs to imply communist sympathy. They wore dark sunglasses even indoors and at night and dangled a lit cigarette from a corner of the mouth.

Another postwar group of nonconformist social outcasts were motorcyclists or "bikers," who were "for the most part lost souls: disoriented and disillusioned WWII veterans, functioning alcoholics, unemployed factory workers, and a few rebellious teenagers, all of whom found solace in the radiated strength of big bikes." These marginalized young men, "feeling cast out of normal society, embraced the motorcycle not only as a recreational diversion but [also] as a weapon against the established order, a raucous, fire breathing barbarian of a contraption."[26] Numerous books on the subject of motorcycles make a distinction between bikers and motorcyclists. The 99 percent of motorcycle owners of the postwar years were ordinary middle-class men (and some women) who simply enjoyed riding whenever they could find the time. Bikers, though, were the 1 percent—outlaws and hellions who were often engaged in dangerous criminal activities, violence, and general mayhem. This reputation stemmed from a July 4, 1947, gathering of bikers in a small town in California, during which the bikers "terrorized its citizens, paralyzed its police force, and created an indelible image of outlaw bikers that would last for decades, perhaps even to this day."[27] The outlaw image gained mass notoriety a couple of weeks later when *Life* magazine featured a report on the incident, including a staged photo of a model appearing "drunk" astraddle a motorcycle with empty beer bottles strewn at his feet. "Police arrested many for drunkenness and indecent exposure, but could not restore order," sensationalized *Life*. The police chief declared the event as "one hell of a mess."[28]

In 1953, Hollywood used the story as a scenario for the movie *The Wild One*, reinforcing the rebellious, nonconformist cachet of the biker. (Figure 3.3.) The movie starred Marlon Brando as the leader of a one-percenter biker gang that

Figure 3.3 Another group of nonconformists in the 1950s were bikers, whose reputations ranged from hellions causing general mayhem to outlaws engaged in criminal activities. Marlon Brandon in *The Wild Ones,* 1953.

invades a small town where they cause accidents and destruction, and intimidate the townsfolk. The movie depicted the macho masculine identity and dress of the 1950s biker fairly accurately. The gang, called the Black Rebels, wore leather jackets screen printed on the back with their club "colors," meaning an emblem or logo, not hues. Their colors featured a large, stylized skull above crossed pistons resembling a pirate's flag. Among the more common colors of real bikers of the time (and since) was a "1%" or "1%er" of various type fonts in a diamond shape. The clothes of the gang were mostly well-worn jeans with long cuffs turned up several inches, crewneck T-shirts or sport shirts, and scuffed black work boots. None of the gang wore helmets, but some donned visored caps. A few of the members had not shaved in a few days, and Brando sported sideburns.

Playboys

As nonconformists, the Beats, beatniks, and bikers combined were a negligible sliver of postwar American society. They were easily identifiable by their dress and accoutrements, making them a containable threat to the American way of life. Beatniks were centered in bohemian urban settings such as Greenwich Village in New York or North Beach in San Francisco. They were seen as benign social objectors, not actually communist agitators or revolutionaries as sometimes portrayed in popular culture. Bikers made their presence known upon arrival anywhere through the noise of their vehicles, and local police and authorities could respond quickly. But a new nonconformist masculine identity of the era came to be regarded as far more threatening to social norms than beatniks and bikers—that of the playboy bachelor.

In the postwar years, US marriage rates spiked and men married younger and started families earlier than before the war. In this social environment, a bachelor beyond a certain age was viewed with suspicion. Something had to be wrong with a man who deliberately chose to remain unmarried. "Bachelors exhibited arrogance and selfishness, because they stubbornly refused to marry." They were regarded as "misfits, misanthropes who purposely rebuffed all civilizing influences, especially those virtues presumably instilled by the sacred institution of marriage." Or perhaps, confirmed bachelors "had no choice but to remain single because they were physically or psychologically unacceptable to women." Whatever the circumstances, bachelors were considered "useless to both family and society"; they "seemed to be individuals who had slipped their social mooring and were drifting in an open sea."[29] Furthermore, postwar single women were wary of the bachelor past his mid-twenties. As the *Ladies' Home Journal* warned women in 1951, the "perennial bachelor" was a "menace to happiness . . . He enjoys dating and may 'go steady' with one girl after another. Feminine companionship is essential to him—but he doesn't want to marry to get it." Not only does he monopolize a woman's time, but he also "prevents her meeting more desirable men," meaning husband material.[30] Even in popular culture, the idea of a bachelor of a certain age was a social curiosity worthy of a Hollywood comedy. In the 1948 film *Every Girl Should Be Married*, the theme throughout was actually every *man* should be married. Cary Grant plays a 30-something pediatrician who is targeted and stalked as a potential husband by Betsy Drake. At a women's club meeting where he is speaking, she stands to ask him:

> Don't you think there would be more of these happy marriages if some men didn't hang onto what they call their precious freedom so long as they close their eyes to everything else? Maybe if they'd let go, maybe they'd find they're in love with somebody and not even know it. Somebody who'd make them a wonderful wife and mother . . . Where would parents come from if every man made a lot of excuses and alibis just so he could go on living in a dumpy little apartment full of moose heads and punching bags and stuffed fish instead of accepting his responsibilities and having a nice little home somewhere?

In other words, Grant is irresponsible, or as he says later, "a villain," for remaining a bachelor rather than having achieved the masculine norms of a husband and a father.

In 1953, entrepreneur Hugh Hefner set about changing the negative perceptions of the American bachelor with the launch of *Playboy* magazine. "We aren't a 'family magazine,'" wrote Hefner in the introductory editorial of the first issue. Instead, "you will find articles, fiction, picture stories, cartoons, humor and special features . . . to form a pleasure-primer styled to the masculine taste."[31] Hefner challenged the broadly accepted domestic ideology of the conformist suburbanite breadwinner and head of a nuclear family by presenting an alternative masculine identity. "*Playboy* promoted an image of the young, affluent, urban bachelor—a man in pursuit of temporary female companionship and a good time, without the customary obligation of marriage or fatherhood . . . The magazine joined a broader chorus of anxiety and dissatisfaction voiced by both men and women over so-called traditional gender arrangements and idealized suburban life."[32] Part of *Playboy's* challenge to Cold War societal norms included frequent attacks on the social pressures to marry early, monogamous marriage, and sanctions against premarital sex.

In addition to advocating singlehood and sexual liberation for American men, *Playboy* "affirmed the centrality of consumption to postwar society, but in the guise of the well-heeled bachelor," making "the individual, rather than the family, its centerpiece."[33] To offset the complaint of many social observers of the era, such as William H. Whyte and David Riesman, that consumption feminized men, *Playboy* instead showed men how to be a consumer and yet retain a masculine identity. "We like our apartment. We enjoy mixing up cocktails and an hors d'oeuvre or two, putting a little mood music on the phonograph, and inviting in a female acquaintance for a quiet discussion on Picasso, Nietzsche, jazz, sex," avowed Hefner in his first editorial.[34] Recurring lifestyle features such as "The Playboy Advisor" included advice on gourmet food and fine dining, cocktails and mixology, music and entertainment, travel and exotic vacations, layouts of bachelor pads, upscale technology for the home, sports cars, and style advice and color charts for the latest men's fashions. Manufacturers and retailers targeting the playboy bachelor produced sophisticated ads that reinforced his goals of pleasurable consumption. (Figure 3.4.) Additionally, ad placement in the magazine followed the publishing model established decades earlier with women's magazines where ads were placed adjacent to articles relevant to the products. Through the editorials and reports on consumer goods combined with slick, alluring advertising, *Playboy* served as a consumer guide for hedonistic bachelors.

Playboy also jolted American society by providing a mass forum for open and informative discussions of male sexuality. When Hugh Hefner died in 1999, press and news headlines around the world referred to him as the "leader of the

Figure 3.4 The playboy of the 1950s was a young urban bachelor who preferred dating a variety of women and having a good time rather than conforming to an early marriage and a ranch house in suburbia. The bachelor's "pleasure primer" was *Playboy* magazine, as publisher Hugh Hefner called his publication when launched in 1953, that promoted the carefree masculine lifestyle. Ad, 1959.

sexual revolution." But Hefner helped popularize, rather than initiate, the sexual revolution, which arguably began with a research report published in 1948. As Hefner noted in *Playboy's* first-issue editorial in 1953, "We believe, too, that we are filling a publishing need only slightly less important than the one just taken care of by the Kinsey Report."[35] What Hefner referred to here was the best-selling book *Sexual Behavior in the Human Male* by social scientist and professor Dr. Alfred C. Kinsey. The Kinsey Report was a compilation of 15 years of research that challenged conventional understandings about men's sexuality, and included data on controversial topics such as infidelity and homosexuality. The book, and its counterpart *Sexual Behavior in the Human Female* released the same year *Playboy* was launched in 1953, became instant best sellers and opened discussions about sexuality beyond scientific circles. Kinsey's findings suggested that Americans engaged in a wider variety of sex and with greater frequency than traditionally believed. Some critics of the time challenged Kinsey's methodology while also recognizing Kinsey as "a pioneering scientific researcher in an age of moral hypocrisy, a tireless investigator of human desire and intimate behavior." On the other hand, moralistic critics viewed Kinsey's work as "unmistakably the most antireligious of the time. . . bent on shredding the moral fabric of the nation by wrecking the family."[36] Both sides of the Kinsey coin—a revealing report on the vitality and variety of American men's sexuality and a strike at moralistic hypocrisy—were admired and welcomed by Hefner and most *Playboy* readers. After all, they had grown up in the conservative 1930s, in which Victorian puritanism remained a core value of American society. Their Depression-era Middletown parents had instilled in them the religious axiom that "sex was given to man for purposes of procreation, not for personal enjoyment." Consequently, "sex is one of the things Middletown has long been taught to fear. Its institutions—with the important exception of the movies and some periodicals it reads, both imported from the outside culture—operate to keep the subject out of sight and out mind as much as possible."[37] But now, Hefner brought sex as entertainment, as a fun pursuit of the healthy, normal American male, into the public arena in a big way. And men, both single and married, increasingly became adherents to the magazine's influence and guidance. The first issue of the magazine sold out the full run of 53,000 copies, and by the end of the 1950s, circulation was more than a million per month.[38]

But unlike the broad variety of men's sexuality in the Kinsey Report, *Playboy* focused principally on the single, white heterosexual career man. The unmarried male in American society, though, had come under intense scrutiny in the early 1950s from politicians, mass media, and popular culture. The Lavender Scare (see next section) was a national hysteria about homosexuality that emerged in February 1950 with the first reports of purges by the US government. Because this antigay fervor went hand-in-hand with the era's anti-communist Red Scare, demagogues like Senator Joseph McCarthy made political use of the furor by conflating the communist and the homosexual as equal threats to national security. To offset any doubts or questions about the heterosexuality of bachelor readers of *Playboy*, Hugh Hefner began including photos of nude young women known as Playboy Playmates from the second issue on. "There's something wrong with some guy . . . who isn't interested in pictures of pretty girls," Hefner remarked in a 1957 interview.[39] The inclusion of the Playmate nude photos was an assertion that single men who read *Playboy* were unequivocally straight. Equally important to the magazine's editors, "the women that interested the playboy should not be seen as sexually delinquent or deviant, and certainly not as unfeminine."[40] Rather, the Playmates were portrayed as the pretty girl-next-door, and editors claimed they were not professional models but were "discovered talent" with a name and an everyday biography (both fake). Moreover, because the *Playboy* reader was presumed to be a cut above the ordinary American male in taste and income, the photos of the nude women were in color on glossy paper, including a foldout, as a contrast to the typical black and white photos in men's girlie magazines. Despite criticisms from religious groups and especially feminists about the nude photos, the magazine's quality of writing by big-name contributors such as Ernest Hemingway, Gore Vidal, Kurt Vonnegut, and Ian Fleming, among others, coupled with the high design and printing production standards gave *Playboy* an aura of respectability. Unlike the "dirty" pulp magazines of the era, which were hidden under the bed or in closets, *Playboy* was put on the coffee table. For visitors of single men, this display was an affirmation of his masculine identity as a straight, sophisticated American male.

"Lavender Lads"

The Lavender Scare was a national panic in the 1950s about homosexuals, commonly referred to as "perverts" or "deviants" in the press and sociopolitical dialogue of the postwar years. The use of lavender as a descriptive slur by journalists, police, and politicians was chosen because the soft, feminine color pink had been appropriated as a description for communist, as in "pinko."[41] David K. Johnson's study of the Lavender Scare details how the discussion of homosexuality came to be so prevalent in public conversation at the time. Between the conclusions in the 1948 Kinsey Report, which suggested a significant percentage of men engaged in same-sex sex of varying degrees, and the push by Republican politicians to find ways to undermine the Truman administration, the subject was frequently in the press and even on radio and television news programs, such as *Meet the Press*. Prior to the Kinsey Report, though, homosexuality was not a topic for polite society. Neither the 1929 nor the 1937 Middletown studies by the Lynds even mention the word "homosexual." Similarly, during the Second World War, when screening military recruits, induction medical examiners sometimes chose mental health terms such as "schizophrenic" or "psychotic personality" as the reason for a homosexual's 4-F rejection rather than branding the candidate with the label of pervert.[42]

But in the Cold War era, the idea of an overt, openly homosexual man was yet another aspect of the crisis in American masculinity. Ordinary people were suddenly confronted with a masculine identity they could not fully grasp. They wondered what had happened to American manhood where there could be a flourishing of such nontraditional masculine behavior. In 1956, psychiatrist Robert Lindner included an entire chapter on "homosexuality and the contemporary scene" in his book on conformity. "The plight of the homosexual in the modern world . . . is a phenomenon, affecting millions, that presents the major contentions of our era in the clearest possible terms. It relates directly to the basic issue of man versus society, of individualism versus conformity." From Lindner's "scientific" perspective, the question of nature versus nurture was fundamental—"the annoying issue of inversion as an innate disposition, as an inborn deviation . . . given at birth" was an "absurd notion." Instead, the answer was not in genetics but rather solely with a child's upbringing by "sex-distorted elders." With that as a given among those in the field of psychology, a man burdened with homosexuality could be "amenable to treatment" with "the hope it can be eradicated." Discredited in the twenty-first century as "reparative" or "conversion therapy," the suggestion in the 1950s that a man could reject his homosexuality, but chose not to, contributed to the "hostility for the invert and his way of life and the same abhorrence of him as a person that have been traditional in Western society."[43]

The public discussions about homosexuality in the Cold War era were kept at a fever high by politicians and religious leaders. In 1950, a senate committee headed by North Carolina Democrat Clyde Hoey was charged with the task of investigating the security risks of homosexuals in government. Conducted in closed-door sessions, the committee interviewed psychiatrists, military and government agency officials, local police, and security experts. After months of hearings, not a single instance was found where a homosexual had provided state secrets to a blackmailer. Nonetheless, the final Hoey Report asserted that "sex perverts are not proper persons to be employed in government for two reasons; first, they are generally unsuited, and second, they constitute security risks." The unsuitability was explained with several assertions:

- "It is an accepted fact among intelligence agencies that espionage organizations the world over consider sex perverts who are in possession of or have access to confidential material to be prime targets where pressure can be exerted."

- "Persons who indulge in such degraded activity are committing not only illegal and immoral acts, but they also constitute security risks in positions of public trust."

- "Aside from the criminality and immorality involved in sex perversion such behavior is so contrary to the normal accepted standards of social behavior that persons who engage in such activity are looked upon as outcasts by society generally."
- "There is an abundance of evidence to sustain the conclusion that indulgence in acts of sex perversion weakened the moral fiber of an individual to a degree that he is not suitable for a position of responsibility."
- "Another point . . . is his tendency to gather other perverts about him."[44]

The greater part of the report dealt with the criminality of same-sex sex—statutes, prosecution, penalties, arrest records—and for the most part, ignored the mental disorder aspect. Considering the number of psychiatrists and other medical professionals who testified before the committee, the notion of homosexuality as a disease was a missed, logical reason for excluding gays from government service. After all, homosexuality would remain on the list of clinical mental disorders by the American Psychiatric Association until 1973. Even disregarding the mental health angle, with the imprimatur of the US Congress, the widely distributed 26-page report was regarded as an official fact and became the go-to source for excluding homosexuals from government work on any level.

With ever-increasing press coverage and exaggerated editorials and scandal stories through the first half of the 1950s, ordinary Americans came to link homosexuals with communism. It was an idea that was easier to understand than psychiatric or legal jargon. Homosexuals could be recruited by communists through blackmail. Homosexuals were thought to be sympathetic to communism since the ideology advocated a classless society where everyone was equal, and the homosexual was presumed to be allowed the same social standing as a straight, married man. The press and politicians' speeches fueled public fear that homosexual men had infiltrated the US government along with hundreds of communists. In the minds of most Americans, that meant all homosexuals were a potential recruitment target for Soviet spies, making the gay man subject to manipulation or blackmail. By the mid-fifties, Eisenhower's Bureau of Security increased investigations and purges of homosexuals from governmental agencies, and expanded the witch hunts into private industries that had contracts with the US government. Even straight, married men who associated with gay men in any way came under scrutiny from the zealotry of investigators.

But even if the gay man was not a likely candidate for communist recruitment, he was nonetheless still considered a menace to society. He was a criminal by law nationwide, mentally ill by medical science, and a sinner by religious dogma. In the 1950s, the homosexual joined the list of those who were regarded as the "other," along with Jews, Catholics, immigrants, racial minorities, and most other non-WASPs. Then, too, there was the threat that the homosexual could "turn" straight men gay. "These perverts will frequently attempt to entice normal individuals to engage in perverted practices," speculated the Hoey Report.[45] This myth persisted for decades among the medical professionals. For example, during the Peacock Revolution of the 1960s, psychiatrist Robert Odenwald asserted that young men's long hair and colorful, sexualized clothing caused the "inevitable result" of "a definite increase in the number of homosexuals in the United States."[46] These episodes of antigay hysteria would erupt every few years with the same arguments and furor of the 1950s Lavender Scare, but with new demagogues making headlines ranging from a former beauty pageant contestant to the usual politicians.[47]

Yet, even as the Lavender Scare reached a fevered pitch in the early 1950s, an embryonic gay rights movement began to emerge in the postwar years. In 1951, sociology professor Edward Sagarin published *The Homosexual in America: A Subjective Approach* (under the pseudonym Donald Webster Cory). Sagarin informs the "uninitiated reader . . . that homosexuals are called *gay,* heterosexuals *straight*." Further, he suggests that "homosexuals are a minority group" since they "are constantly aware of something that binds them to others and separates them from the larger stream of life." Even so, they are

> a group without a leader, without a publication, without an organization, without a philosophy of life, without an accepted justification for its own existence . . . Seldom has anyone ever told the sociologists, the legislators and judges, the novelists and psychiatrists—except in confidential conversations that can never become part of the public domain—what it feels like to be a homosexual, living with a constant awareness of the existence of something inescapable, and how this affects every aspect of life, here, today, now, in the middle of the twentieth century in America.

As a gay man, Sagarin understands and deeply feels this assertion. He cites the findings of the Kinsey Report, published in 1948, and determines that if the "conservative estimate of 5 per cent [of men in America being homosexual] is taken, then the three million mark is reached." From this premise, he questions why gays should not serve in the military, and he even explores the ideal of gay marriage.

> Millions cannot be excluded from government and private employment, from participating in the armed forces, from educational opportunities, without creating a social problem of major dimensions . . . In the millions who are silent and submerged, I see a potential, a reservoir of protest, a hope for a portion of mankind. And in my knowledge that our number is legion, I raise my head high, and proclaim that we, the voiceless millions, are human beings, entitled to breathe fresh air, and enjoy, with all humanity, the pleasures of life and love on God's green earth.[48]

It was a sentiment and a challenge that was heard by homosexuals all across America, especially on the West Coast, where a group of gay intellectuals and activists began to organize the potential and reservoir of protest that Sagarin anticipated.

In 1951, a group of gay men met in Los Angeles to establish a discussion group to talk about their personal experiences in an oppressive society. After a few meetings, they decided to name the group the Mattachine Society, a term based on a medieval Dance of the Fools (Les Mattachine) held during a French spring festival. Costumed, masked dancers would speak truth to the king and the church, questioning laws and challenging their oppression by the elites. "Thus the pyrrhic mime of Les Mattachine portrayed in vivid drama, for all to understand and take courage from, the ancient imitative ritual of initiation made militant and political—that the lowly and oppressed would rise again from their despair and bondage by the strength of *their own faith* and *their own self-created dignity*."[49] The group and later subsidiaries in eastern cities were careful to refer to their organization as "an educational and research endeavor," not a club or activist group that might draw a raid from the vice squad or investigation by the FBI. Despite Sagarin's assertion that homosexuals were a distinct minority group, the Mattachine Society mission initially was "the integration of gay men and lesbians into mainstream society" for "eventual acceptance, not separation in any form—as a cultural minority or a political force."[50] Yet, by its nature, the Mattachine Society was proof of a cultural minority, even if not yet a political force.

Although the Mattachine Society and other early gay advocacy groups of the 1950s and 1960s avoided activism, protests, and public confrontations that later would hallmark the gay rights movement of the 1970s, the Society achieved two landmark milestones with the launch of its monthly magazine *ONE: The Homosexual Viewpoint* in 1953. First, this publication answered Sagarin's complaint that American homosexuals were "without a publication, without an organization, without a philosophy of life, without an accepted justification for its own existence." Second, although the magazine was careful to avoid erotic content, the US Post Office seized all issues once in 1953 and again in 1954 on grounds of obscenity. The publishers took the Post Office to court. Simply because the content was about homosexuality, the federal district court judge, followed by the Ninth Circuit Court of Appeals, ruled against the magazine. In January 1958, though, the US Supreme Court reversed the rulings of the lower courts (without comment). The magazine immediately published an editorial declaring, "By winning this decision ONE magazine has made not only history but law as well and has changed the future for all U.S. homosexuals. Never before have homosexuals claimed their rights as citizens. ONE magazine no longer asks for the right to be heard; it now exercises that right."[51]

Conclusion

Following the Second World War, journalists and social scientists began to assess what they perceived as a crisis in masculinity for the American male. During the previous couple of generations, a redefinition of manhood had developed in which the ideas of individuality and self-determination of earlier generations were replaced by a standard of conformity, consumption, and complacency. Beginning at the end of the nineteenth century, urbanization and industrialization increasingly brought men from farms and rural craft workshops to cities to work in regimented factories, service sectors, and offices. Instead of autonomy and independent control of their time and labor, men became economic dependents of companies and businesses. In addition, because these city workers no longer crafted items for themselves, their homes, and their families, they became consumers of the mass-produced goods of the rapidly expanding Second Industrial Revolution. For the generations of American men over the previous two centuries, dependency and consumption were women's traits. For modern man, they were regarded as emasculating influences.

Through the first half of the twentieth century, men's sphere evolved into a masculine domesticity that combined the traditional roles of breadwinner and patriarch with his interests in his suburban home. Critics referred to his pursuits of materialism and consumerism to make his private space ideal for himself and his family as the feminization, or womanization, of American manhood, further adding to the idea of a crisis in masculinity.

For the postwar white middle-class man who had achieved the American dream of a good job, marriage and children, and a ranch home in suburbia, the stress of success led to another aspect of the crisis in masculinity. To climb the corporate ladder, and hence be able to move to a bigger house in a better neighborhood, and consume more and more, he had to conform to what social critics of the time like William H. Whyte called a genial like-mindedness, and *Esquire* called a "cult of the group." This conformity to the culture of a company required him to compromise his autonomy, the legacy of the pioneering spirit of individuality of his ancestors. In addition, the need to excel in the workplace demanded time away from his family, whether overtime at the office or bringing work home for evenings and weekends, which caused marital problems or misbehavior from the children. As a result, increased stress from the job and family strife often led to serious health issues. Hence, the loss of patriarchal control at home and the weakening of manliness by ailments all contributed to the crisis in masculinity for the postwar American male.

Adding to the crisis in masculinity for American men was the notoriety of certain nonconformists. The aggressive individuality of the Beats, beatniks, bikers, bachelor playboys, and even homosexuals was a sharp contrast to the conventional manhood of the conformist suburbanite. The Beats were writers who expressed their ideology of nonconformity in best-selling books, public performances, and interviews. The beatniks were stereotyped in American popular culture as rebellious youth rejecting the conventions and conformity of their elders. Bikers embraced their image of outcast nonconformists without apology. Playboy bachelors flouted the social norms of marrying young and monogamy by emphasizing singlehood and indulging in sexual freedom and pleasurable consumption. And homosexuals shockingly began to come out openly and challenge antigay laws and policies in government, religious bigotry, and society's opprobrium.

The solution to the crisis may have seemed simple enough to critics—regain individuality. "For men to become men again," advised *Esquire* in 1958, "their first task is to recover a sense of individual spontaneity . . . A man must visualize himself as an individual apart from the group." To achieve this, the American male should develop a "disdain for existing values and goals, a reaching out for something more exacting and more personal, an intensified questing for identity."[52] For the most part, though, the men of the 1950s were not willing to attempt such a radical departure from well-established norms and comfortable conventions. But ironically, their baby boom children took up that challenge when they came of age as the youthquake generation in the 1960s.

4
MEN'S DRESS FROM IVY LEAGUE TO CONTINENTAL TO MOD

Ivy League style

With the end of wartime rationing of materials used in clothing production and textile mills roaring back to full production, men's wear makers introduced new, fuller cuts and shapes of suits, sport jackets, and outerwear. The athletic Superman silhouette of the padded, drape cut jacket that had prevailed since the late 1920s through the war was replaced around 1947 with a loose-fitting, straight-hanging style made with natural shoulders and wide lapels. Trousers were likewise more capacious, and pleats were revived. The new suit style came to be called the Ivy League look because it was quickly adopted by collegians and young college-graduate businessmen. (Figure 4.1.)

In November 1950, *Esquire* referred to the significant change in men's suits as a "fashion tornado" featuring "that comfortable, custom look that you've been waiting for in your apparel: straight-hanging lines; restrained colors; . . . narrower shoulders." The Ivy League suit was "a strictly new and masculine" look "to make a man look taller, trimmer, and always in perfect taste."[1] The natural shoulder was key to the Ivy League style, from which the tubular cut could hang. Jacket lapels initially continued the broad, rolled spread through the late 1940s, with peaked styles extending outward almost to the sleeve, but around 1953, lapels narrowed and lay flat, emphasizing the natural shoulder. By then, the Ivy League suit was described in the press as the "new male uniform."[2] The "Ivy Cult," as *Men's Wear* called it, "made men 3-button-, vent-, lap- and [pocket] flap-conscious."[3]

Figure 4.1 The men's Ivy League suit featured a boxy, straight-hanging jacket with natural shoulders and wide-legged, pleated trousers. In the mid-1950s, the jacket became trimmer with narrowed lapels, but remained shapeless, and trousers were more slim. The Ivy style endured as the corporate man's uniform from the late 1940s through the mid-1960s. From Montgomery Ward: left, 1950; right 1956.

The preferred color for the Ivy League suit was gray. In 1951, *Esquire* recommended that every man should have a gray suit. "Gray has a knack of giving you assurance, a manner that can best be described as satisfying and if you are pleased with yourself, the rest comes naturally." Gray, in its various shades, was an optimal suit color for men of all hair colors—blonde: blue gray; dark brunette: dark gray; brown: mid-tone gray; red: gray or grayish-brown. Only the "doctor, lawyer, business chief" with gray hair might opt for dark blue instead.[4]

The somber gray Ivy League suit was so ubiquitous as the representative of white, middle-class masculine identity in the 1950s that it inspired the best-selling novel *The Man in the Gray Flannel Suit* by Sloan Wilson (1955). The title character was a suburbanite family man who was discontented with his work and was constantly nagged by his wife to make more money to improve their social mobility. The title became symbolic in American popular culture for compromised manhood—the stodgy, conformist corporate man who lacked imagination and was content with the herd mentality at work and with the staid social conventions of suburban married life.

Usually overlooked by the fashion press and retail copywriters of the 1950s was the change in men's trousers for the Ivy League suit. The narrow wartime L-85 leg widths of 18 1/2 inches expanded with the Ivy style to a billowing 25 inches at the knees with a slight taper to 23 inches at the cuff.[5] The waistband remained high at just above the navel, and pleats and cuffs were once again permitted, adding to the fullness and straight-hanging volume that complemented the cut of the Ivy League jacket.

Continental suits

In the mid-1950s, American men's wear began to be influenced by Italian styles. In the years just after the war, tourists flooded into Italy, which had escaped much of the devastation suffered by most of Europe. In Milan, Naples, and Rome, visitors found an abundance of luxury items, especially exceptional leather goods and clothing of fine wool and sumptuous silk fabrics, while Paris and London still struggled with shortages and lingering rationing. Equally important, Italian designers, tailors, and craftsmen produced high-quality fashions and accessories that cost a fraction of similar items north of the Alps or in America. In addition to word-of-mouth from tourists bringing home Italian-crafted goods, trade shows throughout Italy in the early 1950s gained notoriety in the international fashion arena. In 1952, Italy's first Men's Fashion Festival was held in San Remo, on the Italian Riviera near Monaco, and made headlines in the global fashion press.

The influence of Italian style on American men's fashion had actually come full circle. Before the war, Benito Mussolini and fascist nationalists advocated simplicity and austerity in men's clothing, especially shapeless garments made from coarse, Italian-made fabrics. But during the Allied occupation and years just after the war, streets were filled with tall, youthful American GIs and college students, striding with a "rolling gait" and "a certain swagger" in their L-85 khakis and jeans.[6] Italian tailors and ready-to-wear makers quickly adopted the American styles of trim, plain-front, cuffless pants as a modern break with their prewar fascist past. This sexualized masculine identity especially complemented the machismo of Italian men.

The Italian styling of American men's suits, introduced in the 1956–1957 season, came to be known as the Continental look. The new silhouette featured a jacket length about an inch shorter than Ivy styles, natural shoulders, high-cut armholes, a rounded cutaway skirt front, angled besom or welt pockets, and a two-button closure. Some were without the chest pocket. The jacket was trimly shaped with a suppressed waist at the side seams and darts in the front. (Figure 4.2.)

Figure 4.2 In the second half of the 1950s, young men's suits were influenced by Italian styles and came to be called the Continental look. Jackets were cut with a tapered waist, shortened skirt with a pronounced rounded opening, and narrow lapels. Trousers were slim with an unpleated front. Left, shawl collar Continental suit from Andrew Pallack, 1959; right, Continental suit from GGG Clothes, 1959.

Sleeves tapered to the wrists, some with narrow cuffs piped around the seams to stand out. Trousers were without pleats and cuffs, and trimmed to about 20 inches at the knees, tapering to 17 inches at the cuffs.[7] Pockets were often angled and set forward. Men's magazines such as *Esquire* and the newly launched *GQ (Gentleman's Quarterly)* as well as tailors' guides repeatedly provided comparison descriptions and graphics of the Ivy versus Continental styles between 1956 and 1958.[8] American suit makers introduced the new silhouette not as a replacement for the Ivy League style but, instead, as an alternative look for a specific segment of consumers. Young, hip men who worked in New York's uptown ad agencies of Madison Avenue adopted the Continental suit, while men in the downtown Wall Street brokerages continued the gray flannel Ivy tradition.

By the end of the 1950s, *GQ* observed that the Continental suit was sufficiently well established for American suit makers to "experiment with its basic design," such as a three-button closure and a double-breasted style.[9] The "Jivey Ivy" suits[10] combined various elements of Continental and Ivy League looks for the college graduate who wanted to enter the corporate world but not dress like his dad. Three- and four-button closures were adapted to the Continental from the Ivy look, and Ivy pocket flaps were applied to the Continental angled pockets. Some Jivey jackets even added a second, smaller "ticket pocket," also angled, on the right hip. Similarly, some variants of the straight-hanging Ivy jacket were constructed with a slightly suppressed waist and a two-button closure while retaining the longer Ivy skirt and were paired with trim, plain-front, cuffless trousers—a look preferred by President Kennedy. More extreme experiments with the Continental suit included the unconventional jacket by Andrew Pallack shown in Figure 4.2, which was made with a "hidden front button closure," a shawl collar, and side vents, and came in "daringly bright" colors such as gold, periwinkle blue, plum red, burro tan, and olive.[11] Such styles on the cusp of the 1960s forecast the designs that were beginning to transform men's wear in Britain and would hallmark the mod styles just a few years later.

Accessories

The change in men's suit styles from the athletic drape cut of the war years to the straight-hanging Ivy League styles of the late 1940s was a dramatic shift in the dress of American men. The transitioning new silhouette was declared "The Bold Look" by *Esquire* in 1948. An illustration of a man in a transition suit and Bold Look accessories included a red-letter header: "*Here's a Man—with the Bold Look!*" As *Esquire* explained, "The Bold Look is the first real new-from-the-ground-up note in men's clothes since pony-express days." The new postwar suits and accessories

> used big patterns, bold colors, more colors—but none of them go overboard in the matter of color or design. And each accessory is related to the outfit as a whole . . . There's a definite relationship between these accessories—they're selected not just for their own sakes but because of the way they complement each other. That's important, because the Bold Look isn't just a shirt or a necktie or a hat—it's in the complete overall appearance.[12]

The postwar Bold Look in men's wear was reported by *Esquire* through several issues of 1948 and 1949 and picked up in headers and sales copy by men's ready-to-wear and accessory makers.

The business shirts that were developed for the Bold Look featured subtle but distinct construction differences from previous styles rather than new colors or fabric patterns. An ad for the Whitney brand shirt by Wachusett in 1948 defined the "Bold Look" of their styles as "the first new shirt fashion in years; widespread, stayed collar, bold stitching set a half-inch in from the edge, bold center pleat, bigger ocean pearl buttons, [and] longer, wider French cuffs."[13] Called

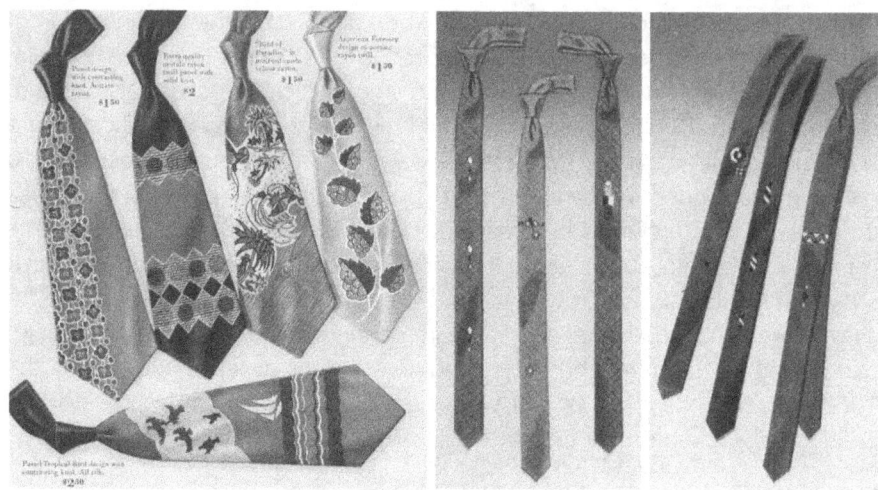

Figure 4.3 Among the more dramatic changes in men's fashions of the 1950s were neckties. The "Bold Look" of the late 1940s and early 1950s included 4-1/2-inch-wide ties in vibrant colors and patterns. In the second half of the 1950s, the skinny necktie of about 2 inches at the tip complemented the trim, youthful Continental suit. Left, acetate rayon ties from Cheney Cravats, 1949; right, embroidered mohair ties by Wembley, 1958.

a "command collar" by *Esquire*, the points were 3 1/2 inches long and could be sharply pointed, rounded, or button-down, so long as the spread was wide enough for a Windsor knot and the stitching was distinctly a half-inch from the edge.[14]

By the mid-1950s, though, as the gray flannel Ivy League suit became the masculine identity of conformist corporate men, the Bold Look was discarded in favor of ordinary white dress shirts. About the most radical the corporate man might venture was a short-sleeved white shirt in summer—a shirt style that had been introduced to his grandfather around 1905.

The key accessory for the Bold Look was the necktie. As they had been since the plain white cravat was replaced by colorful and patterned neckwear in the 1830s, ties (along with vests) were the best options for men to express a bit of individuality and personal style when wearing a suit. Not since the Jazz Age of the 1920s had the colors and designs for men's ties been as exuberant as styles of the late 1940s into the early 1950s. (Figure 4.3.) For a few seasons at the end of the forties, a popular Father's Day gift was the vividly hand-painted tie, especially depictions of tropical sunsets and hunting scenes. As *Esquire* suggested in 1951, "If you've an overwhelming urge to toss caution to the winds, express it in your tie."[15] Blades of the four-in-hand ties were a broad 4 1/2 inches wide at the flared end until around 1952, then narrowed to 3 1/2 inches where they would remain as the conservative Ivy League standard through the late 1960s. Bow

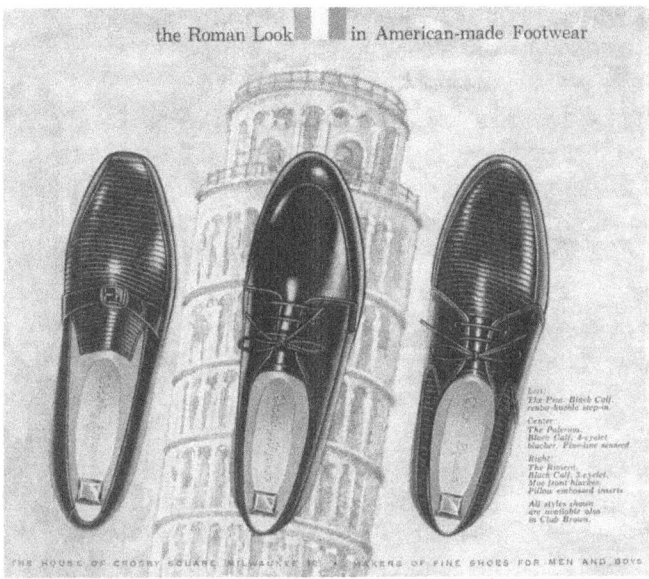

Figure 4.4 Men's footwear of 1950s was influenced by Italian styles, including the new squared toe for the Continental suit. "The Roman Look" in men's shoes from the House of Crosby Square, 1959.

ties were a slim 1 3/4 inches wide and, although colorful, were too narrow for the types of Bold Look designs and patterns of the broad four-in-hand ties.

With the introduction of the slim, fitted Continental suit in 1956, some varieties of neckwear were trimmed to a narrow 2 to 2 1/2 inches at the flared tip to complement the look. Colors remained vibrant, but patterns and prints were reduced in scale, such as the embroidered examples in Figure 4.3. For sport coats, straight skinny knit ties with a squared end were revived from the 1920s and favored by teens. In a cross-over influence at the end of the 1950s and into the early 1960s, collegians adopted the skinny tie for their Ivy League suits. Older men continued to prefer the traditional tie width of 3 1/2 inches.

Men's shoes of the 1950s were largely the same shapes and designs of prewar styles. The Bold Look required men to think about the colors of shoes and socks as part of the whole outfit. Perforated wingtips and medallion tips were in keeping with the bold statement of style. The thick-soled constructions of the war years, for longer-lasting wear, continued through the late 1940s. Italian influences revived sleek pointed-toe footwear in the 1950s. For Continental distinction at the end of the decade, the toe tips were bluntly squared. (Figure 4.4.)

Socks, too, took on new importance with the Bold Look. Vertical ribbed and all-over knit textures were popular, but especially distinctive were socks with decorative clocking down the ankles. For color, the two options remained as always with men's hosiery—harmony or coordination. For harmony, a color of the same palette as the trousers ensured a continuous visual line to the shoe. For coordination, the color of the socks could be a sharp contrast with the trousers but coordinate with the color of the tie or pocket square.

Even the Bold Look made little allowance for men's jewelry, the extent of which largely included only a wristwatch, wedding band, tie clip, and possibly cuff links. Minimal and subtle were the watchwords for men's jeweled adornment through the 1950s. The flashiest piece of jewelry for the man in the gray flannel suit was likely a wristwatch with a wide gold-tone or silver-tone bezel and metal-link bracelet band. For evening wear, a matched set of jeweled tie clip and cuff links might be dared.

Men's hats of the postwar years continued the styles of the 1930s. The wide-brimmed fedoras and porkpies were preferred for business suits and casual sport coats. With the popularity of the trim Continental suit in the second half of the 1950s, hats were pared down as well. The 1959 telescope crown fedora was lower than the earlier pinch-front style, and angled more to the back. Continental brims were narrowed to about 2 1/8 inches from the 3-inch widths of 1950. Beginning in the early 1960s, though, young men increasingly began to appear outside without a hat, following the look of the newly elected president John F. Kennedy, who had often campaigned bareheaded. The fashion press and especially hat makers and retailers took note of the influence of Hatless Jack, as the president was dubbed. "While people love Mr. Kennedy, they are not all following his headwear example," *Men's Wear* declared wishfully in 1962.[16] Retailers understandably advocated for the hatted man. "Men should learn that their wardrobe is incomplete without a hat," recommended an Oregon men's wear shop owner in 1964. "Put one on their head when they stand in front of the fitting mirror. If they see themselves this way often enough, they won't feel right bareheaded."[17] Even scare tactics were attempted in editorials, asserting, "Going hatless does NOT help the hair. Going hatless is actually DAMAGING to the hair and its growth" (from dust, soot, and exposure to the sun).[18] Nonetheless, the youthful style influence of the president and the arrival of the youthquake in the mid-sixties ended the centuries-old masculine hatted tradition.

Sportswear

The cuts of Ivy and Continental suits had cross-over impacts on men's sportswear in the 1950s. The sport jacket was a popular alternative to the business suit for casual occasions where a tie might be worn, such as cocktail parties, travel, or spectator events. By the end of the 1950s, sport jackets were available in both the straight-hanging Ivy League and the trim, shaped Continental styles. Both varieties of sport jackets were made in striking colors and textile patterns, particularly madras plaids, providing men with a bit of personal expression in dress compared to the banal ubiquity of the gray flannel suit. In addition, sport jackets made of imported nubby silk became a trend in the late 1950s. (Figure 4.5.) Previously associated primarily with women's clothing, silk for men's sport coats and sport shirts was promoted in the fashion press and advertising as a fresh, modern masculine look. For example, a 1958 ad from the International Silk Association asserted, "Silk leads a man's life . . . He relaxes in silk sportswear, cuts a dashing figure in the very new odd jacket of silk tweed with a bulky or smooth texture, and makes a confident entrance by night in silk dinner clothes."[19]

Although Ivy suit jackets and sport coats of the early 1960s still hung loosely from natural shoulders, trousers were now cut with trim, narrow legs that tapered to about 15 1/2 to 16 inches at the cuff.[20] The slim cut of trouser legs "would have made dandy thermometer cases," complained an old-school editor in 1962.[21] The waistband of young men's trousers was also lowered about 2 1/2 inches on the hips compared to ordinary men's trousers.[22] These Italian influences of the trim cut and lower waistline were especially evident in the increasingly snug fit of young men's casual slacks. In 1962, Levi's introduced their "13's" slacks in Sanforized twill and midwale corduroy. The hip-, thigh-, and calf-hugging cut tapered to just 13 inches at the cuffs and had to be worn shorter than most standard cut slacks. (Figure 4.6.) Other makers branded their slim-cut slacks with names such as the "Tapered Man" by Asher, "Trimster" from H.I.S., and "Snug Duds" from Haggar.

A related young men's trend of the early 1960s that spread from the West Coast across America was the hugely popular Levi's white jeans. The look was popularized by several beach party and surfer movies of the time, such as *Where the Boys Are* (1960), *Beach Party* (1963), and *Bikini Beach* (1964). In 1962, a song titled *White Levi's* was a hit by the Majorettes, who sang about their boyfriends "wearin' white Levi's and his tennis shoes and his surfin' hat and a big plaid Pendleton shirt" (worn untucked and usually open like a jacket over a T-shirt or sport shirt). Levi Strauss & Co. bought thousands of the records to give away in a 250-city promotion for their white jeans. (Figure 4.7.) "It's the surfer look," explained *Men's Wear* in 1963. "A native costume" of "southern California's surfer fraternity" that "the teen man digs."[23] The jeans were constructed with a waistband lower than regular sportswear pants, and the legs were slim but not quite worn skintight the way they would be a few years later.

Another Italian fashion influence on the American youth market of the early 1960s was the fit of shirts. The 1962 ad from Truval Shirts shown in Figure 4.8 promoted the "new dimension" of the "contour tapered shirt." "The baggy look is out, the tapered look is in," and the "tapered tailoring" of the "trimmer waist" was the "key to the young man's market," the ad advised retailers.[24] Shirts in vivid colors likewise increasingly became significant in young men's business wardrobes. *Men's Wear* reported in 1964 that ready-to-wear production of white dress shirts had dropped from 80 percent to 40 percent.[25]

Figure 4.5 Another men's wear influence from Italy in the late 1950s was the silk shantung sport jacket in the trim Continental style. Ad, 1959.

Figure 4.6 By the early 1960s, the trim cut of Continental styles inspired the snug fit of casual pants for teenagers and collegians. In 1962, Levi's introduced the narrowest pants yet, called "13's," with a lowered waistband and slim legs that tapered to just 13 inches at the cuff. Ad, 1962.

One of the experiments by men's ready-to-wear makers in the mid-1950s was knee-length city shorts as a hot-weather business dress option. City shorts were adaptations of walking shorts, better known as Bermuda shorts, that had become popular for golfing and weekend leisure time in the 1930s. For a few summer seasons during the mid-1950s, the fashion press reported, "Invading the business hours more each year, are the walking shorts with perfect slack-tailoring."[26] Worn with a coordinating sport jacket, dress shirt, tie, and knee-high socks, the city shorts were a cool alternative to wool trousers on hot pavements and in downtown buildings without air conditioning. The idea was not a fashion trend, but as *Life* magazine noted in 1953, "wearers of knee-length Bermuda shorts were cropping up, not frequently but boldly and regularly . . . in offices and along scorching streets." Accompanying photographs in the editorial featured men in city shorts on New York's Fifth Avenue, in a Manhattan office, and with a white dinner jacket and black tie at a Chicago country club dance.[27] For most gray-flannel-suited corporate men, though, such a look was too casual and likely prohibited by rigid company dress codes. Even for the "bold" men observed by *Life,* city shorts were relegated back to weekend dress by the late 1950s as more offices were fitted with air conditioning.

In addition to Bermuda shorts, new forms of summer playwear pants for men replicated women's styles. Lightweight cotton beach pants were shortened

Figure 4.7 In the early 1960s, one of the surfer trends from California with broad appeal with teenagers and young men across America was snug fitting white Levi's jeans. Ad, 1963.

MEN'S DRESS

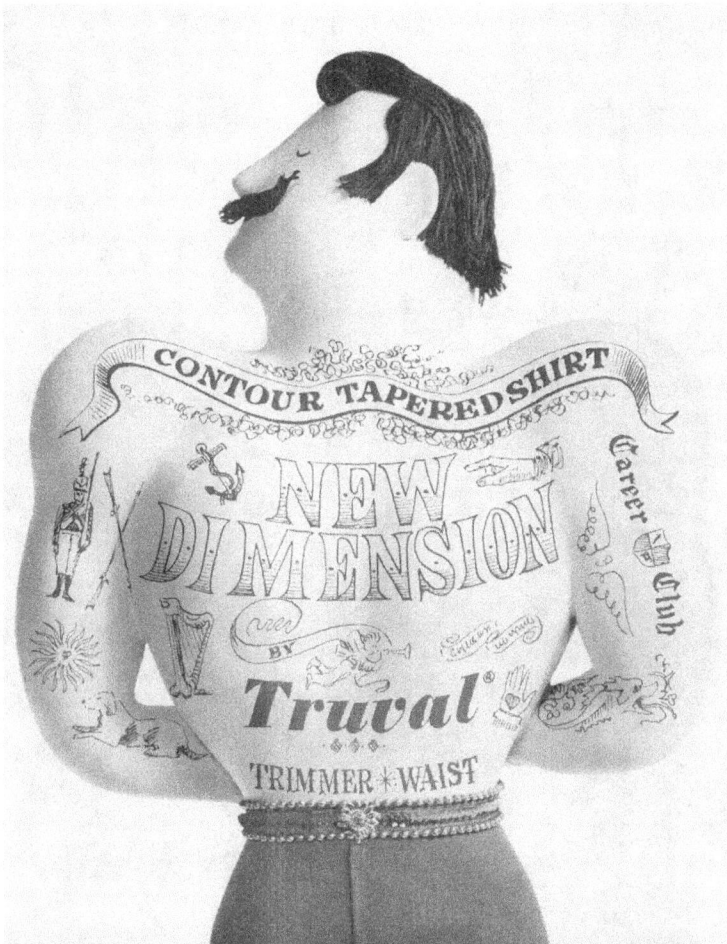

Figure 4.8 The emerging youth market of the early 1960s inspired shirt makers to produce tapered, contouring styles for the trim teenager and young man. Detail of TruVal Shirts ad, 1962.

enough at the ankles to wade in the surf; clam diggers were cropped at mid-calf; and pedal pushers were cut just below the knees, out of danger from a bicycle chain. All were available in bright primary colors, awning stripes, and madras plaids.

Men's casual slacks of the 1950s followed the capacious, pleated cut of Ivy League suit trousers or slim, tapered Continental styles. As shown in Figure 4.9, men's casual pants could additionally include a wide variety of belt loops and pocket flaps. A popular enhancement to men's and boys' slacks of the mid-1950s was the addition of a back buckle strap stitched just below the waistband. Although the back buckle strap style was called the Ivy League trouser, it had a

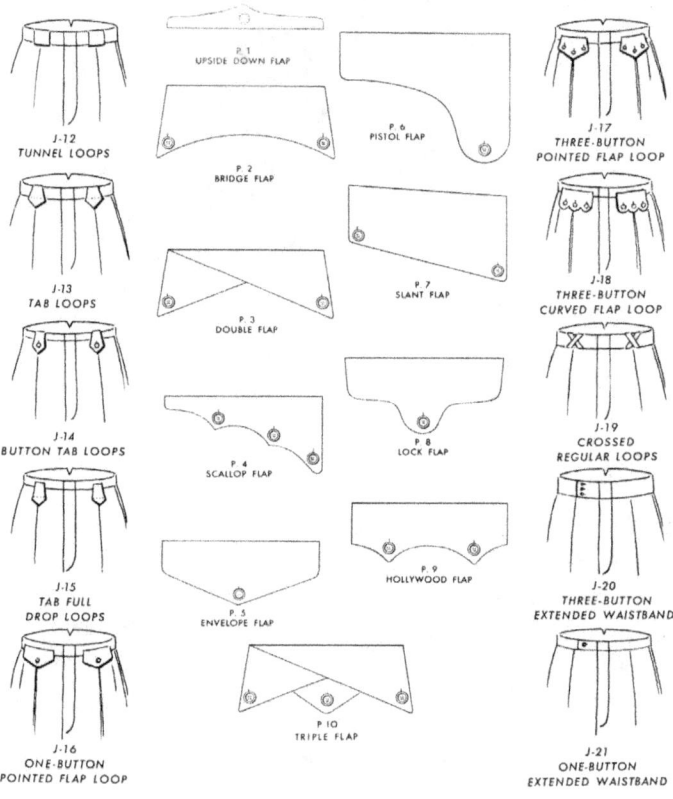

Figure 4.9 In the mid-1950s, men's casual Ivy and Continental pants were available with a wide variety of belt loops and front pocket flaps. Examples of options from Artcraft Tailors, 1956.

plain, pleatless front and was much trimmer than Ivy suit trousers. At the end of the 1950s, some men's wear makers also experimented with new forms of front fly closures. Trousers for the Continental suit by Andrew Pallack shown in Figure 4.2 were made with "a new revolutionary feature . . . the no-fly zipper closure."[28] *GQ* reported in 1959 on this "revolutionary innovation: the hidden fly. This closure has been designed so that the zipper is concealed without the need for an overlapping fly-front. Result: a flat, trim appearance."[29] Contrary to *GQ*'s prediction that "this front will start a new trend in slacks design," the idea disappeared from men's wear editorials and ads after 1960. Similarly, the experimental Velcro fly closure of 1958–1959 was heralded as a gamechanger in men's trousers. The Paxton slacks ad shown in Figure 4.10 explained how the Velcro fly closure worked: "Thousands of minute invisible hooks and tiny eyes mesh and cling like a burr as soon as they touch and never separate until peeled apart." Likewise, a Jaymar slacks ad touted their Velcro fly closure as "the zipperless zipper that holds like magic."[30] Velcro had been used for years on jackets, children's wear, and various accessories, but the idea of a trouser fly closure made with "burrs" and which made a ripping sound when opened evidently was not acceptable to men, and the idea was quickly abandoned by men's wear makers.

Men's sport shirts of the postwar years continued the styles that had emerged decades earlier. The short-sleeved sport shirt had been introduced initially as tennis wear around 1905 but quickly became popularized for casual summer dress (and by the 1910s, acceptable with summer business suits). During the 1920s, the knit polo shirt was appropriated from athletic sports attire for leisure wear at resorts but soon was offered in variations by mail-order mass merchandisers like Sears and Spiegel. In the 1930s, the colorful Hawaiian print sport shirt became a favorite of tourists and Navy servicemen who brought the style home to the mainland where it inspired similar versions by ready-to-wear makers, especially in the postwar years. In 1951, *Esquire* took note of the great variety of the "colorful native-design print shirt"—many of which were advertised in its pages—and recommended for weekend excursions and summer vacations to "leave all ideas of somber, quiet colors at home" since "a riot of color seems to bustin' out all over."[31] For men who spent five or six days a week in gray flannel blandness, the wide assortment of colorful, wildly patterned sport shirts allowed some expression of personality and a break with predictable conformity in dress and identity.

Figure 4.10 Among the innovative but short-lived experiments with men's trousers was the Velcro fly closure of the late 1950s. Velcro continued to gain popularity as a closure for jackets, shoes, sportswear, and bags, but the closure for trousers was quickly abandoned. Ad, 1958.

The dichotomy of desexualized dress and erotic masculine styles

As noted previously, the Superman silhouette of the drape cut suit with its muscular jacket and slim trousers was replaced by the tubular, straight-hanging Ivy League styles and voluminous trousers in the early postwar years. By comparison with the drape cut look, the Ivy League suits thoroughly concealed and denied the male anatomy by a shapeless, baggy encasement of fabric. No fashion editorial or men's wear designer, though, made note of this transformation, let alone suggested that the conservative zeitgeist of the Cold War era had any influence on this desexualization of the American male. In fact, if anything, the fashion press and men's wear advertising asserted that the sack-like Ivy suit was "a new trim look."[32] A 1950 men's suit ad proclaimed the Ivy suits to be "the new shape . . . Its lines dip straight and true from broad, hand-set shoulders to the hips . . . No old-fashioned taper at the waist, no constraining lines anywhere."[33] Another men's wear ad from 1951 similarly avowed that, in the Ivy suit, "You look taller, slimmer, more athletic and more poised."[34]

Yet, by contrast to the baggy, concealing suits, two areas of men's wear provided startling options for overt eroticism—swimwear in public and underwear in private. The evolution of men's swimwear was dramatic in the first decades of the twentieth century.[35] The standard men's swimsuit of 1900 was comprised of a wool knit swim shirt with a modesty skirt that drooped to the thighs over baggy knee-length trunks. During the 1910s and 1920s, men's swimwear became more formfitting in new rib-knit fabrics, and ever briefer as trunks inched to the upper thighs. In the late 1920s, one-piece singlet swimsuits eliminated the modesty skirt, and "crab back" tank tops were opened at the sides and back with large rounded cutouts. In 1932, a new form of elasticized yarn called Lastex was introduced to swimwear, which contoured the body with two-way stretch. Also in the early 1930s, two influences from France further enhanced American men's erotic exhibitionism in swimwear. First was the brief cut with its high leg openings at the hips that lifted and further shaped the genital bulge and buttocks. Curiously, both in Europe and America, the "next to nothing" swimsuits, as *Esquire* called them,[36] were still cut with a high waistband that covered the navel—a design convention that would remain the standard until the 1950s. Second was the elimination of the swim shirt—a controversial look in the 1930s because many public beaches had decency codes against men swimming shirtless.

During the war years, the boxer-style swim trunks in woven cotton or rayon became more prevalent when rubber became a strictly regulated material, making Lastex less available for brief styles. Immediately after the war, though, swimwear makers resumed mass production and promotion of stretch-knit swim briefs. Key design changes in men's swimwear occurred during the 1950s, which made erotic exhibitionism even more pronounced. Beginning in the late 1940s, newly developed elasticized nylon yarns were applied to men's swimwear. In 1959, spandex (an anagram of "expands") was introduced to men's swimwear. Made of elastomeric synthetic fibers, spandex could stretch and recover its shape better than natural rubber. Where rubberized Lastex had molded the body, nylon spandex was even more fluid and sheer by comparison. Equally important to the erotic exhibitionism of a new generation of young men was the increasingly briefer cut. In 1952, Jantzen introduced brief styles with a waistband below the navel. (Figure 4.11.) In addition to a lowered waistband, Jantzen and other makers exposed even more skin by opening the sides with cutouts and lattice strips of fabric. The first men's bikini swimsuit, called a piccolino, meaning "little one" in Italian, appeared on the Riviera around 1950. (The women's bikini had been introduced in Paris in 1946.) The fashion press reported the first examples of the men's bikini at North American resorts in 1955[37] and on California beaches in 1959.[38] Although American men of the Cold War era embraced the swim brief in the new formfitting synthetic knits, the cut of the bikini seemed to be too European and too exhibitionistic. The style was reported in *Esquire* and *GQ* in 1959 and 1960, but then disappeared from men's wear fashion news until the

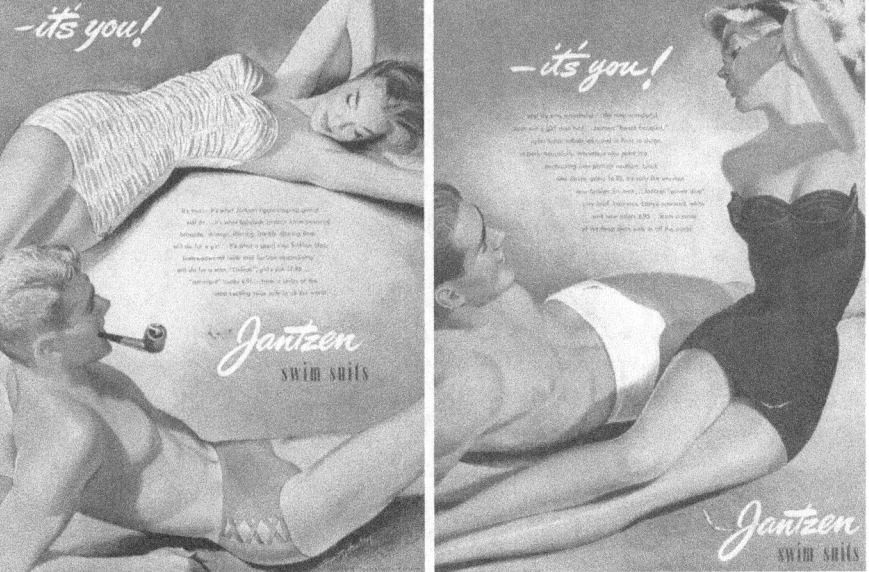

Figure 4.11 One of the dichotomies of men's wear in the 1950s was the popularization of formfitting erotic styles of swimwear and underwear at the same time as the shapeless, anatomy-concealing suits and trousers prevailed. From Jantzen: left "Daredevil" open lattice side swim brief, 1951; right, "Power Dive" white Lastex swim brief, 1952.

early 1970s. The bikini, which had continued to diminish in cut until it was barely an inch wide at the hips in the late 1960s, had become too associated with gay men until the sexual revolution of the 1970s.

For erotic dress in private, the brief style underwear was developed from the brief models of swimwear. Prior to the 1930s, men's underwear was a commodity garment with a practical function. In winter, there were woolen union suits and in summer there were various forms of lightweight short singlets, shorts, and undershirts. In 1934, though, the Coopers knitting mills of Kenosha, Wisconsin, launched a white cotton brief with an elastic waistband based on the shirtless swim brief that had been in the fashion news for a couple of years. The underwear style was branded "Jockey" and became an instant success. "Jockeys are snug and brief, molded to your muscles," declared a 1936 Jockey ad, featuring a photo of a muscular man in the briefs and a tank undershirt.[39] Dozens of competitors soon launched their own versions of the formfitting underwear brief. As with the swim brief, on which Jockeys and its imitations were modeled, the new underwear brief shaped and lifted the genital bulge and contoured the buttocks as no previous type of men's undergarment had. Because ads for the brief style underwear always depicted young, athletic models, the idea of erotic exhibitionism was inescapable.

For the postwar young man, the Jockey style brief was a favorite and widely promoted underwear option. It had remained largely unchanged in cut since its launch in 1935, although makers continually experimented with fly closures, elastic waistbands, and knits in new yarns such as nylon, Dacron, Orlon, and other new synthetics and blends. But in 1958, Jockey made underwear news with the introduction of the men's bikini underwear. Influenced by the European bikini swimsuit, and as a complement to the new trim Continental style suits and slim trousers, the abbreviated underwear was branded as Skants. Made of stretch nylon, the Skants styles were cut low and with a high arc of the leg openings to about an inch of fabric at the hips. The intended eroticism of the new underwear design was clear in the ad copy, which declared the style "molds to your body . . . with a minimum of coverage."[40] In addition, Skants were available in six solid colors and five colors of thin horizontal stripes, a harbinger of what would proliferate in the 1960s as men's fashion underwear.

The British Invasion: From the London Line to Mod

As noted previously, at the end of the 1950s, the Jivey Ivy suit was a hybrid that combined design elements of Ivy League and Continental styles. In the fall of 1961, *GQ* reported on an "avant-garde" new style of suit with a one-button jacket closure. The style was deemed "sensible," since most men "only button one of the usual three anyway." The other details—angled pockets, cuffed sleeves, and waist suppression—were further adaptations from the Continental look. Also new, though, was the reintroduction of shoulder padding, a significant departure from twelve years of the natural shoulder for both Ivy and Continental suits.[41] For the next few years, GQ continued promoting the one-button jacket, including on the cover of the February 1964 issue, declaring it "an American innovation winning support."[42] By 1964, the look of the one-button single-breasted jacket was referred to as the "X-line" because the single button at the center front formed a visual axis.[43] Most of the issues of GQ from 1962 into 1967 also featured ads by American suit makers depicting their versions of the one-button style. (Figure 4.12.) The one-button single-breasted jacket even inspired a two-button double-breasted jacket in 1964 (but with only one-button that fastened low on the right hip).[44] The one-button suit jacket and the short Continental style finally ebbed when men's wear makers rediscovered the shaped drape cut from the 1930s following the hit movie *Bonnie and Clyde* (1967).

Figure 4.12 A variation of the Continental suit of the early 1960s was a one-button closure, called the "X-line" with the single button at the center front forming an axis. Left, one-button suit from Cardinal Clothes, 1962; right, one-button suit from Kuppenheimer, 1963.

In addition to the continued experiments with Ivy and Continental hybrids by American suit makers in the early 1960s, a surge of influences from Britain made news in the fashion press. This was not the youth market that was beginning to develop in Soho's Carnaby Street, which Londoners initially regarded "as renegades of no particular fashion influence."[45] *GQ* called the new suit styles the "London Line"—a "high fashion look . . . inspired by the precepts of Savile Row . . . Classic and conservative enough to appeal to men who shun extremes, yet new and different enough to carry the stamp of fashion." The silhouette featured squared, padded shoulders and a marked waistline, "so that the jacket shapes in, then flares out toward the bottom." The fabrics were "classics rather than high-style innovations," as were the accessories. "The over-all look is manly and mature, tailored rather than loosely casual, simple, nongimmicky and sophisticated."[46]

In 1963, *Men's Wear* similarly reported on the "British flavor" in a "beginning trend toward an additional silhouette" in men's suits that the editors called "body tracing." The cut of the suit jacket "was based on the natural and easy flow of a man's body," a body consciousness that emphasized a broad chest by wider lapels, a defined waistline, and flared skirt with full-sized vents. "With this coat, of course, slim trousers are still in order," the editors advised. The new addition to men's suit styles was not viewed as a replacement of the Ivy or Continental but was "an addition to both of these—actually a variation on a theme."[47]

As the Space Age opened in 1960, the first baby boomers began high school; by mid-decade, half the US population was under the age of 25.[48] It was a youthquake declared a *Vogue* editor in 1965.[49] Much to the dismay of their parents, as the baby boomers came of age in the 1960s, they rejected the conventions, conformity, and materialism of their elders. Instead of embracing the postwar norms of their parents, teachers, and other adult role models, the youthquake generation challenged status quo traditions in their search for their own path in a pluralistic America. They would participate in social revolutions such as the civil rights and student rights movements, the Second Wave Feminism, and, after the start of the Vietnam war in 1965, antiwar demonstrations. They also sought their own dress identity.

The first hints of the influences of the youth market from "Swinging England" began in 1961. *GQ* interviewed London's fashion entrepreneur Alexander Plunket Greene, whose two Bazaar boutiques sold the "off-beat clothes for women" designed by his wife Mary Quant. Greene's "very decided views about men's fashions" were emerging trends for British teens and young men at the time. "Men, like women," suggested Greene, "should aim at sex appeal in their clothes. Trousers should be cut to shape and molded tightly on the figure." The example he wore fitted snugly and low on the hips and was without pleats or cuffs. His fitted jacket similarly was shaped with squared shoulders, a broad chest, and slim contours over the hips.[50]

A year later, in 1962, the American ready-to-wear trade journal, *Men's Wear,* began to take note of something happening in London. The editors advised retail buyers, "London, too, has its orbiting arbiters of fashion . . . They are know as the Chelsea group. They . . . are rebellious to traditional tastes, have their own special opinions about fashions (and life, in general) which runs from the amusing to the very creative." Among the "novelty fashions" from London that the editors suggested were notable included the sharply pointed step-in ankle boots—made famous by the Beatles—and two new looks in men's shirts. "Boldly striped . . . shirts are big in London," some in vivid color combinations that were "very, very strong" and *"sometimes with white collars and cuffs"* (their italics). As a "lift for the dark suits so many men have in their wardrobes," these striped shirts were declared "a real kick in the head." In addition, colorful sport shirts were spotted with unconventional detailing such as sleeve pockets, complex yoke constructions, and bold, double-row top stitching.[51]

As the sexualized tapered fit of slacks, jeans, and shirts became more popular with American youthquake men in the early 1960s, other revolutionary ideas of men's fashion increasingly began to filter into the United States from Britain. Called "mod," for modern or modernist, radically new concepts of men's dress would explode into a Peacock Revolution across America in the second half of the decade. The radiant center of the new ideas of masculine identity and dress was London's Carnaby Street, a narrow alleyway in the Soho theater district. Beginning at the end of the 1950s, entrepreneurs led by "Mr. Carnaby" John Stephen opened specialty men's wear shops along Carnaby Street, which were based on the model of women's boutiques: colorful interiors; eye-catching window displays of trendy fashions; loud pop music; and young, hip sales staff. "A grubby back street has become a prime trading area . . . the liveliest, most colorful, most amusing shopping street in the world," avowed a guidebook of the time.[52] Rapid turnover of inexpensive ready-to-wear and a continual flow of publicity promotions, celebrity appearances, and sales gimmicks ensured crowds of young men would return frequently to buy the new looks in men's wear. "Men's clothing, previously designed for the middle-aged, shifted to the demands for a new style using more color, new fabrics and cut more suited to the youthful figure."[53]

Mod style swept into America with the "British Invasion" of pop culture imports from England led by the music of the Beatles. In 1964, the Fab Four topped US music charts, toured the United States to sold-out concerts, performed on a top-rated Sunday night television program three times, and starred in the movie *A Hard Day's Night*. The mod styles worn by the Beatles, and other British bands such as The Who, Rolling Stones, Animals, Herman's Hermits, and Kinks, inspired teens and young men across America to emulate the dress of their pop idols. Press coverage and fan magazines further promoted the new looks in young men's wear. US ready-to-wear makers took notice and sent their designers to Carnaby Street to buy samples and gather ideas of what youthquake men were wearing. Department stores imported mod fashions from London and set up in-store Carnaby boutiques. By the mid-1960s, the Peacock Revolution in American men's wear was well underway.

The fashions American youthquake men experimented with were gender-redefining looks that shocked their elders. The traditional ideas of masculine identity were foremost shattered when American men began growing their hair long—at first like the cuts of the Beatles at mid-decade, extending to about the collar, but within a couple of years, in long tresses to the shoulder for some.

A second break with gender dress norms was the adaptation of colors and prints to men's wear that previously had been viewed as women's styles. Flower-power prints in pinks, lavenders, and other pastels were applied to shirts, pants, and accessories. Paisleys in all sizes and color combinations were bold, exotic statements in the new permanent-press fabrics. Vividly hued graphics based on Op art patterns and vintage art nouveau posters were fresh and modern for young men. Tie-dyeing and stenciled messages on T-shirts were influences from the street.

The overt sexualization of young men's clothes was as alarming for parents as men's long hair. The trim cut of pants and jeans became painted-on tight, made all the more contouring by new stretch synthetic fabrics and stretch denim. The waistband was lowered to fit as hiphuggers, accentuating slim youthful waists and narrow hips. Rib-knit pullover shirts molded to the body. See-through shirts were made of sheer materials like voile and lace and were worn unbuttoned halfway down the torso.

Accessories, too, crossed gender lines as men tied colorful scarves around their necks, heads, and hips. Unisex jewelry such as necklaces, bracelets, and finger rings were worn by both men and women. Shoulder bags and totes of fringed suede were useful to peripatetic hippies. A few years later, men would further challenge masculine identity norms by adopting high-heeled platform shoes and piercing their ears for studs, small hoops, and dangling earrings. Leather purse-style man bags would be introduced from Italy.

The generation gap between the youthquake baby boomers and their postwar parents dramatically manifested itself visually and defiantly in the fashions—and long hair—the young men chose as their masculine identity in the 1960s.

Conclusion

Following the Second World War, a new form of men's suit was introduced to the American male called the Ivy League style. The cut featured a loose-fitting, straight-hanging jacket and capacious, pleated, cuffed trousers. The ubiquitous

Ivy League suit in gray wool became the masculine dress identity of the white, middle-class corporate man of the postwar years, and defined the 1950s as the era of the man in the gray flannel suit.

In the mid-1950s, influences from the emerging Italian fashion arena resulted in the development of the Continental suit as an alternative to the Ivy style. Continental suits retained the natural shoulders of the Ivy suit but were made with a cutaway front, shortened skirt, angled pockets, and a suppressed waist with darts in the front. The Continental trousers were slim and usually without pleats or cuffs.

At the end of the 1950s, suit makers developed variations that mixed elements of the Ivy and Continental styles in what was sometimes called a Jivey Ivy look. In the early 1960s, an innovative version of the hybrid suit introduced a one-button closure called an X-line, with the single button as the center axis of the silhouette. At the same time, influences from Britain's Savile Row, called the London Line in the press, reintroduced padded shoulders to jackets after an absence of almost 15 years, a more distinct tapered waist, and a flared skirt.

By mid-decade, a British Invasion of pop culture and mod fashions provided the American baby boom male with innovative and radically different looks from the styles of their postwar dads. English rock bands such as the Beatles, Rolling Stones, and The Who inspired American youthquake men to grow their hair long and experiment with colorful, sexualized clothes. From London's Carnaby Street boutiques came mod styles of shaped suits; snug, low-rise pants; and fitted shirts in vibrant colors, patterns, and prints. As the baby boomers came of age in the 1960s, a Peacock Revolution would define the masculine identity of the new generation.

5
ETHNIC MEN'S IDENTITY AND DRESS

The zoot suit

Although this study focuses on the years of the baby boom in American from 1946 to 1964, two periods of distinctive ethnic dress and masculine identity that immediately bookend the baby boom era also should be considered. The zoot suit was an ethnic look of the late 1930s into the 1940s, and a generation later, following the passage of the Civil Rights Act in 1964, African Americans nationwide were inspired to explore varieties of dress that expressed pride in their African heritage. In between these two phases of distinctive ethnic dress, most nonwhite American men followed the prevailing standards of masculine dress, irrespective of ethnic identity. In his 1964 autobiography, Black activist Malcolm X noted that, after his wild zoot suits and yellow "knob-toe shoes" in the 1940s, his dress became conventional in the 1950s. "All of my suits were conservative. A banker might have worn my shoes."[1]

The sociocultural conditions that set the stage for the emergence of the zoot suit as the first distinct masculine identity for African American men had been evolving for decades. Despite the end of slavery in 1865, systemic racism had remained embedded in American culture, sustained in 26 states by Jim Crow laws and sanctioned by the US Supreme Court.[2] In the 1910s and 1920s, more than a million rural Southern Blacks left farms and migrated to industrialized northern cities in hope of factory jobs and a better life free of racial oppression, only to find that even in states where Jim Crow laws were not on the books, socioeconomic segregation was common. In their 1937 Middletown study of Muncie, Indiana, the Lynds found, "The cleft between the white and Negro populations of Middletown is the deepest and most blindly followed line of division in the community."[3] New Deal legislation of the 1930s wrote racial inequality and segregation into federal public policies, including the Wagner Act labor reforms, Social Security Act, and the Home Owner's Loan Corporation, helping to sustain what Black activists referred to as the Jim Crow North. In liberal cities across northern states, "racial discrimination and segregation operated as a system, upheld by criminal and civil courts, police departments, public policies, and government bureaucracies. Judges, police officers, school board officials, PTAs, taxpayer groups, zoning board bureaucrats, urban realtors and housing developers, mortgage underwriters, and urban renewal policy makers created and maintained the Jim Crow North. There did not need to be a 'no coloreds' sign for hotels, restaurants, pools, parks, housing complexes, schools, and jobs to be segregated across the North."[4] These conditions were made even worse with the economic crisis of the Great Depression, which especially hit the industries of the north, where unemployment for whites surged to 25 percent, but for Blacks, soared to 60 percent.

It was during these hard times of the 1930s that early versions of the zoot suit first appeared in the jazz clubs and dance halls of New York City. Unlike most fashions, which since the late nineteenth century largely had come from the seasonal collections presented by designers in Paris, New York, and London, the exaggerated zoot suit instead was a youth street style that developed with Black urban working classes. A number of possible sources for the origin of the zoot suit have been suggested by scholars and fashion historians. Claimants for creating the style included a list of tailors and men's wear retailers from New York, Chicago, Memphis, Detroit, and Washington, DC. Possible inspirations for the look of the zoot suit range from the men's costumes in *Gone with the Wind* (1939) to immigrant Filipino or Mexican folk dress.[5]

One claimant to the invention of the style was Harold C. Fox, a Chicago jazz band leader and men's clothier who claimed to have created the zoot suit in 1939. He previously had designed wild styles of costumes for jazz bands and took the zoot suit one step further with the extreme silhouette of a padded, long jacket and voluminous pegged trousers. The name zoot suit, Fox asserted, was also his, derived from jive talk of the swing era. The highest compliment that could be said of anything was "the end to end all ends." To Fox, the letter Z was the end, and the word "zoot" rhymed with suit. Even the long swag of the key chain in front was claimed by Fox, who said he had added a broken toilet pull-chain to a customer's suit on a whim.[6]

But the emergence of the zoot suit was probably even earlier than Fox's 1939 version. In New York City, Cab Calloway led Depression-era jazz bands in Harlem's Cotton Club, wearing exaggerated custom-made tailcoat suits with padded jackets and baggy, pegged trousers. These precursors of the zoot suit, called "drapes," were made nationally famous by Hollywood when Calloway and his flamboyant suits were featured in films such as *Hi-De-Ho* (1934) and *Jitterbug*

ETHNIC MEN'S IDENTITY AND DRESS

Party (1935). In the 1943 movie *Stormy Weather,* Calloway substituted his stylized tailcoat suits for a full-on zoot suit of white wool, with a knee-length coat, enormous harem-style trousers, white bowtie with slim wings extending about 8 inches wide, a keychain swag to the ankles, and a broad-brimmed white hat.

By the end of the 1930s, the basic silhouette of the zoot suit was a jacket with wide shoulders and long skirt worn with capacious pegged trousers. (Figure 5.1.) There was no specific standard for any of the zoot suit features. In some instances, the suit and trousers were made of different fabrics and contrasting colors. Men who went to tailors for custom-made zoot suits usually had specifications in mind for every inch of the jacket and trousers. A semi-drape

Figure 5.1 From the late 1930s until 1943, many young, urban, working-class African Americans and Latinos adopted the zoot suit as a unique ethnic identity. The exaggerated style featured a jacket with padded shoulders and a long skirt worn over wide-legged, pegged trousers. Photos 1942–1943.

zoot suit was a modification of the London drape cut business suit that had been the prevalent style since the late 1920s. Semi-drape zoot jackets were padded a bit more than regular business suits, and skirts were about knuckle-length. The trousers of the semi-drape had a waistband rise of a few inches higher than regular styles, and were about the same 22–24 inches at the knees but pegged at about 16 inches at the cuff. Accessories for the semi-drape zoot suit might be regular men's toe-cap oxfords and a smooth derby or a porkpie hat instead of the broad brim version. The keychain swag was omitted.

At the other end of the zoot suit spectrum was the extreme-drape or superzoot—the look favored by Black and Latino entertainers like Cab Calloway and Tin-Tan in the early 1940s. The jacket shoulders and chest were broadly padded and squared, sometimes almost parallel to the floor. Peaked lapels might spread across to the shoulder sleeve seam. Sleeves were full at the upper arms and tapered to the wrist, sometimes completely covering the hands to the knuckles. Skirts were usually about fingertip length but could extend to the knees, and fitted narrowly at the hips with a minimum of flare. Sharpies—men who dressed sharp—bragged about the 28-, 30-, or 32-inch circumference of their trousers at the knees, most of which were pegged to an ankle-choking 14 or even 12 inches at the cuffs.[7] The waistband rise could reach the diaphragm, held up by a 1-inch-wide leather belt. Suit colors for urban African Americans in the east were often vibrant, and patterns such as windowpane checks, plaids, awning stripes, and herringbones were oversized and bold. On the West Coast, Latinos preferred subdued earth tones, particularly shades of brown.

The accessories for the zoot suit differed between the eastern Black youth and West Coast Latinos. Hats were more common with sharpies in the east, especially flat, wide-brimmed, and porkpie styles. The hats were worn straight on the brow, never tilted to the side or pushed back on the crown. A long, colorfully dyed feather might embellish the hatband. Latinos usually went bareheaded to display their thick hair and pomaded pompadour cuts, but some opted for a low-crown porkpie hat in a dark brown.

A necktie was not always worn with zoot suits, especially if the intention of the wearer was dancing the jitterbug; a tight shirt collar and knotted tie was too hot and restricting. Still, for some jitterbuggers, a tie was an extra dash of color and style for the dance floor. For a date or hanging out in a pool hall with friends, a four-in-hand tie was preferred over a bowtie. Because silk was a restricted material needed for the war, men's ties of the time were often of rayon and rayon/cotton blends in wildly abstract prints and vivid colors.

Shoes had to be clean and well-polished. For Blacks, shoes that were eye-catching, such as two-tone wingtips or oxfords in an unusual color, were favored. Malcolm X made note of yellow or orange "knob-toed" shoes he wore with his zoot suits.[8] The knob-toe shoe was actually a square-toe style that became popular with both men's and women's footwear of the war years. (Figure 5.2.)

Figure 5.2 The preferred footwear for the zoot suit for African Americans was the squared knob-toe oxford (left), and for Latinos, the blunt, thick-soled blucher (right). Men's shoes from Spiegel, 1941.

Latinos, though, preferred wide, thick-soled bluchers polished black to a high sheen to wear with their dark-colored zoot suits. For a platform effect, Latinos sometimes took their shoes to a shoe repair shop to have a second sole added.

Grooming was a significant part of the zoot suiter's total look as well. Since on both coasts, the zoot suiter was a young man in his late teens to early twenties, facial hair was usually not an option. For those who may have been on the verge of sprouting some whiskers, they still shaved cleanly. For urban Blacks in the east, the modern look for their hair was called a "conk." Commercial hair straighteners for Blacks had been available since the late nineteenth century. But for many working-class Blacks, a homemade treatment called "congolene" could be made cheaply with a mixture of thin-sliced potatoes, lye, and two eggs. The hair was first teased out and then the scalp, ears, and neck were slathered with a generous amount of Vaseline to protect the skin from the lye. When the burning got too intense, the congolene was washed out of the hair with soap multiple times. The result was straight hair with a reddish tint. As Malcolm X recalled upon seeing his first conk in the mirror, "the transformation, after the lifetime of kinks, is staggering . . . On top of my head was this thick, smooth sheen of shining red hair—real red—as straight as any white man's."[9] In the West, Latinos preferred to be bareheaded, displaying their ducktail haircuts—thick black hair combed into a pompadour on top and swept back from the ears into a short crest in the back resembling a duck's tail (often called a "DA," meaning "duck's ass"). Various hair oils and pomades held the pompadours in place and added a gloss.

Jewelry was minimal. A tie clip might have been added to the four-in-hand necktie to keep it straight and secured to the shirt when dancing or shooting pool. Otherwise, the most notable jewelry piece was the long swag of a key chain. Usually of gold-plated or gold-tone base metal, the chain was often a bonus item offered by tailors and men's wear retailers if the customer bought the full accoutrement of a zoot suit, including shirt, tie, and hat. The chain was sometimes long enough to form a double swag, attached to the belt or trousers waistband at the front right hip and draped around the leg to the back hip pocket. The chain may or may not have keys attached.

Although the zoot suit is historically regarded as an ethnic dress identity, some young, urban white men who liked swing music and jitterbug dancing also wore the zoot suit. For the most part, these white youths went to whites-only events, but occasionally, some also went to Black clubs in Harlem, south Chicago, east Detroit, and similar segregated sections of cities. To whites, the experience was an exciting venture of youthful rebellion and, at the same time, an indulgence in the hip modernity of the time. Black patrons were largely tolerant of the occasional invasion of white tourists, since, after all, they spent money on cover charges, drinks, and tips, which was good business for Black club owners and managers. For other white youth who wanted to attend swing parties and clubs and look sharp, but not dress in the zoot suit, American tailors offered a modified version of the zoot suit without the overt ethnic symbolism. Called a "swank" or "swing" suit, the jacket was constructed with broadly padded shoulders, tapered sleeves, a darted and contoured waist, and knuckle-length skirt. Pleated trousers were slightly fuller than for regular drape cut suits but were distinctly pegged with a shortened hemline. (Figure 5.3.) The moderated swank suit was available in most tailors' stylebooks and catalogs for a few seasons in the early 1940s but were removed after the US government implemented restrictions on fabric use and set L-85 garment standards in 1942.

The social significance and cultural meaning of the zoot suit

By the beginning of the Second World War, the zoot suit was commonly seen at jazz clubs and dance halls nationwide. For African American and Latino urban youth, the zoot suit served three important functions. First, the zoot suit was an experience with high-style fashion for a segment of marginalized, poor Blacks and Latinos. These working-class youngsters were usually excluded from the fashion statuses of their middle- and upper-class neighbors and classmates whose wardrobes were current and abundant with trends featured in magazines, shops, and retail catalogs. Moreover, the zoot ensemble with its various accessories was a statement of consumption and leisure, both of which were indulgences of the affluent. Tailor-made zoot suits were expensive. Malcolm X recalled that he had to save up to buy zoot ensembles (including accessories) priced in the $70 to $80 range in 1940,[10] and a New York tailor's apprentice recalled the cost of a full zoot look could exceed $100[11] (at a time when a ready-to-wear worsted

ETHNIC MEN'S IDENTITY AND DRESS

Figure 5.3 The swank or swing suit was a variation of the ethnic zoot suit worn by some white middle-class youths who went to dance clubs in the early 1940s. The swank suit was tailored with broad, padded shoulders, contoured waist, and knuckle-length skirt worn over full, pegged trousers. Swank suits from Pioneer Tailoring, 1942.

business suit, dress shirt, tie, shoes, and fedora might cost $18–$24.[12]) Hence, "by donning a costly zoot suit, the Black or Latino zoot suiter put his opulence in evidence and announced to the world that he had the power to spend time and money alike."[13] They did not call themselves "zoot suiters" though, but rather "sharpies," as in sharp dressers. And zoot suits were described as "killer diller" looks, jive talk for something exceptional and outstanding, a term derived from the energetic, improvised dancing of jitterbuggers.

Second, the zoot also "signified a new urban identity, being modern, prosperous, and in the know . . . Men found in the style a compelling aesthetic that embodied a new sense of themselves at a moment of possibility and transformation."[14] For some new arrivals to the big city, this transformation provided by the zoot suit was an elevation from provincialism to street-smart sophistication. Malcolm X explained in his autobiography how wearing his first zoot suit and conking his hair allowed him to shed his small-town "country" past and, for the first time, feel a sense of belonging, of being part of a modern male comradeship, and of being sexually attractive to women.[15]

A part of this new urban masculine identity provided by the zoot suit was the idea of performance, a visual spectacle that inspired wearers to effect gestures, jive talk, and public behavior that they would not otherwise demonstrate. In the 1992 movie *Malcolm X,* Denzel Washington wears a sky blue zoot suit, accompanied by Spike Lee, dressed in a boldly checked zoot suit, as they perform the attention-getting "swag walk" down a crowded city street. Likewise, in posing against a wall or pool table, a zoot suiter might twirl the watch chain for attention and effect. "If nonwhite youth were denied their dignity through discrimination, violence, and negative discourse, zoot suiters reclaimed it by asserting control over their own bodies and performing unique race and gender identities."[16]

A third function of the zoot suit was sociopolitical. Although not initially viewed as a political statement in the 1930s, the style became a visual expression of ethnic masculine identity and cultural resistance in the face of oppressive systemic racism and segregation during the war years. Because it was an unconventional look in men's wear, the suit called attention to the wearer—a nonwhite young man dressed in nonconformist clothes that negated norms of masculine identity and behavior, even within their own ethnic communities. "By mobilizing their own bodies and occupying public space, zoot suiters challenged the indignities forced upon them at the same time that they created their own cultural identities and social relations."[17] In the summer of 1941, Duke Ellington developed a musical revue of Black entertainers called *Jump for Joy* "with an overtly political purpose . . . to correct the race situation in the USA through a form of theatrical propaganda."[18] Ellington's stated intention was to produce "a show that would take Uncle Tom out of the theatre, eliminate the stereotyped image that had been exploited by Hollywood and Broadway, and say things that would make the audience think."[19] As a point of pride, the zoot suit was featured in the show as a representation of Black expressiveness, dignity, and freedom, including a skit in a tailor's shop called "Made to Order" in which three sharpies banter in jive talk about the extremes of their zoot suits in cut and color.

The zoot suit riots

The zoot suit became a politically charged symbol for nonwhites in 1942 when the US War Production Board issued its L-85 order of restrictions on the use of materials and the limitations of clothing designs discussed in Chapter 1. The L-85 regulations were not mere suggestions; they were national defense requirements of all US manufacturers, tailors, dressmakers, and retailers, backed by stiff fines and potential prison-time for noncompliance. By the fall of 1942, the zoot suit became a well-publicized target for regulators as an especially egregious violation of L-85 regulations. "Zoot gets boot—jitter garments outlawed; makers face prosecution," warned a war department bulletin in September 1942.[20] That same month, Life magazine described the "scandalously wasteful" excesses of the zoot suit, which included "three to six inches of padding in each right-angled shoulder," the long skirt length extending "to within a few inches of the knees," and voluminous trousers cut "up high to the diaphragm" and legs with a "full 32-inch knee."[21] Yet, despite the national call for conservation of wool and other materials as a wartime necessity and a patriotic duty, a black market for custom tailoring of zoot suits persisted in most large cities, especially Los Angeles.

As Life also reported, the "WPB order ending jive-garb production outrages nation's teen-age jitterbugs . . . Spokesmen for the hepcats in Washington, D.C., a hotspot which ranks with Harlem and Hollywood as a style center for the glad rags of solid-diggers, claimed that the WPB edict was a persecution of a minority."[22] The magazine seemed to be suggesting that teenagers were simply being selfish about the inconvenience of the wartime restrictions, but in ethnic communities, denying the zoot suit was negating a cultural identity. To some young Blacks and Latinos, the zoot suit had become an expression of their ethnic identity that "helped convert their social alienation, economic exploitation, and political marginalization into a sense of security and 'coolness' that enabled them to navigate the highly segregated and discriminatory society in which they lived."[23] The government regulations against what for many ethnic young men was an important representation of their culture and identity seemed to be yet another form of oppression—just one more Jim Crow order to keep men of color in their place. The result was that young Blacks and Latinos ignored the government mandate.

Through that fall of 1942 and into the spring of 1943, ethnic zoot suiters were increasingly confronted in public by white servicemen and police officers who viewed the flouting of the wartime dress regulations as unpatriotic and subversive. On the West Coast, especially, where port cities bustled with war industries and military deployment centers, tensions between servicemen and nonwhite residents intensified into frequent altercations and disturbances. From the perspective of white servicemen, the zoot suit was a declaration of contempt and disrespect for America's military, in general, and white servicemen, in particular. And for some Black and Latino young men, the zoot suit was a way to lash out at a society in which they were treated as second-class citizens. Insults and name-calling from Latinos to sailors often suggested the Navy was filled with homosexuals, a particular challenge to white manhood.[24] To be especially provocative, some Latinos included a Nazi salute with their taunts.[25] In addition, white men especially felt compelled to protect white women to whom ethnic zoot suiters might make lecherous remarks in passing by or cast perceived lascivious glances at them.[26] For Black and Latino men, too, protecting their women was also a flashpoint. White servicemen frequently cruised Black and Latino neighborhoods looking for available women and were just as guilty with their suggestive remarks. Residents of ethnic communities often complained that white servicemen, particularly sailors, acted like they owned the streets.

The police and judicial system likewise contributed to the rising tension and resentment in ethnic neighborhoods. In Los Angeles, the all-white police force regarded the zoot suit as a sign of a Latino gang member, criminality, and deviance. As more and more confrontations between Latinos and white servicemen occurred in 1943, the police increasingly harassed and arrested the Latinos for disorderly conduct, drunkenness, or loitering. During violent mob conflicts, white residents and servicemen sometimes stripped Latinos of their zoot suits, photos of which appeared in *Life* magazine at the time.[27] Some police reportedly even attached razors to their nightsticks to shred the jackets and trousers of Latino zoot suiters.[28] As the police broke up the melees, they often only arrested Black and Latino participants, seldom the white servicemen.

Once in custody, the judicial system was equally hostile to the zoot suiters. At preliminary hearings, the courts refused to allow the young men to change clothes or cut their ducktail hairstyles, since the zoot suiters' looks were viewed as "distinguishing gang characteristics" and evidence in their cases.[29] Prosecutors and judges lectured the youths for their behavior but never acknowledged the contributing roles of police or servicemen.

Particularly problematic were skewed press reports that likened young Latinos to "baby gangsters" and "zoot suit hoodlums."[30] Some newspapers even went so far as to link the unrest in Latino communities to fascist influences fomented by Nazi agents.[31] Rumors and misinformation in both the civilian and the military populations fueled the hysteria. Baseless stories of robberies, rapes, and even murders reinforced racial myths of the hypersexuality and depravity of Latinos and Black men. White fears intensified prejudices and discrimination and spurred vigilantism.

Finally, in June 1943, Los Angeles erupted into several days of violence in what the national press and historians have called the Zoot Suit Riots. (Similar violence between zoot suiters and white servicemen occurred elsewhere at the same time along the West Coast from San Diego to San Francisco and eastward to Philadelphia and New York, even north to Toronto.)[32] Numerous books and essays have been written about the week-long conflicts in Los Angeles, which had escalated from minor skirmishes during the spring into racial mob violence by June. Reports indicated that it all started when a large group of Latinos attacked a smaller group of white sailors in a barrio. The next day, white sailors and accompanying white civilians formed "vengeance squads" of more than a hundred men, sometimes including the police. The lightning rod was the zoot suit, and the target was anyone wearing one, whether Latino, Black, or even a few white jitterbuggers in the wrong place at the wrong time. The white mobs went into movie theaters, arcades, and dance halls to find zoot suiters, and to drag them out into the street where they were beaten and stripped of their clothes. Under pressure from the mayor and city officials, the Navy and Army declared the city a restricted area for enlisted men, and the riots came to an end.[33] "Ultimately, the Zoot Suit Riots were the result of a myriad of political, economic, and social factors that underscored the racial, gender, and sexual conflicts between zoot suiters and servicemen, and consistently marked zoot suiters as a threat to the safety of the general public."[34] Consequently, following the riots, movie theaters, amusement parks, arcades, pool halls, and other businesses banned the zoot suit. Schools posted notices prohibiting the style. Groups of middle-class nonwhites in Los Angeles held "surrender" gatherings with white flags and American flags to demonstrate their patriotism and to denounce the incendiary "zooting." Quickly, the look was abandoned by the end of 1943.

Soul style in the 1960s

Although the development of Afrocentric dress and identity that emerged from the mid-1960s into the early 1970s is beyond the scope of this study, its prelude at the end of the baby boom years should be mentioned because the sociopolitical groundwork for its development occurred during the civil rights movement of the mid-1950s through the early 1960s.

With the passage of the 1964 Civil Rights Act and the 1965 Voting Rights Act, African Americans reevaluated what it meant to be Black in the changing culture of the time. Having achieved its goals legislatively—if not yet socially, politically, and economically—the civil rights movement transitioned into the Black Power movement in the second half of the decade. "Black is beautiful" became a rallying cry for African Americans who wanted to find a modern, visible identity that reaffirmed their ethnic pride and unity.

One of the first challenges for many African Americans was to break the decades-old cycle of denying their ethnicity by straightening their hair and applying skin-bleaching creams. In his "Black Power" speech of July 28, 1966, activist Stokely Carmichael declared, "We have to stop being ashamed of being black. A broad nose, a thick lip and nappy hair is us, and we are going to call that beautiful whether they like it or not."[35] Yet, Carmichael and other advocates of the Black Power movement did not yet have recommendations for how to represent their new pride in self and heritage in the mid-1960s. The search for a way to manifest that idea of Black is beautiful developed slowly through the second half of the 1960s. The ideas of Black beauty that were so familiar to most African Americans—light skin, narrow noses, thin lips, straight hair—remained entrenched for years after Carmichael and other activists made their first Black Power speeches. For example, just a month after Carmichael's speech, the August 1966 issue of *Ebony* magazine celebrated "The Negro Woman," yet contained 15 ads for hair straighteners, "bleaching creams," and "skin whiteners."[36] In addition, an editorial noted, "Modern chemical methods of permanently straightening hair are being used increasingly by Negro and white beauticians." As one hair salon manager explained, "all operators in her establishment are capable of administering both the older thermal, or 'heat' method of straightening hair and the newer chemical hair relaxing process. Twenty-five per cent of her customers prefer relaxers, which have been available at her shop for ten years."[37]

A first step toward a Black-is-beautiful identity was to allow the untreated, natural growth of their hair, a look that came to be called an Afro. The hairstyle, cut in various shapes or teased out into a rounded puff, was initially associated with Black militants, but quickly became a ubiquitous fashion trend. At about the same time as the popularization of the Afro, Black activists also adopted forms of clothing and accessories that reflected their African heritage. The dashiki was a loose, collarless tunic usually made of fabrics that replicated African textiles, especially the multicolored patterns of kente cloth. Both men and women wore dashikis of varying lengths and sleeve types. For some African American women, the Afrocentric styles they adopted included kaftans and towering headwraps. Accessories included slippers, totes, and belts made of embroidered raffia and jewelry of colorful Maasai-inspired beadwork and cowrie shells. These were "symbols of the new awareness," of "black unity," and an identity that expressed the African Americans' "commitment to the struggle for development of the race."[38]

The Afrocentric styles adopted by many African Americans were the first ethnic dress and identity since the zoot suits were put away in 1943. "Black is beautiful" paved the path for what would become "soul style" in the late 1960s into the early 1970s. American ready-to-wear makers found a new market opportunity with the Black power movement and produced lines of shirts and trousers made in African-inspired prints and patterns. The Afro hairstyles would be replaced by more relevant African looks such as beaded braids and cornrows. "Black liberation provided a space for black people to use clothing to not only adorn but also re-aestheticize the black body. In doing so, Africana people believed they were rebuilding their psyches and healing emotional and physical wounds." This "re-aestheticization of blackness . . . created new value and political power for the black body . . . Through their clothing, they projected a sense of sexual freedom, gender nonconformity, and upward social mobility."[39]

Conclusion

On the cusp of the baby boom era, the first distinct dress and identity for African American and Latino men, the zoot suit, emerged in the swing culture of large cities in the late 1930s, culminating in broad, national popularity during the early years of the Second World War. The style of padded jackets with fingertip-length skirts and wide-legged trousers that tapered from a 30-inch knee to a pegged 12-inch cuff became a favorite look of some urban Black and Latino youths to wear to jazz clubs and dance halls. For many young men of color at the time, the zoot suit was more than a faddish fashion; it was a symbol of modernity, a visual spectacle, and performance that inspired jive talking and swag walking. On the dance floor, the zoot suit was also a performance, with its voluminous trousers flapping wildly and the long jacket skirt swirling about the body as the wearer energetically danced the jitterbug.

In addition, the pricey zoot suit and accessories were a statement of opulence. Some zoot ensembles—including a porkpie or broad-brimmed hat, knob-toe shoes, colorfully patterned four-in-hand necktie, and long silver- or gold-plated keychain—might cost in the $70–$100 range at a time when a ready-to-wear business suit and accessories cost $18–$24. As such, a custom-made zoot suit represented a consumption and leisure that marginalized working-class Blacks and Latinos had been denied.

Equally important for many young African Americans and Latinos, the zoot suit was a nonconformist assertion of dignity and resistance to systemic racism and oppressive segregation. The look was their unique cultural identity that challenged the norms of white society in the public sphere.

In early 1942, though, the zoot suit became a target for social opprobrium and eventually violence. As the US government geared up for the Second World War, the War Production Board issued a series of conservation regulations. To ensure war needs were met, the US government placed restrictions on the use of certain materials used in clothing such as wool and silk, and limited the amount of fabric that could be used in the construction of garments. Wearing the zoot suit, with its excesses of fabric and oversized garment cuts, appeared to be an unpatriotic flouting of wartime mandates. Confrontations between white servicemen and zoot suiters in ethnic neighborhoods, particularly in Los Angeles, increasingly led to violent mob actions that reached a peak in several days of race riots in June 1943. With the national press coverage of the conflicts and mass arrests, businesses began to prohibit zoot suits. Soon after, the style was abandoned.

The next distinct ethnic dress and identity would not emerge until the mid-1960s. Following the passage of civil rights legislation in 1964 and 1965, African Americans began to rethink what it meant to be Black in the changing culture of the era. Black activists challenged their people to embrace the physical attributes of their race with a rallying assertion that "Black is beautiful." The first step toward a re-aestheticization of blackness was the natural, untreated hairstyle called an Afro. In addition, Blacks began to wear styles of clothing that reflected their African heritage, such as the dashiki, a loose-fitting tunic usually made of fabrics that replicated African textiles. The Black-is-beautiful idea would continue to develop into the "soul style" of the 1970s in which even more Afrocentric looks were explored, ranging from beaded braids and cornrows to ready-to-wear in distinctly African-inspired prints and textile patterns.

6
WOMEN OF THE BABY BOOM ERA: LESSONS OF YOUTH

Feminine role models and expectations

The lives of most women of the baby boom era, particularly young wives and mothers, often have been viewed by historians as regressive compared to the war years. Young women of the 1950s were children of the Great Depression and grew up with family traditions still rooted in the nineteenth-century notions of separate spheres for men and women. In their 1937 Middletown study, sociologists Robert and Helen Lynd found a general consensus among the townsfolk that "women look after the affairs within the household; they care for the small children, and rear and teach the children, always with male authority in the background in the form of the father who comes home at night or the male superintendent of schools."[1] The message from the government, media, and popular culture of the Depression era was that a married woman should stay home and focus her attention on her husband, children, and housekeeping. A 1930 promotion by the *Ladies' Home Journal* announced a "new word . . . not yet in the dictionaries—homemaker." It was defined as a feminine noun: "One who makes a home, who manages a household, cares for her children, and promotes the happiness and well-being of her family."[2] A vast number of women in the 1930s who had obtained higher education or vocational skills, established careers or job tenure, and developed some degree of social and economic independence now came under pressure to set all that aside and be a homemaker exclusively. Women who worked during the Depression were often accused of stealing jobs from unemployed men. "All wage-earning women, whether in sales or clerical work, in the ill-paid sweatshop, manufacturing, and lesser service jobs that made up the bulk of female employment, or even, in rare cases, the professions, implicitly challenged notions of feminine moral purity and the companion ideal of family-as-vocation."[3] After Franklin Delano Roosevelt became president in 1933, his wife Eleanor was required to set an example for the nation and gave up her job teaching at a New York private school for girls as well as her membership in sociopolitical organizations such as the League of Women Voters.

> In the breadline climate of the 1930s, many turned to the old argument that woman and work [outside of the home] was a contradiction in terms . . . Working women, especially married ones, became the scapegoats of a movement to reassert the separate sphere thinking of past decades . . . Working women were carrying the baggage of a lingering Victorianism concerning their physical and moral fitness for work.[4]

From these pervasive sociocultural conventions, the baby boom era woman had been inculcated through her childhood in the 1930s with the singular identity goal as a married homemaker.

Yet, despite the social pressures of the time, millions of women continued to work or took their first jobs. Over 22 percent of the labor force, or about 10 million, was women in 1930, increasing to 25 percent, or about 12 million, by the end of the decade.[5] Most single women, widows, and many head-of-household women had no choice but to work outside the home to earn a living. Women with college degrees or vocational training continued with their careers as teachers, nurses, stenographers, beauticians, and the like. Also, some married women took jobs to supplement the reduced hours and wage cuts of their husbands. Still others became the family breadwinners when their husband's unemployment lingered or the men left to search for work far from home.

Unlike with men, the job was not the identity of women wage-earners. If their role was as family breadwinner, it was likely viewed as a temporary condition in hard times that could be remedied by a husband's reemployment or an improvement in his wages. Single working women were considered in transition from school to marriage and, in fact, upon marrying, would likely lose their jobs anyway due to pervasive company marriage bars. As such, Depression-era women's dress and identity were less linked than those of men. A man's drape cut business suit, whether worn by a bank clerk or a bank president, was integral to his identity—a uniform by which those he might encounter in the public sphere would identify him as a family breadwinner. For women, though, the white bow blouse and navy or charcoal wool skirt might indicate that the woman on a streetcar or a downtown sidewalk was employed, but the clothing was not integral to her identity—which remained that of a potential housebound wife, mother, and homemaker.

Women's dress of the 1930s shifted significantly from the previous decade when the flapper bobbed or shingled her hair short, abandoned girdles, and wore loose-hanging chemises with a dropped waistline at the hips. But beginning in 1929 and lasting through the 1930s, women's clothing became more curvaceous with a defined waist returned to its natural position. Dress silhouettes contoured the breasts and hips, and slim, long skirts accentuated thighs and buttocks. Whether in a $500 design by a Paris couturier or a $1.98 ready-to-wear dress from a mail-order retailer, these tenets of style hallmarked women's dress of the Depression era.

The new silhouettes of the 1930s also contributed to a revival of girdles and corsets. Figure-control foundation garments that had largely been worn by matrons in the 1920s now became essential for shaping the figure even of young women. Improved circular knitting techniques of elasticized yarns made tubular shapewear more comfortable, and the innovative addition of zippers to girdles and corsets made them easier to put on. Bras were reengineered to better support and shape the breasts, and the introduction of alphabet cup sizes in 1935 ensured the best fit. Nylon yarns, developed in 1938, were a more durable and affordable alternative to silk in intimate apparel, especially hosiery.

In women's sportswear, the emerging popularity of slacks paved the path for what would become a safety need for wartime workers. The legacy of trousers for women dated to the 1850s, when a few daring feminists such as Amelia Bloomer experimented with the idea. The bicycle craze of the 1890s expanded the variety of women's trousers in the form of knicker suits. As a fashion, a type of trousers called jupe-culottes was a brief fad of a few couturiers and avant-garde women in Paris, London, and New York in the early 1910s. The more practical need of trousers for women, though, came during World War I, when women in Europe and America went to work in munitions and armaments factories to backfill labor shortages while men were in the military. Through the 1920s, voluminous, colorful pyjamas (not to be confused with sleepwear pajamas) for women were increasingly seen at summer resorts as beach and casual afternoon attire. In the mid-1930s, Hollywood stars such as Katherine Hepburn and Marlene Dietrich led the way for the middle classes to wear slacks by appearing in movies and publicity photos dressed in comfortable versions for daytime activities and leisure. By the end of the decade, *Life* magazine reported that "American women find it's fun to wear pants [and] spend millions a year for them . . . Each year, new merchants add slacks to their stocks [and] the demand has forced manufacturers to turn them out in sizes up to 44. American women like to wear pants."[6]

When the United States entered the Second World War, women's fashions again changed significantly. But for more than five million American women who entered the labor force, new varieties of dress meant more than keeping current with hemlines, hats, and hairstyles. Wartime needs required redefining gender roles and identities that dramatically altered prevailing conservative social norms.

American women during World War II

The Second World War began in September 1939 when Nazi Germany invaded Poland, and by treaty with Poland, allies Britain and France immediately declared war on Germany. For the following two years, before Japan attacked the United States at Pearl Harbor, Hawaii, in December 1941, America remained neutral. But the US government and industries responded with a massive aid program for Britain called Lend-Lease, in which millions of tons of weapons, ammunition, aircraft, ships, tanks, transport vehicles, military equipment, and supplies such as steel, cable, chemicals, oil, and canned food were exported to the besieged nation. In addition, the Roosevelt administration began preparing for an inevitable entry into the war by stockpiling materiel at home. Almost overnight, the Great Depression came to an end as American industries converted and expanded operations to a war footing. Unemployment dropped from a high of 25.2 percent at the peak of the Depression in 1933 to only 1.2 percent in 1944—a reduction from 12.8 million unemployed (of a labor force of 51 million) down to 670,000 (of a labor force of 66 million).[7]

In 1940, the United States began planning for a national labor force to include an increase of women workers, most of whom had never worked outside of the home or were just finishing school and preparing for their first job. The Analysis Division of the US Department of Labor compiled a report of readiness as well as recommendations for mobilizing the surge of new workers.[8] In 1940, nearly 13 million women worked outside the home full time (out of a population of 65 million women), mostly in the service sectors such as restaurants, hotels, laundries, and retail (75 percent of workers were women), and in certain manufacturing like textile mills and apparel production (65 percent of the workers were women). Both government and industry leaders anticipated when the United States entered the war, "Undoubtedly, appeals to patriotism would cause many women to seek war employment. Nevertheless, some means will have to be found to relieve women homemakers of part of their family obligations before they can assume work outside the home."[9] Among the government's recommendations for employers were part-time shifts and staggering hours, and providing daycare services. Once hired and trained, to keep the women employees, factories also were advised to consider improving sanitary and healthful working conditions. And most importantly for the war effort, training programs had to be implemented for jobs that had usually been exclusively male domains, such as welding, electronics, vehicle assembly, shipbuilding, aircraft fabrication, and machine and heavy equipment operation, among many others.

To achieve the wartime workforce and defense production goals, the Labor Department further advised employers on how to hire women, publishing a series of bulletins covering topics ranging from "effective industrial use of women" to preparing "washing and toilet facilities for women in industry." To prepare for the "great influx of women into jobs previously marked for 'men only,' the Women's Bureau provided factory employers a guideline of ten points based on experience of women working in industry":

First—Sell the idea of women workers to present employee staff—the foremen and men workers.

Second—Survey jobs to decide which are most suitable for women.

Third—Make adaptations of jobs to fit smaller frames and less muscular strength of women.

Fourth—Provide service facilities in the plant to accommodate anticipated numbers of women.

Fifth—Appoint a women's personnel director to organize and head a women-counselor system.

Sixth—Select women carefully and for specific jobs.

Seventh—Develop a program for the induction and training of women.

Eighth—Establish good working conditions.

Ninth—Supervise women workers intelligently.

Tenth—Give women equal opportunity with men.[10]

Some of these guidelines were fairly complex and required reengineering shops with automated production steps such as installing conveyor belts and air-operation wrenches, reducing the size of shovels and carts, or replacing manual levers and wheels with push-button controls.

Other guidelines required basic psychology. One suggestion that had proven effective in finding women replacements for men who may be leaving for military service or changing jobs within a plant was to ask the male workers "to bring a woman relative whom he regarded as capable of holding his job. It became a matter of pride on the part of each man to have the woman substitute succeed, so no effort was spared in teaching her his work."[11]

The government propaganda posters, movie newsreels, radio public service announcements, and other media calls for women workers were effective. The surge of women into the labor force between 1941 and 1945 was almost 5 million for a total of 19 million working women.[12] But women workers were needed for much more than defense production. With 10 million men in the military, a broad range of routine civilian jobs also needed to be filled by women. In 1942, *Time* acknowledged, "The most striking evidence of the still incomplete social revolution wrought by World War II can be found in the new occupations of American women," which included highway steam roller operators, railroad track gangs and brakemen, blacksmiths, traffic cops, streetcar conductors, casket carriers and hearse drivers, and garbage collectors. "There is hardly any job—truck driver, mechanic, cobbler, oyster shucker, engineer, bartender, butcher, baker, or candlestick maker—that women cannot get if they want them and more and women are getting them."[13]

Among other preparatory measures the US government initiated ahead of the influx of new women workers in factories and heavy industries were recommendations for the types of clothes that would ensure the best safety. In 1941, the Labor Department produced the booklet *Safety Clothing for Women in Industry*. The first principle was "Work dress must suit the job to be safe . . . Designers have in mind first safety, then convenience, wearability, comfort, cleanliness and coolness. Attractiveness is given due consideration."[14] Many safety aspects of women's attire likely had not been considered by clothing makers previously, such as spark-proof shoes made with wooden-pegged soles for working where explosives were manufactured or wooden-sole clogs where chemical spills might occur. In some industries, special safety equipment had been required for years, such as goggles, gloves, aprons, or rubber coats and boots. Since most of these were made with easy-fit adjustments, special sizes for women were not necessary for factories to stock.

Women's long hair was especially hazardous around machinery, requiring special visored caps that fully encased the hair and shaded the eyes, or various types of headwraps and scarves, which not only held the hair in place but also protected scalp and tresses from dust and airborne chemicals. Hair nets were a common solution for keeping hair close to the head, a look that inspired milliners to revive the snood as a fashion look. Hairstylists responded to the trend of working women pinning up their hair and developed updated revivals of their grandmother's Gibson Girl pompadours. Actress Veronica Lake, famous for her long blonde "peek-a-boo" hairstyle (worn down over one eye), provided a movie newsreel demonstration of the "victory roll" arrangement, which was tightly pinned up in the back, forming a V-shape. Many women, though, simply opted for the convenience of short haircuts.

Jewelry, too, was forbidden. "The useful wrist watch, the frivolous earrings, necklaces, rings, and bracelets, though attractive in themselves, have no place in the factory," forewarned the *Safety Clothing* bulletin. "Companies make definite rules that no visible jewelry may be worn."[15] The preferred women's safety clothing for most defense plant work was pants and a short-sleeved blouse, or a short-sleeved jumpsuit. (Figure 6.1.) These outfits became the dress identity of the patriotic working woman during the war—an image celebrated in advertising and popular culture, notably Norman Rockwell's 1943 depiction of "Rosie the Riveter" for a cover of the *Saturday Evening Post*. Women were cautioned against any frills, cuffs, or excessive fabric that could get caught in machinery. Even rolled-up long sleeves formed a bulk of fabric that was a safety hazard. Cotton was recommended for comfort and easy laundering,

WOMEN OF THE BABY BOOM ERA

Figure 6.1 The recommended safety clothing for women working in war defense factories was pants and a short-sleeved blouse. Reliance ad, 1942; Pan-American Coffee ad, 1944.

while rayon and similar cellulose textiles were to be avoided as dangerously flammable.

All women's clothing styles of the war years were subject to government restrictions in the use of fabric and garment construction. As noted in Chapter 1, the L-85 regulations from the US War Production Board (WPB) were issued in

April 1942 with the intention of reducing the amount of fabric used in apparel. Prohibited immediately in women's wear were turned-back French cuffs; double material yokes; balloon, dolman, or leg-of-mutton sleeves; all-over tucking, shirring, or pleating (minor trimmings remained acceptable); patch pockets of wool cloth; and linings of wool cloth. Skirts could no longer be made with attached overskirts, aprons, or petticoats. For coats, attached capes, hoods, scarves, and accompanying accessories such as handbags or hats were prohibited. Specific measurement limits for various types of garments were specific in length, width, or sweep depending on the garment size. Skirts, for example, were shortened to 28 inches for a size 16 with hems no more than two inches. Jackets were shortened to 25 inches from the nape of the neck to the hem for a size 16 and could no longer include back vents, Norfolk-style pleats, or sleeve cuffs. Trousers were narrowed to a taper of 12 inches at the hem. Self-belts were limited to two inches in width. Multigarment ensembles sold as a one-unit price were curtailed depending on the fabric.[16] Illustrations in the L-85 Limitation Order showed examples of before (prohibited) and after (conservation-compliant) designs. (Figure 6.2.)

The WPB apparel industry committee was headed by Stanley Marcus of Neiman-Marcus Department Store and included a number of fashion experts and editors. Everyone was concerned with stifling creativity in the fashion industry by overly strict, government-imposed dictates on designing. But after the L-85 regulations were issued, Marcus and the committee were reassured by the National Retail Dry Goods Association, "There will be no stagnation in fashion designing as a result of these rulings . . . The government has worked very thoughtfully in drafting the new rulings. With great wisdom they have avoided the kind of arbitrary checks that would be a hindrance to creative design."[17] For most women of the war years—factory worker or homemaker—wearing the new shorter, trimmer fashions was representative of two duties: patriotic conservation and support of the civilian economy. Any woman wearing a fully pleated wool skirt or jacket with leg-of-mutton sleeves not only appeared to be out of style but also was regarded as unpatriotic in her extravagant waste. In *Vogue*'s "view of law-abiding clothes," the editors reassured readers in May 1942, "We chose the clothes in this issue because they're pretty, practical, and right for these times. As it turns out, they're right by conservation standards, too. You can be pretty and patriotic, at one and the same time."[18]

In addition to taking new jobs in defense plants and backfilling a wide variety of other civilian jobs, more than 400,000 women also volunteered for newly formed auxiliary military corps. The first US military organization for women was the Women's Army Corps (WAC), established initially in 1942 as an auxiliary service unit, but the following year converted into an active-duty branch of the Army. These women worked as aircraft mechanics, installed radios in tanks, managed requisitions and records, and trained men in field artillery, among many other responsibilities. In 1944, WACs were sent abroad into dangerous support

Figure 6.2 During World War II, the US government implemented the L-85 restrictions on the use of materials in clothing production. Official bulletins sent to manufacturers in 1942 included illustrations of prohibited styles (shown as figures 1: coats with dolman sleeves, fully pleated skirts, and patch pockets) next to conservation-compliant adaptations (shown as figures 2).

areas behind combat troops around the globe from Normandy to Manila. As the press noted in 1944 of "those wonderful G.I. Janes," the WACs in the European theater "have been called 'Eisenhower's secret weapons.'" They "have proved able and willing workers . . . doing a thousand and one different jobs they never dreamed of doing when they joined up." (Four had even received Purple Hearts at that time.)[19] A war correspondent from the Italian campaign reminded stateside readers in April 1944, "Up front where tents, mud, and the ability to slide quickly into the nearest fox hole are essential to living, a platoon of WACs is proving that soldier girls can take the front line in stride . . . 'We couldn't—and wouldn't—do without them,'" declared General Mark Clark.[20]

The success of the WACs inspired the organization of women's units for the other branches of armed services. Women volunteers for the Naval Reserve were called the WAVES (Women Accepted for Voluntary Emergency Service), and for the US Coast Guard were called SPARS (Semper Paratus—Always Ready). They served in US shore stations but were never allowed on board ships or sent abroad other than Hawaii and Alaska. For the Air Force, women recruits were the WASPS (Women Airforce Service Pilots) and WAFS (Women's Auxiliary Ferrying Squadron). These women were licensed, experienced pilots who flew aircraft from factories to US airbases, assignments which freed hundreds of male pilots for combat duties overseas.

The dress identity of women in these volunteer organizations was a uniform. As a recruitment booklet advised potential volunteers:

> A WAC wears a uniform for the same reasons Army men do—it's efficient for the work she has to do. It identifies her as an Army person—a person who has accepted the full responsibilities of an Army job . . . The Army outfits you completely. Supplies you with equipment and clothing that would cost you about $250 if you were to buy these things in a store at retail prices. You get winter and summer uniforms. Clothes for working [such as slacks, jumpsuits, overalls, aprons, and safety garments depending on the assigned tasks]. A serviceable handbag. Underwear and shoes.[21]

The uniforms, raincoat, overcoat, and rayon "victory blouse" of the WAVES and SPARS were famously designed by couturier Mainbocher and were described in the press as "womanly, workmanlike."[22] Advertisers and popular culture media honored the sacrifice of these women with depictions of them in uniform or at work in the field. (Although women of color were accepted into some of these women's corps, they were commonly segregated, given menial assignments, and largely kept out of sight.) The 1944 Fashion Frocks ad shown in Figure 6.3 depicts the uniforms of a WAC and WAVE with copy that reminds women of a totally new, patriotic identity available to them: "Your WAC or WAVE uniform tells people you are in the Army or Navy—not merely wishing but working for Victory.

WOMEN OF THE BABY BOOM ERA

Figure 6.3 Women's wartime identities expanded dramatically with the introduction of female volunteer service organizations. Their uniforms represented these new, patriotic identities not only within the service branches but also to the public. Ads, 1943–1944.

When you become a WAC or a WAVE, you will be serving your country, enjoying a thrilling new life, going new places, making new friends . . . The experience and training you will get pave the way for better opportunities in postwar days."[23]

Similarly, Tangee Cosmetics featured WASPS preparing to fly a fighter plane dressed in the same functional jumpsuits and safety equipment that combat pilots wore. These women are not fashion plates, although Tangee reminds readers that "American women are still the loveliest and most spirited in the world. The best dressed, the best informed, the best looking." The US government agreed with Tangee that "a woman's lipstick is an instrument of personal morale," and preserves "the precious right of women to be feminine and lovely"—not only for themselves but for the men in wartime America.[24] Consequently, cosmetics were regarded as essential civilian needs by the War Production Board and were exempted from many conservation restrictions of raw materials, such as oils, petrochemicals, and dyes used in lipstick and makeup product manufacturing.[25]

The dress identity of American women working in war industries or service branches ranged from unflattering but necessary work clothes, headwraps, and safety equipment to couturier-designed uniforms and matching accessories. On sight in the public sphere, these women were recognized as patriotic workers doing a duty for the war effort—a necessary but temporary role for the duration. At the same time, social conservatives and traditionalists also often expressed concerns about what these wartime feminine identities were doing to America's young women both in the moment of the war years and in the long run.

Sociocultural changes for women during World War II

The women defense workers in slacks and jumpsuits and women service members in uniforms may have been acknowledged as patriotic citizens for the duration of the war, but even then, in some circles they were also regarded with suspicion and disdain by many Americans. Some men working in jobs that had previously been solely a masculine domain resented the presence of women, even if the labor need was acute. This misogyny was rooted in the Victorian notion of separate spheres—men were the breadwinners and women stayed home in the kitchen and nursery. To have women doing the same work as men, often side-by-side with men, in their eyes, diminished their masculine identity. Suddenly, men found their workplaces renovated with the addition of women's bathrooms and locker rooms. Machines and equipment were modified with push-button controls, conveyor belts, and chain pullies to ease heavy lifting and operations that men had otherwise managed with brawn. In many instances, men had to modify their workplace behavior and language with women present.

Women in the military, even those restricted to stateside postings, were even more resented. Most Americans considered a "skirted army" as a social experiment they were not ready for, regardless of the wartime needs. The "asymmetrically gendered relationship between the male 'protector' and the female 'protected'" was deeply ingrained in American culture. The female soldier was viewed as "a figure whose potential sexual and economic independence from men subverted the 'natural order' and whose position as a female protector usurped men's status and power, both within and outside of the home."[26] It was one thing for nurses to care for convalescing soldiers in military hospitals, and perhaps for some women civilians to volunteer time as telephone operators and clericals in military base offices, as had occurred during World War I, but to actually recruit women into the Army, with the same pay and benefits as male servicemen, was unacceptable for many, including army leadership. Allied Supreme Commander Dwight Eisenhower later admitted when initially faced with the proposal of women in the military, "like most soldiers, I was violently against it."[27] To most Americans, military service, even more so than breadwinning, was a man's job. Moreover, some argued that women in the military might displace young men who wanted to enlist, thereby costing them the opportunity to prove their manhood with an honorable discharge.[28]

Many of the arguments against the formation of the first US women's auxiliary corps were the same as against working women in general; the separate spheres of men's and women's domains and roles in society would be undermined. During the debate on the legislation in Congress, Representative C.E. Hoffman insisted, "Who then, will maintain the home fires; who will do the cooking, the washing, the mending, the humble, homey tasks to which every woman has devoted herself; who will rear and nurture the children?"[29] In addition, there were family economic considerations as well, since women leaving the home for the military, whether young daughters who just completed school or young working women living at home and contributing to their parent's economic status, meant a household's loss of domestic labor or income. Generations of gender role norms were suddenly challenged, and this cross-over of women into military service meant possibly questioning other gendered conventions. Especially vocal against women in the military were religious groups. In 1942, one Catholic publication declared the formation of the women's corps as "an opening wedge, intended to break down the traditional American and Christian opposition to removing women from the home, and to degrade her by bringing back the pagan female goddess of desexed, lustful sterility." Especially alarming for many of these groups was how the acceptance of women in the military might lead to other sociocultural shifts and be "used as a means of fixing a national pattern [of women soldiers] on American community life."[30]

Part of the sociocultural fears of traditionalists was the sexual autonomy that young women would have while out on their own, away from parents, teachers, pastors, and similar chaperoning elders. Being their own women in the military, earning their own money, and achieving personal and professional goals might also encourage sexual exploration. After all, these young women would be surrounded by battalions of good-looking, fit young men in uniforms. In 1944, *Ladies' Home Journal* asserted, "On the plane of sexual morality, most traditional barriers against women are gone . . . They may drink and smoke in public, be as free as they like in extremes of dress and adornment, and may even be sexually promiscuous, provided they are fairly discreet about it."[31] Like the *Journal* editors, most people conflated sexual autonomy with sexual promiscuity, which allowed opponents of women in the military to spread misinformation, rumors, and blatant lies about the morality of women who joined the military corps. Through much of the war, the WAC had to endure accusations "that its members were prostitutes, 'loose' women, or predatory lesbians." Gossip was rampant about the promiscuity of military women in both civilian and military circles. Among the falsehoods about women in the corps that made the rounds were that these women were recruited specifically as "companions" to soldiers to service their sexual needs, and, as such, virgins were rejected by medical examiners. Another refuted slander was that these women were so promiscuous that the military had to provide contraceptives to minimize pregnancies. In actuality, "the WAC had to go beyond behavior to manage the sexual reputation of the WAC . . . WAC leaders took extraordinary steps to guarantee that the corps was—and was perceived to be—a 'respectable' institution that neither harmed its members' reputations nor undermined their femininity."[32] Women entered the corps with a full understanding of rules governing all aspects of their behavior, including their sex lives.

As for women going overseas into the theater of war, another question in the minds of many Americans was a woman's physical capabilities and potential for enduring the hardships of makeshift camps and the dangers from enemy planes and bombs. Forgetting the history of America's women pioneers, most Americans regarded women as the weaker sex, who would therefore weaken the effectiveness of the military. "We may be serving shoulder to shoulder with American men—but we're still the weaker sex," avowed a 1944 Tangee Cosmetics ad. (And as such, "it's still up to us to appear as alluring and lovely as possible.")[33] Detractors further insisted that weaknesses of women—physical and moral—not only diluted the strength of the army but also put at risk soldiers who needed to count on the training, skill, and strength of their comrades in arms.

Nonetheless, tens of thousands of American women enlisted in the various military services, thousands of which went to war in North Africa, Europe, and the Pacific. At the end of the war, corps women received high praise from throughout the military command. The debate about women in the military was renewed when proposals were made for allowing women to continue to serve as reservists. Surprisingly, the head of the WAC was against the idea since "so many women reservists would marry, have children, and thus be unable to serve on active duty when they were needed." She believed that most Americans "wanted their servicewomen returned home promptly to reknit family life."[34] Between 1945 and 1948, Congress debated and revised bill after bill to allow women to serve as both Army reservists and regulars. Finally, in 1948, as the Soviets began their Cold War aggressions in Central Europe, Congress passed the Women's Armed Services Integration Act, and in June, President Truman signed the bill into law.

Conclusion

The young wives and mothers of the baby boom era had grown up during the 1930s with family traditions and norms rooted in Victorian ideas of separate spheres for men and women. Men were the breadwinners and head of the family, while women were homemakers and child caregivers. A working married woman in the Depression years likely held a job out of necessity—the single young woman just out of school awaiting marriage, the widow needing an income, or the working-class wife supplementing the family finances. Employment was not an identity for them, the way a job often was for men. Exceptions were rare, such as women with advanced degrees whose job was a profession such as a doctor, lawyer, or professor, for whom certain forms of dress identified them as distinct from the masses of their sisters. For the most part, working women in the 1930s were viewed with skepticism. They were often stigmatized as neglecting their duties as wives and mothers, even if the income was necessary for the family's well-being. They were also criticized for stealing jobs from men and thus undermining the masculine identity and role of a man as family head.

This pervasive attitude toward working women changed dramatically during the Second World War. With more than 10 million men serving in the US military, labor shortages were acute. Government and industry called for women to help as their patriotic duty, and tens of thousands went to work outside the home for the first time in their lives. Now, a woman's work was her identity, especially when hallmarked by her dress in trousers and headwraps as a defense worker or by her military uniform.

But Rosie the Riveter was regarded as a temporary wartime anomaly in American culture. When the war ended, many of these women quit their jobs to return to their roles as full-time wives, homemakers, and mothers. Many other women, particularly if married, who may have wanted to continue working, were instead fired as companies revived marriage bars that prohibited women under the age of 45 to be employed or hired.

These were the lessons of gender norms, feminine identity, and societal expectations that postwar young women had learned as girls growing up in the Depression and war years. These were the lessons that the majority of postwar young wives and the mothers of the baby boom generation understood, accepted, and applied to the roles and identities that defined their lives.

7
WOMEN'S IDENTITIES IN THE BABY BOOM YEARS

Marriage reunions at the end of the war

Women who married before or during the war were anxious to reestablish relationships with their soldier husbands and to acclimate young children to fathers who had been away for two or three years. Wives looked forward to demobilized husbands finding jobs with better incomes than the military paycheck had provided, and reestablishing their roles as the head of household and family breadwinner. If their men were known to have been in combat, the long periods of worry were over. For wives whose husbands were posted stateside but far from home, bringing their men home meant an end to their loneliness and tedious waiting.

For many women, though, the marital adjustment was a challenge. Tens of thousands of married women had been living autonomous lives, sometimes for three years or more, making their own decisions, earning their own money as defense workers, managing finances, and being a head of household. Now they were to revert to the role of dependent wife, which many were happy to do but only with a significant effort. "They've got a job of reconverting too," cautioned *Ladies' Home Journal* in December 1945. "They've got to stop being independent and get used to having a full-time boss around the house. They've got to adapt themselves to the male ego after being comfortably female for several years." Women were forewarned, "Just as it takes six months to make a husband into a soldier, so it takes six months to unmake that soldier and turn him back into a family man again." The editors acknowledged that during the war, many young wives achieved a "mental and emotional maturity" that would have a significant impact on their reunions:

> For them, reconverting to a domestic pattern is a major step in which they feel they are doing all the giving. Trading eight hours of clean methodical work

at a factory to go back to a sixteen-hour day of mopping floors, washing dishes and cooking, with no pay check at the end of the week, strikes them as an unfair and unattractive exchange . . . If GIs come home with the same definition of a wife they went away with—and all indications confirm that they will—then there are rocks ahead for a vast number of marriages.[1]

Married women were further advised by the *Journal* that they would need to be especially patient with husbands who had been on the front lines of war. "A combat soldier, whose constant emotion has been fear for two or three years, [cannot] immediately become a home-loving husband upon discharge." During his time at war, instead of "the love of home, his wife and children, he has had to substitute buddy love, company love, and fear, fear, fear."[2] Readers were advised that the readjustment to civilian and home life for the veteran could take months.

Another significant readjustment for married couples after the war was economic. Many thousands of women who had taken war defense jobs wanted to continue earning a paycheck. Some families needed the income since many GIs opted for a year of unemployment benefits during their readjustment to civilian life or chose school instead of a job. But tens of thousands of women who had taken war defense jobs suddenly faced the reestablishment of marriage bars by companies large and small that banned the employment or hiring of married women under the age of 45, or in some cases, married women of any age.[3] Women workers who married while employed also were usually required to quit by company policy. For many couples, this loss of income was yet another stressful adjustment to married life after the war.

For many other women at the end of the war who were terminated and told to go home and focus on husbands, children, and homemaking, they were content to do so. In 1945, *Ladies' Home Journal* profiled a "demobilized housewife" who, during the war, "had two babies, helped build fifty-five submarines, and earned twice the salary of her [Navy] husband." Like many young women defense workers, she had

> worked too hard, slept too little, ate on the run, and when the final whistle blew came home to stacks of clothes to be washed, floors to be scrubbed, hungry people to be fed. The weariness and strain on their faces were not paid for by the money they made, and the mark on their spirits was as real as any foxhole fatigue.

When she was no longer needed to weld submarine components, she was more than glad to return full time to her role as housewife and mother. Her Navy husband was discharged and planned on attending commercial art classes. "'I want some sleep, some time to love my husband,' says this ex-welder, glad to be home."[4]

Postwar newlyweds

As discussed in Chapter 2, following the end of the Second World War, US marriage rates spiked significantly from a Depression era low of 7.9 percent to 16.4 percent of the population, with 2.2 million couples getting married in 1946.[5] Also, the median age of newlyweds in the postwar years was younger than before the war—for women, dropping from age 21.5 in 1940 to 20.1 in 1956.[6] The nation was anxious for a return to normalcy, which included a restoration of family stability, traditions, and gender norms. Marriage was idealized by government propaganda, advertising, movies, romance magazines, and other forms of popular culture. "The twin specters of communism and atomic war also called for national sobriety and a responsible mature citizenship . . . Fears of communism and nuclear annihilation prompted a turn to the comforts of home and family."[7] In addition, returning servicemen were given incentives to get married through the GI Bill that provided VA-guaranteed loans for the purchase of homes and businesses. The booming wartime and postwar economies further encouraged young couples to marry. Single women working war jobs who were fired when factories retooled for the production of consumer goods and to make way for returning soldiers found marriage a way out of financial straits. Also, single young women, newly from school, saw marriage as a way to escape from parental authority and to enter the world of adulthood.

For many young newlyweds of the postwar years, though, the adjustment to marriage was often a struggle. With the adult privileges of independence from parents, self-determination as a couple, and spousal intimacy also came unfamiliar adult responsibilities. Many of these postwar couples were still in their teens or barely in their twenties and had a great deal of physical and emotional maturing to undertake. For the first time, they had to think of someone other than themselves. Compromise was necessary for marriage to succeed, and, for women, that burden was usually on their shoulders. As *Ladies' Home Journal* advised in 1951:

> When a woman becomes a wife, she undertakes an entirely new role. Since her principal occupation will be running the house, in a sense marriage is a change of jobs. Adapting to this change successfully requires many of the attitudes that would be needed in any new job . . . A secretary takes for granted her obligation to carry out her employer's wishes, to make allowances for his mistakes and weaknesses while doing her utmost to enhance his talents and abilities. She approaches her job with optimism, determination and willingness to learn.[8]

Adaptation was a key word for newlywed women in the 1950s—much more so than for men. Historian Elaine Tyler May reflected that baby boom era wives were "more willing to make sacrifices for the sake of the relationships and eager to define their marriages as workable and successful, even if imperfect." The success of their marriage hinged on their capacity for flexibility—"adapting to their husband's needs and adapting their own goals and aspirations to fit the marriages they had created . . . Most seemed to agree that a less-than-ideal marriage was much better than no marriage at all, and that marriage itself offered benefits that compensated for the shortcomings of their husbands." Foremost among those benefits were a "secure, stable, and materially comfortable life" and eventually, motherhood.[9]

Along those lines, decision-making was frequently deferred to the husband. "Married women in the 1950s may have been members of a team, but their husbands called the plays. Wives were in the peculiar situation of being equal, but less than equal."[10] Even *Vogue* entered the marriage advice arena with similar traditionalist views. As the editors looked at future fashion trends in 1959, they also glanced backward to notions of Victorian separate spheres. "In marriage both sexes are equal, only one, the male, is more equal than the other . . . The man should be the undisputed head of the house."[11] In certain areas of the marriage, though, men allowed women free rein, usually regarding decisions in which they had little interest to begin with. Home décor was commonly women's domain, except when expenses for major purchases such as large appliances or furniture were considered. Childcare was also viewed principally as a woman's decision prerogative, unless disciplinary punishment needed administering, or significant expenses such as orthodontics were involved, and then Dad stepped in.

This male privilege legacy of the Victorian separate spheres sometimes required women to scheme and to manipulate their husbands into thinking that an idea was theirs, especially if the man of the house had previously made known his opinions to the contrary, or if finances beyond the household allowance were involved. These "power plays" of manipulative wives were often a theme in TV dramas and comedies of the 1950s, notably *I Love Lucy* and *The Donna Reed Show,* where the housewife mother was the focal character.[12]

Besides having to grow up fast and adjust to the compromises of marriage, many young couples confronted financial troubles for which they were not prepared. Thousands of young husbands who had served during the war opted for the education benefits of the GI Bill to go to college or trade school full time rather than get a job. Young wives sometimes had to take on the role of breadwinner for a few years. They had to postpone having children, or worse, had to deal with raising small children while working outside the home, housekeeping, and supporting a husband student. In other instances of financial strain, the young woman who managed to escape from her parents as a bride instead had to return home with a husband whose wages or starter salary was not adequate, to live cramped in her old childhood room or a makeshift apartment in the parent's basement, attic, or garage. In addition, the newlyweds also might have needed loans or supplemental allowances from parents, forestalling their progress toward maturity and adult independence.

If the wife of a husband student also had intentions of completing her education or attending college, she likely deferred that goal in favor of the husband's educational pursuits. The number of women completing college degrees for the ten years between 1951 and 1961 actually dropped from a high of 496,000 conferred degrees in 1950.[13] In addition to the demands of putting their husbands through school, a number of other roadblocks deterred postwar married women from seeking a higher education. College admission policies of the era gave priority to veterans, and in some institutions married women were barred entirely. Women of color, single or married, faced even greater exclusion. Sociocultural pushback from social scientists, women's magazines, and popular culture continually suggested that education for women was largely a waste of time and money, and could actually impede their roles of wife and mother. "Since the role of women as wives and mothers will prevent them from enjoying any of their intellectual or cultural interests . . . a college education in the liberal arts is said to be either unnecessary or potentially harmful," affirmed a 1959 study of women's higher education.[14] A firsthand example of this attitude came in a letter to a married woman applying to Harvard's Graduate School of Design in 1961, in which she was advised, "Our experience, even with brilliant students, has been that married women find it difficult to carry out worthwhile careers in [urban] planning, and hence tend to have some feeling of waste about the time and effort spent in professional education."[15] Furthermore, this decline in the college enrollment of women in the 1950s caused "a general erosion of the respect and prominence of women on college campuses. The attitude on campuses became apathetic, even hostile in some cases, toward women."[16] Only when the first baby boomers were old enough to attend college in the early 1960s did the enrollment rates of women begin to climb again.

As a consolation for some young wives of husband students in the 1950s, when their husbands graduated, women's support groups and even colleges handed out Ph.T "degrees," meaning "Putting Husband Through."[17] Citations printed with raised-letter type fonts acknowledged the wife's patience and loyalty while her husband attended school: "assisting him with studying, turning the radio low so that he might concentrate, . . . keeping the baby quiet, preparing coffee for midnight cramming sessions, arranging textbooks, filling pens, ironing coats, cancelling party plans, answering midnight telephone calls, working to supplement his income and intuitively providing spiritual encouragement."[18] Some women accepted the award as acknowledgment of their self-sacrifice, but for others the parchment token was a reminder of their own deferred or lost ambitions. "The wife who puts her husband through, winds up through. By the time he acquires the significant degree and she is awarded the sop to her pride, the relationship of peers has been fractured. At this point, he takes up the earning responsibility as a professional, while her profession becomes marriage."[19] In one instance, the Ph.T diploma was used in a divorce case as evidence of the wife's contribution to the marriage.[20]

Postwar marriage: Not happily ever after

As the US government, social scientists, and religious groups applauded the surge in young marriages at the end of the war, they were likewise shocked and dismayed at the spike in divorces. As early as December 1945, wives of returning veterans were forewarned by the *Ladies' Home Journal* that they, too, had "a job of reconverting" to a postwar life, and the adjustment could be demanding and difficult. Just in the few months since the end of the war in Europe, the *Journal* noted, the divorce rate had already climbed significantly. "Service centers, community counseling bureaus and the Red Cross report an overwhelming succession of veterans and veterans' wives seeking divorce information."[21] In 1946, the US divorce rate of 4.6 percent was over three times what it had been in the 1930s. During the 1950s, the divorce rate leveled off, but remained at 2.1–2.6 percent, or double what it had been in the Depression era.[22]

The reasons for the high divorce rates, even as numbers of marriages and the baby boom soared, were topics of sociocultural studies and analyses all through the postwar era. As discussed earlier in this chapter, for couples married before or during the war, the return of veteran husbands in the months after the war presented challenges of readjustment that were often overwhelming. Many wives found that the husbands they had seen off to the military had changed significantly during their time away. Women were told by counselors, magazine articles, and social peers that they needed to be patient, perhaps for months, while their veteran husbands adjusted to civilian and home life again. Most wives took on that burden willingly, but for others, patience wore thin.

The adjustment for many couples also included a new, unexpected test. Some young couples had been married only a short time before or during the war and did not really know each other well to begin with. For the young wife who became a war worker during her husband's absence, her newly acquired self-reliance, autonomy, and financial independence helped her mature rapidly. For that wife to give up her autonomy to resume a dependent role of wife and homemaker seemed regressive and demeaning to some women. For the returning husband to find a different wife than the one he thought he had left behind was a further disappointment to the dream he may have had of his homecoming, and an additional challenge to the readjustment process.

Still, for thousands of postwar married couples, the adjustments were unbearable and divorce was the only solution. In 1947, Dr. Marynia Farnham wrote in *Modern Woman, The Lost Sex,* "For whatever else divorcing persons may be, it will be conceded that they are not happy . . . Reasons assigned for the sharp rise in the divorce rate are numerous, but whatever they are, it is clear that good relations between divorcing persons have ceased. They have not become indifferent to each other so much as actively hostile."[23] In 1956, a panel of psychiatrists for *Life* magazine examined "the causes of our disturbing divorce rate." From their analysis, divorce was "the failure of men and women to accept their emotional responsibilities to each other and within the family—as men and women, male and female . . . Increasingly, sexes in this country are losing their identities." In essence, psychiatrists of the time determined that modern American men and women suffered from "sexual ambiguity." That is, "men are designed by nature to sire children and women to bear them," from which comes "their differences in emotional needs." The "primary feminine qualities—receptivity, passivity and the desire to nurture—color a woman's entire emotional life. For the male, the sexual role requires aggressiveness and a certain degree of dominance, even of explosiveness—the desire to utilize others for one's own advantage." Instead, the roles seemed to be reversed in many marriages in the mid-1950s. The "career woman" especially was often determined to be at fault. "She is independent and assertive . . . She dislikes housework, she never learned how to cook, she turned the children over to [caregivers] . . . A large number of young mothers . . . work not because they really have to but because they are rejecting the role of wife and mother." The career woman "may find satisfaction in her job, but the chances are that she, her husband and her children will suffer psychological damage, and she will be basically an unhappy woman."[24] These role reversals, as determined by the *Life* panel of psychiatrists, led to conflicts, neglect, arguments, perhaps too much drinking, and ultimately divorce.

Despite these evaluations by *Life's* experts in the mid-1950s, a great many working women had successful, happy marriages and managed to balance their job, homemaking, and child nurturing with great satisfaction for themselves and their families. More importantly, only about 30 percent of married women worked in the 1950s.[25] That meant the high levels of divorce in the baby boom era largely came from the 70 percent of stay-at-home wives, particularly the suburbanites who may have suffered from the "suburban syndrome" discussed in the next section.

As noted previously, making a successful marriage required much more of an adaptation for women than for men. Similarly, a divorce was commonly viewed as a failure of the wife to adequately adapt—even in the case of a husband's infidelity. In 1951, psychologist Clifford R. Adams provided for *Ladies' Home Journal* points of advice that "*every* wife" should keep "constantly in mind . . . to avert or meet the threat of divorce." She was cautioned to examine "continuing friction about money, in-laws, religion, household management or personal relationships." If her husband was having an adulterous affair, she was advised not to "verify the involvement of another woman" since that would "put him on the defensive and convince him that divorce is the only answer." Instead, she was to further adapt, to compensate. "All other aspects of the marriage must be made especially satisfying and pleasant to offset the negative factor." In addition to the psychologist's advice, the *Journal* offered a questionnaire for wives to evaluate the couple's "mutual respect and trust." The eleven questions were all about the husband's behavior, with a subtext of how well the wife adapted to him. She was asked to consider if he: trusted her, talked over problems with her, admitted his mistakes, lent her a hand when things went wrong, and noticed and praised her efforts to please him. If the score was low, the couple was "not sharing properly and working for the same things." In the end, if divorce was still likely, the *Journal* concluded, "The causes for divorce are never one-sided. Though you may believe that he is solely to blame, somewhere along the way you failed. Unless you accept that fact, you will lack the spirit and willingness to try to maintain the marriage . . . Only unselfish devotion will hold him—or win him back."[26]

Although the marriage may not have been a happily-ever-after story, many couples chose to remain together for a variety of reasons. Foremost was usually for the sake of the children. The damaging effect of a "broken home" on children was a dire warning for parents of the 1950s from physicians, psychiatrists, marriage counselors, social workers, and parental guides. In 1953, for example, child psychiatrist Dr. Juliette Louise Despert published *Children of Divorce,* in which she asserted, "'For the sake of the children' was often the clinching argument . . . to maintain the form of marriage though the spirit might be quite dead." Among the consequences that parents who were considering divorce heard from experts was that children of divorce "may join the throng of the delinquent or the mentally ill . . . We have been told repeatedly that divorce is a major cause of juvenile delinquency," a significant social concern in the 1950s. Moreover, Despert told parents, for children of divorce, "childish rebellions exploded into temper tantrums, an inquiring mind became an erratic one, and liveliness was transformed into violence." Children unable to cope with their parents' divorce might ultimately become runaways or, in extreme instances, commit suicide. Divorce could even cause "permanent scars" that children could carry into their adult lives, "for they pay not only in present unhappiness, but also in future maladjustment and perhaps the failure of their own marriages to come."[27]

Another factor in avoiding divorce was financial. Women who married young straight out of school and were never employed feared the prospects of a reduced economic status from alimony (if any) or child support (if any). Finding a job with no employment history or skillsets other than those of a housewife was another fear that forced many women to remain in an unhappy marriage. Similarly, when arranging a divorce settlement, men often ignored or denied the contributions a wife made to accumulated assets of the family. Most husbands were in charge of the family finances, and as a divorce seemed inevitable, they might hide assets or transfer them out of the reach of the wife. The cost of the divorce was also a deterrent for many men. During the lengthy divorce proceedings, couples sometimes separated, requiring the additional cost of an apartment and living expenses for the husband. Lawyers' fees and court costs were ordinarily paid by the man. In addition, many states required reconciliation processes called "therapeutic divorce," or pejoratively, "coercive conciliation," before a divorce hearing was set.[28] These reconciliation processes often included the additional cost of marriage counseling or sessions with a psychologist or psychiatrist, also paid by the husband. Once the divorce was granted, the usual 50/50 split of assets left both spouses feeling diminished. A house might be too expensive for the woman to afford alone, and if the house had to be sold, the man saw an immediate loss in equity as half went to the ex-wife.

Of special consideration for couples considering divorce was the emotional strain. Besides facing the failure of the marriage, the humiliation of airing personal details of the breakup in the public arena before strangers in the legal process was excruciating. This indignity was further compounded by those courts that required a therapeutic divorce procedure, in which couples initially were sent to marriage counselors or even psychologists and psychiatrists. "Legal and social science experts viewed most divorce-seekers as 'sick' couples whose freedoms should be curtailed because of the adverse social consequences of their contemplated action." For a couple to be told by a judge that they were "mentally ill" or in "an aberrant mental state" for pursuing a divorce came as a profound shock.[29] Such added humiliation sometimes achieved the court's goal of a reconciliation as the couple opted to stay together just to bring an end to their embarrassing ordeal, even at the cost of remaining irreconcilably unhappy.

For those couples for whom the court-mandated therapeutic steps proved useless, the court had to assign fault in the failure of the marriage. In some particularly hostile breakups, the accusations of who was at fault might cause divorce-seeking spouses "to be squared off like prizefighters in a ring" resulting in "an unfortunate legacy of indignity, hostility, bitterness and aggression."[30] In most cases, though, couples obtained their divorces through mutual consent with one of the spouses accepting responsibility for the breakdown of the marriage. This collusion was commonly tolerated by most courts through 1969, when the fault-based process became obsolete with the introduction of the first no-fault divorce laws.

One final reason that many couples chose to remain in an unhappy marriage rather than divorce was the stigma of the label "divorcée." Although the term applied to both men and women (sometimes spelled "divorcé" for men), the identity had a different significance to each. As noted in Chapter 2, instead of feeling ashamed of the failed marriage, a young man may have felt liberated. He could take risks with a career change and leave a tedious job that was steady and had been necessary for his role as the family breadwinner, but now he could explore careers that possibly paid less but promised to be more fulfilling. Divorce also meant the freedom to come and go as he pleased, and to date as many different women as he liked without any emotional investment or commitment. After the launch of *Playboy* magazine in 1953, many divorced men shed the identity of divorcée for that of playboy with a bachelor pad in an urban apartment set up to his liking.

To most women, though, a divorce branded them as a failure in one of their two roles—wife and mother—demanded of them by society. The label of divorcée was a humiliating accusation, and according to many examples from popular culture previously cited, an indictment of their shortcomings as a wife and as a woman.

> Marriage remained an important goal for women, even if their particular spouses turned out to be disappointments. So powerful were the imperatives to achieve a successful family that even when marital happiness was obviously lacking, some individuals were not even willing to admit the fact to themselves, much less to venture into the realm of social deviance through such a drastic measure as divorce.[31]

Postwar suburban wives

In the postwar years, housing developments expanded into farmlands and woodlands surrounding cities across America at a rapid pace. Into these planned communities moved tens of thousands of young, white, middle-class families in the traditional mold of breadwinner father, homemaker wife, and school-age children. By all socioeconomic standards of the baby boom era, these families were living the American dream. Suburbanite women were continually targeted by every form of popular mass media—advertising, magazines, novels, movies, television—with affirmations of their life choices as a housewife and mother. As Betty Friedan expressed in her landmark 1963 book, *The Feminine Mystique*:

> Over and over women heard in voices of tradition and of Freudian sophistication that they could desire no greater destiny than to glory in their own femininity. Experts told them how to catch a man and keep him, how to breastfeed children and handle their toilet training, how to cope with sibling rivalry and adolescent rebellion; how to buy a dishwasher, bake bread, cook gourmet snails, and build a swimming pool with their own hands; how to dress, look, and act more feminine and make marriage more exciting . . . They were taught to pity the neurotic unfeminine, unhappy women who wanted to be poets or physicists or presidents. They learned that truly feminine women

do not want careers, higher education, political rights . . . All they had to do was devote their lives from earliest girlhood to finding a husband and bearing children.[32]

Millions of American women embraced these messages that came at them from all directions and eagerly adopted the identity of a suburbanite housewife. Many of these young women were newlyweds and still held the romantic promises of happily-ever-after fiction they had read in *Ladies' Home Journal* or *Woman's Day*. Wives of soldiers home from the Second World War or Korean War were excited that the GI Bill made possible a new home in a new neighborhood. Young mothers were happy to have modern schools and safe, nearby playgrounds for their children.

With their new identity as suburbanites came adjustments to lifestyles that may have been unfamiliar to them. Newlyweds were still adjusting and adapting to marriage and now had the added challenges of setting up a new household in an unfamiliar community. Former urbanites often left behind a close-knit neighborhood of friends, shopkeepers, and peer social groups with which they had interacted daily, instead, to start anew in suburbia. In 1956, sociologist William H. Whyte wrote about the "educating process" during the adjustment period for new suburbanites. That is, new arrivals, particularly recently married wives, were "particularly quick to pick up the cues from college-educated girls" when it came to how suburbanites should dress, furnish their ranch homes, and behave. "Merchants are often surprised at how quickly their former customers in city stores discard old preferences when they arrive in suburbia." To sustain the conformist homogeneity of their white, middle-class community, continued Whyte, neighbors of the newcomers would "go out of their way to make [them] feel at home and, through a sort of osmosis, to educate [them] in the values of the group."[33]

One of the foremost community standards most suburban developments enforced was racial segregation. The suburban developments of the postwar era were specifically planned to be all-white, middle-class communities. Suburban covenants in purchase applications, mortgages, and homeowners' association policies specified who would be admitted to the community and who would be excluded. Nonwhites, and sometimes white Jews and Catholics, were directed elsewhere.[34] Even before couples were allowed to view the homes for sale, they were "screened" by sales agents and realtors.[35] These segregationist covenants not only barred nonwhite buyers but also prohibited a white owner from later renting or reselling the property to nonwhites. Likewise, mortgage lenders followed "redlining" guidelines initially provided by federal agencies decades earlier such as the Federal Housing Authority (FHA). Redlining was "the practice of arbitrarily varying the terms of application procedures or refusing to grant a mortgage loan within a specific geographic area."[36] Underwriting guidelines and industry maps with areas outlined in red were used to steer lenders away from neighborhoods of predominantly minority, ethnic, and low-income residents where properties were deemed poor investment risks.[37]

For the newly arrived suburbanites, the home was the immediate focus. Many of the homebuilders offered fully equipped kitchens, washers, and even television sets with the new house. That allowed the young couples to direct discretionary spending toward other acquisitions for the home—new furniture, window treatments, hi-fi consoles, and perhaps improvements for outside like a patio, barbeque, outdoor furniture, and landscaping. Manufacturers of consumer goods and mass-market retailers saturated magazines, newspapers, direct mail, and television with enticing ads featuring white, middle-class suburbanites enjoying the good life in their well-accoutered homes and backyards. (Figure 7.1.) Everything had to be new for suburbanites. Homemakers compiled wish-list scrapbooks filled with color clippings of products for the home and family from magazine editorials and ads. The semiannual thousand-paged wish books from mail-order retailers such as Sears, Penney's, and Spiegel were eagerly perused by housewives who marked pages with dog-eared corners for future purchases.

The real estate developers of these planned communities also made shopping convenient for consumer-driven suburbanites by building adjacent shopping centers and leasing space to a variety of retailers and services. The first enclosed shopping mall opened in 1956 in the suburbs of Minneapolis, followed quickly by similar retail complexes embedded into suburbs across America. Upscale department stores like Macy's and mass merchandisers like Sears competed to anchor the best entrance corners of these malls to ensure the most foot traffic from the parking lots. Displays in store windows and merchandise placement along aisles were planned with the woman shopper in mind. This suburban "feminization of public space . . . created the equivalent of a downtown district dedicated primarily to female-orchestrated consumption."[38] Since the Second Industrial Revolution of the nineteenth century, manufacturers and retailers recognized that women controlled the purse strings for the home and family, and directed much of their marketing efforts toward women. By the mid-twentieth century, marketing research confirmed that women not only purchased almost everything for the home and children but also most goods for men as well. In the mid-1950s, women reportedly bought about half of men's suits, two-thirds of men's shirts,[39] and almost 80 percent of men's underwear.[40] Makers of men's clothing and accessories developed ads that targeted women as the consumer and filled pages of women's magazines with those ads. (Figure 7.2.) Even fashion magazines like *Vogue* featured ads for men's suits, sportswear, hats, ties, and sleepwear.[41]

The incessant consumption and materialism of suburbanites in the baby boom era were driven by several factors. Family needs and wants were foremost, especially if there were children. Baby boom parents had grown up during the

WOMEN'S IDENTITIES IN THE BABY BOOM YEARS

1954

1957

1958

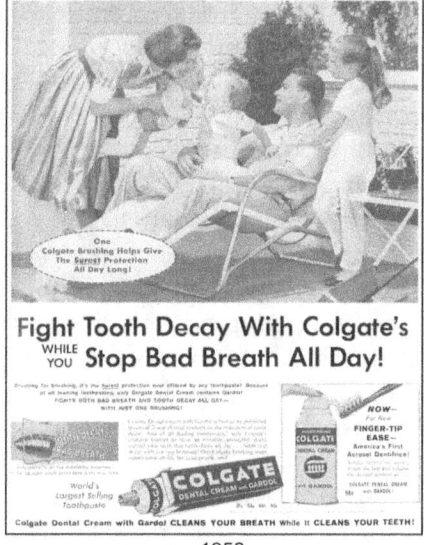

1958

Figure 7.1 In the consumer-driven economic boom of the postwar years, advertisers represented the white, middle-class family enjoying the good life in suburbia as the American dream.

stark days of the Depression and came of age during the rationing and privations of the Second World War. As part of the American dream, they wanted to ensure that their children enjoyed better childhoods than most of them had experienced.

For most suburbanites, making a better life also included continually spending for home maintenance and improvements. Middle-class women stocked their homes with all the modern labor-saving appliances and equipment to more efficiently store and cook food and to scour and clean every inch of the house. And then, they upgraded those for new-and-improved models in coordinating decorator colors. Home sewing machines were made with all sorts of operating options, encouraging women to make clothing for the family and replace curtains and home linens with regularity. (Figure 7.3.) Women's magazines and daytime television homemaking programs provided creative ideas and instructions for home sewing projects. Similarly, men accumulated power tools and built workshops in the garage or a backyard shed for do-it-yourself home projects. Coupled with the mass production and mass marketing of processed foods, toys and games, ready-to-wear clothing, and countless other consumer goods, this mass consumption fueled a booming postwar economy that lasted through the 1960s.

Along with this affluence and materialism developed a drive for social mobility for many suburbanites. Housewives urged their husbands to climb the corporate ladder or improve their businesses to make more money. An increased income would mean a move up the social scale and the means to display a higher economic level, perhaps, than the Joneses next door. "It is the mover—the restless, never-satisfied, status-seeking, job-hopping, climbing middle-class consumer—who has been the backbone of American growth," avowed Richard Gordon in his assessment of the "split-level trap" in 1960. "By fighting for more money and more houses and more social standing, by keeping up with the Joneses, by migrating in mass from the lower to the middle classes, from farm to city to suburb, the movers have built themselves an opportunity for good living that is absolutely unparalleled in world history."[42] These suburbanite housewives and their driven husbands were "upward strivers," suggested social critic Vance Packard in 1957. "At the very center of American life . . . is the most motivating force in the lives of many of us—namely what we call social mobility, the aspiration drive, the achievement drive, the movement of an individual and his family from one level to another, the translation of economic goods into socially approved symbols, so that people achieve a higher status."[43]

But, as Richard Gordon noted, all this consumerism and materialism became a trap for many suburbanites, especially the stay-at-home wives. In many cases, the new arrival in suburbia likely would find "herself alone in a house, surrounded by a sea of strangers in an alien world . . . She is not naturally thrown together with her new neighbors" and "may have little in common with them, little to talk about."[44] To compensate, many new suburbanite women

WOMEN'S IDENTITIES IN THE BABY BOOM YEARS

Figure 7.2 As consumers, women were targeted by manufacturers and retailers as purchasers not only for themselves, the home, and their children but also for their husbands. Lee Hats ad, 1956; Hanes ad, 1959.

Figure 7.3 Through the 1950s, makers of home sewing machines continually improved the ease of operation and technological sophistication of sewing options. The suburban homemaker was encouraged by advertisers, women's magazines, and daytime homemaking television programs to make clothes for the family as well as curtains and linens for the home. Ad, 1959.

fell into the consumerism trap as a way to "justify their existence, even while they deplore their wasted lives . . . These possessions, which apparently offer magic to subdue discontent and boredom, must in many cases be bought on the installment plan: television sets, new cars, all manner of those household appliances which often only make possible a dangerous amount of added and misdirected leisure."[45]

Between the isolation and the boredom from monotonous housekeeping, many suburbanite women became discontented with their lives. Betty Friedan called this "strange stirring, a sense of dissatisfaction, a yearning that women suffered in the middle of the twentieth century . . . the problem that has no name."[46] Yet, others writing of the "woman problem" in the baby boom years called this condition the "suburban syndrome." As a consulting panel of psychiatrists for *Life* magazine observed in 1956, "There is such a thing as 'suburban syndrome' . . . To be 'just a housewife' is to be degraded: she announces her position to the census taker with an apologetic flinch." From her "disgruntlement . . . she may become morbidly depressed," and consequently, "she can work as much damage on the lives of her husband and children [as on] her own life." The solution, said *Life*'s panel, was basically more of the same. "Married women in the child-rearing ages . . . have fully equipped minds and should use them in every feasible way, from potting geraniums to writing books or making political speeches . . . so long as their primary focus of interest and activity is the home."[47] What the psychiatrists for *Life* advocated for women was the prevailing ethos for a generation of young women in the two decades following the Second World War. Only with the emergence of the women's liberation movement in the late 1960s did American women more broadly begin to explore alternatives and possibilities other than the gender-as-destiny roles of wife and mother.

Motherhood in the baby boom era

The young wives of the postwar years had spent their childhood during the Depression when Americans had regressed into a conservative backlash against the social upheavals of the First World War and the 1920s Jazz Age. Girls of the 1930s were inculcated with revived ideas of the Victorian traditions of woman's sphere by parents, teachers, guidance counselors, and pastors. As sociologists Robert and Helen Lynn observed in their 1937 study of *Middletown in Transition,* children were rigorously taught gender identity "on the assumption of contrasting temperamental characteristics and aptitudes of men and women . . . Men are expected to perform certain social functions and to behave in certain ways, and another set of expectations rules the lives of women." Eventual motherhood was at the top of the list of expectations for all girls. The Lynds found that to Middletowners, "A marriage without children is regarded, according to the tradition of their culture, as incomplete, and healthy couples who choose to remain childless are alternately sympathized with, gently coerced, or condemned as 'selfish' . . . A woman who does not want children is 'unnatural.'"[48] Throughout their childhood and adolescence, young women of the postwar years had heard the relentless sociocultural demand that their primary purpose in life was to marry and have children.

With the marriage spike of 2.2 million couples in 1946, the baby boom surge got underway, with more than 70 million babies born between 1946 and 1964.[49] Manufacturers of baby and children's products idealized motherhood with print ads and TV commercials depicting happy mothers enjoying their

Figure 7.4 With more than 70 million babies born between 1946 and 1964, manufacturers and retailers of children's products had a steady market of parental consumers. Ads and TV commercials commonly depicted happy mothers enjoying their babies and children. Ad, 1951.

gendered roles. (Figure 7.4.) In addition, for millions of first-time mothers, child care advice was abundant in newspaper and magazine articles, and numerous books by medical professionals provided guidance for most aspects of parenting. Dr. Benjamin Spock became a household name in the baby boom era with his best-selling *Common Sense Book of Baby and Child Care,* first released in 1945 and revised in 1957. From the start of the book, Spock tells mothers to "trust yourself . . . You know more than you think you do . . . Bringing up your child won't be a complicated job if you take it easy, trust your own instincts, and follow the directions that your doctor gives you."[50] And for the new mother, Spock outlined the basics for child care from infancy through the teen years:

Equipment and clothing
Medical and nursing care
Feeding, diet, and schedule
Daily care (bathing, sleep, play)
Infant problems (crying, digestion, rashes)
Childhood issues (school, bedtime, discipline)
Inoculations, first aid, illnesses
Toilet training
Puberty development and "The Facts of Life"

For most new moms of the postwar years, many of these practical aspects of motherhood were instinctual or learned from their mothers and grandmothers without the need of manuals. What was particularly new and powerful for mothers of the baby boom era, though, was the addition of child psychology that medical professionals like Dr. Spock, Dr. Farnham, and Dr. Gesell now offered the average American mom. Spock noted that earlier psychiatry was centered on treating the insane, "but as psychiatrists have learned how serious troubles usually develop out of mild ones, they have turned more and more attention to everyday problems."[51] Some of this guidance could be alarming to parents who were warned that psychological problems their child may develop were their fault and the well-being of their child might be compromised at their hands. "The spawning ground of most neurosis in Western civilization is the home," challenged psychiatrist Marynia Farnham in 1947. "The basis for it is laid in childhood." For Farnham, three types of mothers were problematic to raising children. (1) The "rejecting mother" substitutes harsh discipline and indifference for nurturing to her children. "Unconsciously she never wanted them." The child is doomed to rarely please his mother and, on the other hand, may become overachievers in school and manners or, on the other hand, become rebelliously hostile and aggressive. (2) The "overprotective mother" can be "over concerned about the rate of the child's development" and consequently, "retards him by oversolicitous concern to prevent every possible injury." This prolongs a child's dependency and may "instill in the child many fears," possibly causing hypochondria and passivity as adults. (3) The "dominating mother" is in a "constant need to obtain and retain control over everything and everybody . . . Children come to be a psychological extension of themselves through which they may find expression and over which they are permitted to exercise absolute domination." She becomes dictatorial toward her children by "planning every facet of their lives and intervening constantly." In reaction, the dominated children become bullies and lash out in ways they can dominate others. The failings of all these types of mothers, concludes Farnham, "produce the delinquents, the difficult behavior-problem children, some substantial percentage of criminals and persons who, although moving in socially approved channels, are a trouble to themselves, to close associates and often to society."[52]

"Mother-blaming" was not new to 1947. In the nineteenth century, Sigmund Freud and his followers looked to the parents, particularly the mother, as the cause of so many mental ailments of children. In 1942, Philip Wylie popularized the idea to a mass audience with his book *Generation of Vipers,* in which he coined the term "momism" as a criticism of overprotective mothers. Wylie saw smothering moms as dangerous to the security of America because they produced weak, dependent sons who were unfit to be soldiers let alone fight in the Second World War and, in the 1950s, to defend the nation during the Cold War.[53] The idea of mother-blaming increasingly became a recurring theme in popular culture as well as psychiatry. "Mother love is said to be sacred in America, but with all the reverence and lip service she is paid, mom is a pretty safe target, no matter how correctly or incorrectly her failures are interpreted," concluded Betty Friedan.[54]

In 1946, psychiatrist Edward Strecker published *Their Mothers' Sons,* in which he took up the idea of momism. "Mom" versus "mother" was a distinction for Strecker with profound impacts on their children. The idea of a "mom" was "an indictment of the woman who has failed in the elementary mother function of weaning her offspring emotionally as well as physically . . . A mom does not untie the emotional apron string—the silver cord—which binds her children to [her]." A mother, on the other hand, "does everything in her power to make her children stand on their own feet. She prepares them for an adult life." A mother "uses the emotional ingredient sparingly and wisely. Her major purpose is to produce a proper balance of give-and-take in her children, so that they may attain full-statured personal and social maturity and lead reasonably constructive and happy lives." Like Farnham and others, Strecker also defined categories of momism, ranging from the "pollyanna" mom and "self-sacrificing" mom to the "protective" mom and "pseudo-intellectual" mom. As with other medical professionals and social scientists of the period, Strecker, too, blamed moms (along with "progressive education") for a myriad of childhood problems and adult neuroses—everything from insubordination and nonconformity to antisocial or even criminal behavior. Even more, Strecker avows, momism in the postwar years "asks for more than the nation can afford to give—the sacrifice of the maturity of the new generation and the loss of the hope of its youth becoming participating and contributing citizens."[55]

Particularly notable was the frequent accusation of mothers for contributing to what was perceived as "an increase in male homosexuality" in the baby boom era,[56] a widespread concern triggered in part from the findings on the subject by Alfred Kinsey in 1948.[57] In 1956, *Life* magazine reiterated that the characteristics of "the overwhelming mother" are "bad for her, but . . . worse for the children, especially the boys. The children are her responsibility: Daddy is busy, he understands business, she understands children. So she proceeds to take up this role with a vengeance and to become an overwhelming mother . . . The sons she raises tend to be more or less infantile in their relations with women and to be immature human beings," or in other words, "emasculated males" who "had lost the male image."[58] To Lundberg and Farnham, the "over-affectionate" mother can cause a son to become "mother-fixed" and, as a result, become a homosexual.[59] Spock cautioned parents that "a boy doesn't grow spiritually into a man just because he's born with a male body"; with a disinterested or disapproving father, "he is apt to draw closer to his mother and take on her manners and interests."[60] Strecker more directly warns that a smothering mother who is incapable "of freeing him gently but firmly and guiding him along the path of normal sexual development which ends in mature heterosexuality, often sows the seed of latent or even overt homosexuality in her son."[61] So accepted was mother-blaming for male homosexuality that even Betty Friedan asserted in 1963 that

> the mother whose son becomes homosexual is usually not the "emancipated" woman who competes with men in the world, but the very paradigm of the feminine mystique . . . who attaches her son to her with such dependence that he can never mature . . . The love of men masks his forbidden excessive love for his mother; his hatred and revulsion for all women is a reaction to the one woman who kept him from becoming a man.[62]

In 1952, the idea of mother-blaming crossed over from social science studies to the movies in Leo McCarey's film *My Son John*. In the movie, recent college graduate John (played by Robert Walker) is a nonathletic, bookish intellectual who has gone astray, becoming an atheist and a communist, causing family conflict. His mother is depicted as a pill-popping neurotic who is doting on her son to the point of flirtatious. Although the intent of the movie was a statement of anticommunism in the era of McCarthy, a strong undercurrent of momism prevails, leading to not only John's political deviance as a communist but also an implication of his sexual deviance as a homosexual.[63]

Mother and daughter relationships were less fraught with psychological and pathological pitfalls than those with sons. Mothers of the baby boom years had their own girlhood upbringing and experiences as points of departure in the gender role socialization of daughters. It was an era of conservatism and conformity following the sociocultural disruptions of the Second World War. As discussed in the previous segments of this chapter, postwar American women were urged and cajoled by government, society, and popular culture into centering their lives on the home as wives and mothers. Millions of women embraced their separate sphere place in the kitchen and nursery and, consequently, instilled these same gender role principles into their daughters. Mothers were the role models for daughters and led by example in standards of identity, behavior, and dress. The 1959 illustration on the cover of this book says it all: the rambunctious boys in their comfortable, casual playwear clamor over their dad, while the mother in her cinched shirtdress stands in the background. Mom makes a silencing gesture at the daughter, who primly wears a pink dress, pristine white socks, shiny shoes, and hair barrettes, and likewise demurely stands back in deference to the males. In public schools, the curriculum for teenage girls often required home economics classes in which they were taught cooking for a family, preparing a home, and caring for children; sex-segregated school clubs such as Future Homemakers of America (FHA) and Daughters of the American Revolution (DAR) further emphasized traditional feminine activities to prepare girls for their expected adult roles. See Chapter 9 for more on children of the baby boom era.

TV wives and mothers of the baby boom era

Television became an integral part of American family life in the 1950s. Antiseptic programs such as family sitcoms "influenced their morals, virtues, and values; in many situations, television became their mentor."[64] Week after week, television networks presented audiences with the American ideal as white, middle-class families living in a safe, clean suburban world free of the Cold War threat of nuclear annihilation, racial strife, political divide, disease, poverty, or even bad language.

TV moms such as Donna Stone (*Donna Reed Show*), June Cleaver (*Leave It to Beaver*), Harriet Nelson (*Adventures of Ozzie and Harriet*), and Margaret Anderson (*Father Knows Best*) moved cheerfully through these dreamscapes, cooking, cleaning, and caring for their families with a minimum of effort. They were all stay-at-home moms; none of them were employed outside the home. Any activities other than shopping that took them away from the home were social and limited in hours and scope so as not to interfere with their housework, meal preparation, and presence in the home when the children got home from school.

The dynamics of TV family programs, though, were largely patriarchally centered. Even *The Donna Reed Show*—featuring an Academy Award-winning movie star—many times subordinated Donna's role as a principal parent to that of her husband. A common script ploy for 1950s melodramas was for the father to have the children all to himself for chats, sharing, counseling, or doling out verbal discipline while the mother was elsewhere in the house. But it was Mom who regularly set and enforced the rules for the children—"wash your hands," "eat your peas," "say 'thank you.'" She was what the postwar psychiatrist Edward Strecker called "the ruthless thwarter and frustrator."[65] Dad was usually oblivious to the children's little transgressions and got to be the fun parent. Dads could play with and love the children, while mothers were strict wardens of behavior, manners, and bedtime.

Conflicts and arguments between TV spouses were tame and usually were presented as persuasion discussions rather than contests of will. In instances such as on *I Love Lucy,* Desi constantly had to put his foot down when Lucy wanted to spend money beyond her allowance or enter show business or otherwise stray from the traditional path of wife and mother. Lucy would concede, temporarily, but then scheme to get around her husband's mandate, and hence the crux of the episode's comedy. In TV family melodramas, the husband was unequivocally the primary authority as head of the household, and his decision was final—unless he could be persuaded or manipulated into changing his mind.

The pursuit of outside activities by TV moms was sometimes a theme for episodes of TV family melodramas. The clichéd formula was usually an external influence from a neighbor, friend, or a women's club making a suggestion that the mom take on a new role, which savvy audiences knew would ultimately spell disaster. For example, when Donna Reed is encouraged to run for city council, her family is initially encouraging and supportive. But, predictably, soon the "household is in disarray: the kids are fighting, Dad can't sew on a button, and they all burn their breakfasts."[66] Ultimately, she withdraws her candidacy to return to full-time wife and mother.

Audiences also expected TV moms to look as tidy and well-scrubbed as their homes. They were usually dressed in neatly ironed shirtdresses or plain blouses and skirts—often with a frilly apron tied on—and for special occasions, simple New Look suits. Frequently they did housework and cooking in high heels, and Harriet Nelson often wore a strand of pearls around the house (claiming in interviews that TV lights caused a deep shadow in the pit of her neck, which the necklace concealed). For really dirty chores, such as gardening or painting a door, jeans were acceptable to viewers, but never shorts or swimsuits, let alone lingerie. Not until the 1960s was a TV mom allowed to wear slacks with regularity when Mary Tyler Moore as Laura Petrie, Dick Van Dyke's TV wife, broke the barrier with her capri pants. Even then, though, she was criticized by traditionalists because the formfitting styles accentuated her slim, youthful dancer's figure.[67]

"In the end, the only thing TV housewives can be accused of is being good—gifted—at their chosen profession, that of homemaker. They were accomplished in running their households and caring for their families."[68] TV audiences knew that such exceptional standards of goodness in a wife and mother and such perfection in homemaking were impossible to attain. As such the depictions of TV moms were not thought to be reflections of true life. However, many aspects of the TV families may have been aspirational to some degree for white, middle-class suburbanites, such as polite social decorum and especially consumerism when it came to the well-accoutered modern home. But for most viewers, the thirty-minute programs were simply an entertaining escape from realism, a reprieve from Cold War threats, racial unrest, McCarthyism, divisive politics, and other such real-life drama that daily headlined the six o'clock news.

Working women of the baby boom era

During the Second World War, the number of American women entering the labor force increased by almost 5 million, from 14.6 million in 1941 to 19.3 million in 1945.[69] Most of these women had never worked outside the home and were answering a call to patriotic duty and national defense in a time of crisis. They viewed their status as war workers as temporary and fully expected to return to the kitchen and nursery afterward. But millions of other women wanted to continue to work after the war, only to be fired to make way for returning veterans. When they tried to find other jobs, they often encountered newly revived marriage bars whereby companies refused to hire married women, especially those with school-age children, despite their financial needs. In addition, social attitudes toward working women dramatically shifted as government propaganda, mass media, and popular culture repeatedly drove the message that a woman's place was in the home.

But by the second half of the 1940s, the very definition of woman's sphere had changed in ways for American women that their mothers and grandmothers could not have imagined. During the two world wars and the years in between, millions of American women who went to work outside the home had experienced competition in the public arena, gained financial rewards of work for pay, enjoyed pride in their accomplishments, developed self-reliance and self-confidence, and achieved a sense of individualism. These feelings of self and accomplishment remained with them after they switched identities of working women for those of stay-at-home wife and mother. Throughout the 1950s, social scientists, psychiatrists, and sociologists recognized this mental and emotional contrast as a contributing factor to women's discontent.

> On the one hand, [American women] were educated as equals and trained for the same independent, autonomous role as that assumed by men. On the other, they were expected after their school years to revert to the 'lonely,' unstimulating role of homemaker—a role allotted little prestige or value and depicted by advertisers as a bore from which the lucky housewife could escape with the right kind of automatic stove or dishwasher.[70]

Anthropologists such as Margaret Mead and Florence Kluckhohn concluded from their research that the woman who worked outside the home was better off than the housewife who fretted and brooded in her frustration, boredom, and discontent. Similarly, sociologists such as Mirra Komarovsky and Peter Berger pushed back against the traditionalists' suggestions that discontented American women were psychologically maladjusted because they did not adequately embrace their predestined feminine roles of wife and mother. Instead, from the perspective of these and other social scientists, men's and women's spheres had increasingly overlapped so rapidly between 1917 and 1945 that the status of working women was in such stark contrast with the social norms of feminine roles, that many women felt constant confusion and anxiety about who they were supposed to be or wanted to be. "Passing in and out of each world daily, they experienced understandable ambivalence and insecurity about their identity."[71]

In 1947, *Life* magazine examined the postwar "American Woman's Dilemma." The married "working girl" had three options, suggested the editors:

1. Continue her full-time career "combined with motherhood." This choice would "likely be very hard when her children are young and need her attention, but it will leave her well-rounded in interests and experience when she has reached the free years after 40."

2. "Full-time housework," which "has compensations when her children are small," but because "a mother's schedule is so filled with routine tasks" she will soon find "she cannot keep up with her husband's interests."

3. "Combine part-time work with housekeeping while she is young and use this experience more fully when her children have left home."[72]

Despite the barrage of messages from traditionalists that for young married women option 2 (full-time housewife and mother) was the only meaningful way, US census statistics indicate that options 1 and 3 (full- or part-time employment) were increasingly pursued by American women. From 1946 through 1965, the increase of working women steadily climbed from 27.8 percent to 34 percent.[73]

Through the entire baby boom era, though, the sociocultural pressures against working women were relentless. In 1954, journalist Elizabeth Longford cautioned career women about the "self-deception" that working full time could be managed while keeping family as a "number one priority." Because family life can be "flexible" but work schedules are "rigid," "it needs great ingenuity and firmness as a mother, and not too great ambition as a career woman to make the compromise work . . . Even then, with the best intentions in the world, you may not succeed . . . for careers have a way of encroaching."[74] With a more ominous tone, a 1956 *Life* magazine assessment of working women insisted that the "career woman . . . may find many satisfactions in her job, but the chances are that she, her husband and her children will suffer psychological damage, and that she will be basically an unhappy woman." Women work outside the home, suggested the editors, "because they are rejecting the role of wife and mother."[75] And similarly, in their 1947 study *Modern Woman, The Lost Sex,* journalist Ferdinand Lundberg and psychiatrist Marynia Farnham warned that when a woman tries to combine home and child care with a career, "it is inevitable that one or the other will become of secondary concern and, this being the case, it is certain that the home will take that position . . . No one can find and hold remunerative employment where the job itself doesn't take precedence over all other concerns." The pursuit of a career "is essentially masculine because exploitative," and "her work develops aggressiveness, which is essentially a denial of her femininity." The result for the career woman, then, Lundberg and Farnham conclude, is a "masculinization" in which she will "develop the characteristics of aggression, dominance, independence and power" in order to compete with men.[76]

Despite these dire warnings from traditionalists, the postwar economic boom needed a substantial labor force to keep up with increasing consumer demands for ever more goods and services and the need to be ready for national defense from the threats of the Cold War. In April 1951, the National Manpower Council was established at Columbia University by a group of business, education, and labor leaders with links to the federal government and sponsored by General Eisenhower. Their goals were "identifying and evaluating areas of significant manpower wastage, determining methods of improving the utilization of human resources, and recommending ways of developing potential resources."[77] The council periodically provided policy papers and sponsored conferences to present their research and recommendations. Yet, despite the intentions of the Manpower Council, the group did not even begin to evaluate *womanpower* until 1955. Even then, participants were at odds on goals and ideas. At meetings of the council, women resented men explaining the low levels of women workers as a result of their lack of training or ambition rather than institutionalized sex discrimination. Among those discriminations that women faced at the time were marriage bars prohibiting the hiring of young married women with children. Similarly, many companies instituted policies that designated "men's jobs" versus "women's jobs," precluding women from applying for jobs and promotions for which they were otherwise qualified. The council, along with women's groups and labor unions, emphasized the need of protective legislation to guarantee equal pay for equal work, but as members were repeatedly told, employers would continue to hire men over women if the pay had to be equal. And of course, broad discriminations nationally against women of color were acknowledged as a further deterrent to expanding the labor force with women workers.

Despite the research, policy papers, conferences, and efforts of the council and its subcommittees to improve America's womanpower in the work force, most participants gave deference to the prevailing sociocultural norms of women's roles as wives and mothers. A 1955 report reasserted that "its proposals for broader participation of women in employment or other areas of the public arena must not detract from the importance of their roles as wives and mothers."[78] At a council conference in 1957, Secretary of Labor James Mitchell concluded in his keynote address that "the fundamental job of the American woman remains . . . being a good wife, a homemaker, a mother."[79] As a work-around for these assumptions of women's essential purpose, council reports suggested that women work outside the home before having children, assume their stay-at-home roles while the children are preschool age, and then return to the labor force once the children are in school. In addition, the council explored ways of encouraging older women to return to employment. At the end of the 1950s, the council reported that most of the members "saw the growing participation of wives and mothers in the labor force as an essential part of the story of the continuous growth in real income, as a major factor in improved living standards, as an influence for rich fuller lives for America's children, as responsible for lifting families from the bottom of the income scale and increasing the proportion of middle-income families. Moreover, there was a strong feeling that the new pattern of work in women's lives is positively related to the expansion of individual freedom of choice," an argument that would be a touchstone of Second Wave Feminism a decade later.[80] Despite the findings and recommendations of the National Manpower Council and other labor and women's advocacy groups, workplace policies and federal legislation lagged behind. Consequently, the participation of American women in the labor force would linger in the 30 percentages well into the 1970s.[81]

Feminism in the baby boom era

In its "Special Issue on the American Woman" in 1956, *Life* magazine observed, "'Feminism' as such became moribund after women received the right to vote [in 1920] and it now seems as quaint as linen dusters and high button shoes." Other articles in the magazine referred to the "dead issue of feminism" and the "outdated term of feminists." To these journalists, and most Americans in the 1950s, a feminist was the suffragette of the late nineteenth and early twentieth centuries whose goal was an "incomprehensible scuffle to prove herself the equal of man." But, concluded *Life,* for modern, postwar American women, "there is an increasing emphasis on the nurturing and homemaking values . . . Because these women are better informed and more mature than the average, they have been the first to comprehend the penalties of 'feminism' and to react against them."[82] Antifeminists like psychiatrist Marynia Farnham saw no use for feminism in modern American society because women had

> won the right to emulate men . . . On the legal plane, American women can now do just about all the things they once could not do. They can vote, own and manage their own property. They can pay taxes, serve on juries and hold public office. They can give themselves in marriage or declare for a divorce, and claim exclusive jurisdiction over the children . . . Both the follies and the great achievements of men are alike open now to women.[83]

Contrary to the assertions that feminism was dormant and unnecessary in modern America, feminism had endured past the implementation of the Nineteenth Amendment in 1920, but now in the postwar years focused on expanding women's rights and opportunities in education and the labor market. Leading feminist voices included Susan B. Anthony II, great-niece of her famous suffragist namesake. Her 1943 book, *Out of the Kitchen, into the War*, advocated for greater inclusion of women not only in the labor force but also in labor unions. But because some of these feminists were affiliated with the American Communist Party, they and their ideas were largely reviled as anti-American and dangerous, especially during the McCarthy years. Also, the Communist Party turned out not to be a good fit for American feminists since the party's ideology "emphasized the primacy of class over gender, celebrated the heterosexual nuclear family, and refused to support the Equal Rights Amendment [introduced in Congress in 1923] . . . Communists accepted traditional notions about women's natural submissiveness and subordination."[84] Resistance to feminists' advocacy for working women from employers, labor unions, and traditionalists remained formidable through the 1950s and 1960s resulting in little progress.

Some feminists then directed their activist experience into the civil rights movement or antinuclear cause. But even then, they were largely marginalized in the sociopolitical arena throughout the era. Others turned their attention and writings toward women's history. In 1959, feminist Eleanor Flexner published *Century of Struggle, The Women's Rights Movement in the United States*, in which women's history was presented as a tool of change. To Flexner, understanding the history of sociopolitical forces in the women's rights movement might help in coping with problems confronted by women and men of her time, and even into the future. "It was a goal that made sense in the context of unusual societal hostility to feminism and the existence of an elite and isolated group of women continuing to work explicitly for women's rights." The activities and books of baby boom era feminists "reflected the conviction that women's history was more than academic: that education . . . could be a tool to mobilize women and help bring about change."[85] Although the feminists' work toward race and gender improvements in the postwar years had little impact, it laid the groundwork for a new generation of feminists who would unite in their common purpose of equal rights and organize into a protest movement at the end of the 1960s.

In 1972, history professor William Chafe published *The American Woman: Her Changing Social, Economic and Political Roles, 1920–1970.* He noted that for the mobilization of a protest movement, three conditions must coalesce: "First, a point of view around which to organize; second, a positive response by a portion of the aggrieved group; and third, a social atmosphere which is conducive to reform."[86] The catalyst for what many historians now call the Second Wave Feminism, arguably, was Betty Friedan's 1963 book, *The Feminine Mystique.*[87] Friedan contended that in the post-World War II years, women emerged from their wartime economic independence, self-reliance, and social progress to become victims of regressive, oppressive ideas of a "feminine mystique," which manipulated women into thinking they could only find fulfillment and happiness as a wife and mother. Advertisers of the era relentlessly promoted images of the happy homemaker in her new suburban home surrounded by all the modern conveniences and products of housekeeping and family care. Women's magazines romanticized housewifery and motherhood. Books and essays by psychiatrists and sociologists such as Marynia Farnham and Helene Deutsch insisted that a woman's highest goal was a full-time focus on the home and family, and if discontented with those achievements, she was neurotic and emotionally maladjusted. But contrary to these prevailing and persistent norms, Friedan insisted that postwar housewives surrendered "the essence of their past identity," and "the very condition of being a housewife can create a sense of emptiness, non-existence, nothingness in women." Housewives "who live in the image of the feminine mystique" have "trapped themselves within the narrow walls of their homes," which has become "a comfortable concentration camp . . . They have become dependent, passive, childlike; they have given up their adult frame of reference . . . The work they do does not require adult capability; it is endless, monotonous, unrewarding."[88] Many young, college-educated women who were coming of age in the mid-1960s took up the clarion call from Freidan and mobilized a women's liberation movement, and with it, the launch of Second Wave Feminism.

Of course, not all homemakers agreed with Friedan and feminists. For millions of American women of the baby boom era, their world of housekeeping, cooking, childcare, volunteer work, and socializing with friends was not a life of servitude and tedium, nor did they feel oppressed. And for those who may have felt discontented, most lacked the training, education, and skill sets to abruptly change courses in life and get a job outside the home. Instead, they made the most they could of their identities and roles as wives and mothers.

Conclusion

At the end of the Second World War, American women's identities shifted dramatically from the war years. Millions of women had gone to work outside the home in answer to the nation's wartime need during the labor shortage. These newly employed women had proven their capabilities outside of the kitchen and nursery as they produced armaments and ammunition in dangerous defense factories; built tanks, ships, and submarines; flew fighter planes; drove ambulances and jeeps; and even donned military uniforms in service as WACs, WAVES, and WASPs. They gained newfound self-reliance and independence in taking on jobs and responsibilities thought of as men's work, and they earned their own money.

But as soon as the war ended, women suddenly faced a sociocultural regression. Millions of working women were fired from companies to make room for returning veterans. Businesses reinstituted marriage bars that prohibited married women from being hired. Postwar government propaganda, popular culture, and social attitudes reverted to prewar views that a woman's place was in the home as a wife and mother. For more than 70 percent of American women, the roles as exclusively wife and mother were fully embraced. (Less than 30 percent of American women were employed through the mid-1950s and only rose to 34 percent by 1965.) Marriages spiked in the postwar years after declines during the Depression and deferrals during the war, and a baby boom unlike any in American history continued from 1946 to 1964, when more than 70 million babies were added to the population.

Yet, for millions of women, the identity solely as a wife in the postwar era was a significant adjustment. Many of those who had enjoyed autonomy in making their own decisions and earning a paycheck during the war now became dependents of husband breadwinners. Married career women were disparaged and accused of compromising their primary duties as wives. Young women, newly out of school, had been taught on a fairly level field in the classroom, where often they dominated male counterparts with better grades and academic achievements but now were expected to submit to husbands as masters of their lives. In the rapidly expanding suburbs, for some wives a modern ranch house filled with the housekeeping conveniences of the era was the American dream; for others, suburbia was a trap in which they felt isolated and bored with endless cycles of housekeeping and limited social routines.

In addition, postwar wives continually read and heard from experts that they only could be complete women with children. Innumerable sources and studies from government agencies, medical experts, and social scientists urged them toward motherhood. Best-selling family guide books and mass-market publications such as *Parents' Magazine* outlined every aspect of childcare for modern moms. All aspects of American popular culture emphasized and idealized motherhood. Television family programs depicted stay-at-home wives who were singularly family focused. For postwar American women, the message was persistent: their ultimate gender-as-destiny role was motherhood.

8
WOMEN'S FASHIONS OF THE BABY BOOM ERA

The New Look

During the Second World War, three significant developments impacted American fashions. First were the abrupt shortages and rationing of materials used in the production of clothing and accessories. Wool was needed for soldiers' uniforms and blankets, silk for parachutes, nylon for dozens of uses, leather for boots, rubber for jeep tires, and metals for arms and ammunition. Compromises had to be made by designers and ready-to-wear makers, everything from using recycled wool and more cotton and rayon to reengineering girdles and bras with only inset panels of rubberized yarns.

Second was the implementation of government regulations regarding the use of available materials in garment constructions. As discussed in Chapter 6, the L-85 restrictions narrowed and shortened a variety of apparel, which included women's garments such as dresses, skirts, jackets, and slacks. Many decorative elements such as yokes, turned-back cuffs, balloon and dolman sleeves, tucks, shirring, all-around pleats, multiple patch pockets, and many trimmings were prohibited.

Third was the closing of the borders of France by the invading Germans in June 1940. With no guidance from Paris couturiers, American designers were on their own for the first time. The American fashion industry and press looked to established New York names such as Hattie Carnegie, Henri Bendel, Norman Norell, Adele Simpson, and Claire McCardell to take the creative reins. Through the war years American fashion met the challenge of materials shortages and L-85 restrictions with designs that were simple, functional, and easy to wear, reflecting the casualness of the American woman. The California style of comfortable sportswear was especially prevalent and came to dominate postwar American fashions of the 1950s and 1960s.

In the months immediately after the war ended in August 1945, both European and American fashion industries struggled to find their footing. In America, the L-85 restrictions were lifted, but fabric shortages remained a problem for months as textile mills retooled and restructured manufacturing from war production to civilian consumer needs. Imports of silk from Asia were limited well into the 1950s as the infrastructures of China and Japan were slowly rebuilt.

Fashions from Paris were once again available for export to America, but because European rationing was extended and shortages were severe, couturiers limited their collections to only a few models for the first few seasons after the war. As the fashion press noted at the time, there was "little in Paris to inspire creative effort; no exciting fabrics, no brilliant accessories."[1] For the most part, wartime utility styles lingered—trim dresses and skirts with knee-length hemlines, slim jackets, and minimal surface interest.

In early 1947, though, a seismic shift in women's silhouettes was introduced in Paris. Christian Dior, one of the principal designers for the House of Lelong, was persuaded by a wealthy textile manufacturer to open his own salon, and on February 12, 1947, he made his debut as a couturier. The title of his first collection was "Corolle," which meant flower petals. (Figure 8.1.) In his 1957 autobiography, Dior wrote of his design philosophy, "I designed clothes for flower-like women, with rounded shoulders, full, feminine busts, and handspan waists above enormous spreading skirts."[2] The name of the collection, though, was eclipsed by a declaration from the fashion editor for *Harper's Bazaar* who had rushed to the designer after the show and exclaimed, "It's quite a revolution, dear Christian! Your dresses have such a new look." Dior's New Look made headlines in all the fashion centers and was quickly adapted by all other postwar designers and ready-to-wear makers.

After almost seven years of severe utility clothing during the war, American women were eager for the fresh New Look styles. Dior's fashions were at once revolutionary and at the same time nostalgic. The New Look provided postwar women with a feeling of a return to normalcy, a revival of the trappings of femininity from earlier eras when women's fashion silhouettes were contouring and curvaceous. "Other designers might sidle up to old-fashioned femininity and romance; Dior tackled it headlong," observed *Life*. "I know very well the women," Dior said during his 1947 American tour.[3] The narrow, short styles of wartime utility clothing were supplanted by the return of fashions with yards of fabric and statement details like big cuffs, broad collars, and oversized bows. Skirts swept near the ankles with hemlines just 12 inches from the floor, climbing up to about 15 inches from the floor by 1950.[4] (Figure 8.2.) The boxy, masculine suits of the war years were replaced with fitted jackets and trim, long skirts that contoured the curves of the feminine form. Dior especially emphasized the slim, cinched waist in the early collections (much to the chagrin of Chanel, who had

WOMEN'S FASHIONS OF THE BABY BOOM ERA

Figure 8.1 In 1947, Paris couturier Christian Dior launched his debut collection "Corolle," which featured rounded shoulders, cinched waists, and long skirts with yards of fabric. The ultrafeminine styles were heralded as the "New Look" by the fashion press and would dominate women's fashions into the early 1960s.

prided herself on freeing women from binding corsets and restrictive clothes in the 1920s). To achieve the prerequisite handspan waist, corsets with boning and laces were revived, and other foundation garments were once again made fully of rubberized yarns and fitted with metal zippers.

Suddenly, everything in a woman's closet was démodé, and since L-85 clothing had been made to save material, most garments did not have enough of a hem or a seam overlap to be altered in the New Look silhouette. But American ready-to-wear makers quickly adapted the latest trends from Paris to the mass market, and Dior knock-offs were soon available at a fraction of the cost of an original. In 1948, *Life* magazine photographed two ready-to-wear versions of a $400 Dior

Shirtwaist dress by Lyn Brook, 1948.

Leaf print dress from Diminutives, 1949.

Figure 8.2 Skirts for the New Look remained long through the late 1940s and into the early 1950s when hemlines began to inch up again.

Faille suit from Diminutives, 1949.

dress made by American manufacturers "with less fabric and workmanship," one priced at $45 and the other at $8.95.[5] Of course, ready-to-wear adaptations could not match the perfection of a couturier's hand-done craftsmanship and choice of high-quality materials, but the high style of Paris designs could be simulated for mass consumption. Even simple shirtwaist dresses, one of the most prevalent women's garments of the era, could replicate the New Look silhouette with full skirts, long hemlines, snug bodices, and cinched waists. (Figure 8.3.)

The success in adapting the New Look to the mass market by the American ready-to-wear industry did not go unnoticed at the Chambre Syndicale de la Couture in France. Although some Paris designers such as Chanel, Patou, and Lelong had experimented with some ready-to-wear versions of their fashions as early as the 1920s, most couturiers regarded the mass market with disdain. But during the 1950s, the French fashion industry struggled as fewer wealthy

Figure 8.3 US ready-to-wear makers easily adapted the cinched, full-skirted silhouette of the New Look to the popular shirtwaist dress, a favorite casual style for most American women. Left, cotton print shirtwaist dress by Carolyn Schnurer, 1952; right, cotton print shirtwaist dress by Jamison's, 1954.

clients were willing to pay increasingly exorbitant prices for genuine couture styles. In addition, burgeoning competition from Milan, Rome, and London eroded French dominance. Meanwhile, the booming economy in America and its affluent, consumption-driven middle classes were too tempting of a market to ignore. Beginning in the late 1940s, representatives of the Syndicale and industry businessmen began making trips to the United States to meet with ready-to-wear makers and study their expertise. Gradually through the 1950s, Paris couturiers explored ways of increasing revenue for the house with ready-made fashions called prêt-à-porter. "Though couture retained its glamour and prestige it was rapidly displaced in women's wardrobes by copies and prêt-à-porter."[6] The prêt-à-porter boutiques of the major salons featured the latest styles by the designer with high-quality construction and materials. At the same time, some prêt-à-porter models were also licensed to American department stores, boutiques, and ready-to-wear makers to produce copies at a reduced price, often in different colors or materials from the original, and sometimes with slight design modifications for the American market. Some licensing agreements prohibited the retailer from specifically mentioning the names of the designers of these discounted copies, but euphemisms became well-known in some upscale stores: Dior was known as Monsieur X, Fath as Monsieur Y, and Givenchy as Monsieur Z.[7]

Through the 1950s, the fashion world watched Dior closely. Key to his success as a designer was to subtly evolve New Look styles of the previous collection into innovative variations for the next season. In 1950, his "Vertical Line" collection revived the sheath from the 1930s, only now as a fitted, second-skin style that contoured the hips and bosom and emphasized the cinched waist in the New Look mode. (Figure 8.4.) It was what *Vogue* heralded as the "body line," a next step in the New Look that emphasized "an unexaggerated bosom, a concave middle, a close hipline, a seemingly long leg."[8] Another couturier who was equally influential on American fashions was Cristóbal Balenciaga, who revived the dropped waist from the 1920s as the "middy," tailored in 1951 with a molded-wax-fit in the ultrafeminine silhouette of the New Look. Dior and others quickly adapted Balenciaga's middy into the "H-line" with the horizontal crossbar at the hips. (Figure 8.5.) Another alphabet variation from Dior was the 1954 Y-line, which was a sheath with a sharp V-neckline or top-heavy elements such as oversized collar treatments or sleeves.

Postwar American designers and ready-to-wear makers once again found themselves subject to the dictates of Paris. Because the US fashion press was filled with news of French fashions and the names of French couturiers, American designers were largely ignored. Yet, for American women, the casual California style that had begun to spread its influence eastward during the 1930s and especially in the war years, continued to gain in popularity, particularly with busy suburbanites and the expanding youth market of the 1950s. (Figure 8.6.)

WOMEN'S FASHIONS OF THE BABY BOOM ERA

Figure 8.4 In 1951, Dior's Vertical Line collection revived the contouring sheath and shaped suit from the 1930s. Left, wool sheath by Jay Thorpe, 1951; right wool suit from House of Swansdown, 1951.

Advertising by the major American labels such as Claire McCardell, Pauline Trigére, and Adele Simpson reinforced the idea of American style and fashion innovation. In addition, Hollywood and television helped perpetuate the American casual look. For example, in the 1957 movie *Funny Face*, Audrey Hepburn portrayed a bookstore clerk who was persuaded to go to Paris as a model for a fashion magazine. While there, she is photographed modeling New Look couture styles at the Arc de Triomphe, in front of the Eiffel Tower, and on the grand staircase of the Louvre, but on her own time as a tourist, she wears capri pants, a knit pullover, and loafers.

In the second half of the 1950s, looser-fitting, draped dresses, suits, and coats were introduced by Dior beginning with his 1955 A-line collection. (Figure 8.7.) Other designers and especially American ready-to-wear makers adapted the idea to other loose, hanging designs such as chemises, sack dresses, balloon-back drapes, and the vareuse suit (meaning fisherman's smock top). When Dior died suddenly in 1957, Yves St. Laurent took over the salon and based his first collection on the trapeze, a variation of the A-line that featured a high darted or seamed bust that flared into a wide tent shape. Although the fresh, loose-fitting silhouettes of the late 1950s were a welcome, comfortable change to the sheath,

Figure 8.5 Cristóbal Balenciaga's middy style of 1951 dropped the waistline to the hips but retained the cinched contours. Dior adapted the silhouette to his 1954 H-Line collection, more broadly popularizing the look.

Cocktail dress by Richard Cole, 1954.

Silk shantung dress by Jo Copeland, 1951.

Acetate rayon dress by David Levine, 1955.

Figure 8.6 American women may have preferred ready-to-wear adaptations of New Look dresses and suits, but the casual California look of comfortable slacks and easy knit tops became the suburbanite's daily uniform. T-shirts and slacks from various makers, 1951.

H-line, and other fitted styles, the original tenets of the ultrafeminine New Look persisted with most women's fashions well into the early 1960s in collections from Paris, London, and Rome, as well as the ready-to-wear markets of America.

From the mid-1950s into the early 1960s, a key development in women's changing fashions was the hemline. In the late 1940s, the hemline had dropped from the utility L-85 cut at just below the knee to about 12 inches from the floor. In 1950, the fashion news was the hemline climbing to about mid-calf or 15 inches above the floor. Through the mid-decade, the hemline continued to get shorter until 1958, when the press reported skirts at a substantial, noticeable 2 inches shorter than the previous year.[9] "A new look in American fashion based on the legs," proclaimed *Vogue*. "Not to show the legs is to look very much out of date."[10] The hemline was once again at the bottom of the knee, where it had been during and just after the war.

Cotton chemise from L'Aiglon, 1958.

Figure 8.7 (this page and facing page) In the second half of the 1950s, varieties of loose-fitting dress silhouettes were fresh alternatives to the fitted, cinched New Look fashions. Innovative styles included Dior's A-Line, balloon backs, sacks, chemises, and Yves St. Laurent's trapeze.

WOMEN'S FASHIONS OF THE BABY BOOM ERA

Wool A-line suit by Dior, 1955.

Balloon back dress by Mr. Mort, 1958.

Wool herringbone sack dress by Larry Aldrich, 1958.

Trapeze dress by Yves St. Laurent, 1958.

Mod and the miniskirt

In the early 1960s, fashion remained firmly entrenched in the New Look, only with a shortened hemline. Looking toward a new decade, *Vogue*'s "Changes 1960" in the January issue of that year emphasized the "thoroughly female waistline," "a little waist," "fit of the new fitted clothes," "narrowness of skirt," and "the full-skirted dress,"[11] — in other words, not really "changes," but the decade-old tenets of the New Look lingering from Dior's 1947 playbook. The American fashion icon of the period was First Lady Jackie Kennedy. The young (age 31–33 in her White House years), slender, and beautiful wife of the president was a sharp contrast to her recent predecessors, Bess Truman and Mamie Eisenhower, both in their sixties when First Ladies. Yet, her personal style was elegant simplicity for official functions and American casual for vacations at the Kennedy estate. Jackie exemplified the "American look," which *Vogue* defined as "the clothes that American women live in—fetch the children from school in; go to parties in; shop for other clothes in; look terrific, right, and completely natural in. They are, in a word, the great naturals of American fashion." These clothes, the editors continued, are "suits, separates, little-nothing dresses, carefully tailored pants—in one form or other, they've been around for years and show every sign of going on indefinitely."[12] For day dresses and evening gowns, the First Lady preferred designs by Oleg Cassini. The designer had fled fascist Italy in 1936 for America, where he established his name as a Hollywood costume designer before opening his New York salon in 1952. The American fashion press was obsessed with everything Jackie wore, yet conceded that her clothes "were so unobtrusive that the wearer was far more significant than what was worn . . . We're fully aware that the look being applauded isn't essentially new."[13]

Still, some newness in fashion for the sixties was beginning to emerge in fashion capitals of Europe. "Swinging London," especially, took center stage with designer Mary Quant at the forefront. Well ahead of the Mods and the Carnaby Street scene, Quant opened her boutique named Bazaar in King's Road in 1955. When she could not find the types of young women's ready-to-wear she wanted for the shop, she began designing and making her own clothes. She was inspired by the comfortable clothes she saw on the streets of Chelsea worn by young dance and art students—colorful tights, short skirts, loose-fitting sweaters, and knit tops. Her simple chemises with Op art color blocking sold well, and in 1960 were licensed to an American ready-to-wear maker. By 1962, Quant was so successful that she launched her own ready-to-wear production with her name on the label, and the following year, began exporting collections.

In fashion history, Mary Quant is often credited with creating the miniskirt. As noted previously, hemlines had been climbing throughout the late 1950s, back to the level they had been in 1946 at just below the knee. By 1960, Quant discovered that her young customers often requested the hemlines of her dresses be shortened at least across the knee caps, and sometimes an inch or two above. With her first export collection of 1963, Quant's dresses were cropped to hit above the knee. The term "mini" used for the skirts and dresses of the early 1960s with hemlines just above the knee is thought to have been adopted by the British fashion press from the name of the popular compact cars of the time, the Morris Mini-Minor—commonly called the "Mini."[14] The iconic 1960s look of the miniskirt at mid-thigh, though, was a style change that occurred after 1966 in Europe and not until around 1968 in America.

By the end of the postwar baby boom in 1964, a new sociocultural era was dawning in America. It was a youthquake. The first baby boomers had started high school in 1960 and were now entering college. These young people were in search of their own identity as distinct from that of their parents. The youthquake generation rejected the conformity, social conservatism, and materialism of their parents. America's young were not complacent about the sociopolitical conditions of the nation and set about to make changes. They joined social movements for civil rights and students' rights. Feminism was revitalized to challenge sex discrimination. Thousands joined the Peace Corps, founded in 1961, and went throughout the world to help in education, health care, agriculture, and civil engineering. All of this laid the foundations for later baby boomers who came of age in the second half of the 1960s, some joining anti-Vietnam War protest groups, some taking up activism for Black Power or gay rights, and some becoming flower-power hippies.

As baby boomers explored new identities that were departures from the traditions of their parents, they also experimented with new self-expressions, including music, dance, and especially dress, that were their own. Many baby boomers of the early 1960s were energized by the British Invasion, an import of pop culture that brought to the United States the Beatles and mod fashions. Mod style, though, did not impact American women's dress the way it did men's wear. The men's Peacock Revolution that rocked American society with masculine long hair and vividly hued and sexualized clothes was well underway by the mid-1960s, initiated in part by the Carnaby Street looks worn by the Beatles, Rolling Stones, Who, and other British rock bands. But for women's fashions, the impact of mod styles was not about silhouette drama as it had been with the New Look, but rather was a vivacity of vivid colors and exuberant prints and patterns, especially those influenced by the Pop and Op art movements. Yves St. Laurent's famous 1965 Mondrian dresses replicated in bright primary colors the artist's 1920s canvases. (Figure 8.8.) Promotional disposable paper dresses were printed with depictions of soup cans and giant candy bar logos. Space age technology spurred experimentation with unorthodox materials applied to women's clothes such as vinyl, plastic tiles, metal chain mail, and shiny metallic-looking synthetics. Jeans and pants became increasingly favored by young

Figure 8.8 The first versions of the minidress appeared in London around 1963. The hemlines were just at the knee cap or slightly above, where they remained until 1967 when the first thigh-high styles emerged. Mondrian collection from Yves St. Laurent, 1965.

women, and the first low-rise cuts began to appear in fashion editorials in 1964, forecasting the bell-bottom hiphuggers of the late sixties. For African American women, the passage of the 1964 Civil Rights Act inspired the adoption of some elements of African dress as a tribute to their ancestry, including fabric prints based on traditional kente weaves and bogolanfini mud-dyed patterns, and the natural hairstyle called an Afro.

During the second half of the 1960s, as the second wave of baby boomers began entering high school, the commercialized mod fashions were eclipsed by a myriad of personalized counterculture dress identities that included antiwar protest clothing, hippie multicultural looks, elements of American Indian dress, and handcrafted street styles such as tie-dyeing, macramé, and student art screen-printing. American ready-to-wear makers took these street styles and produced tame versions for the mass market. Hollywood once again began to influence fashion with costumes from movies like *Bonnie and Clyde* (1967) that would launch a trend for 1930s revivals such as the midi skirt and knickers pantsuits for women and the athletic, drape cut suit for men.

Women's accessories of the baby boom years

In the postwar years, the New Look, even in ready-to-wear adaptations, had such great appeal to women because of its abundance of fabric and details. As Christian Dior wrote in his autobiography, "Dresses took up a fantastic yardage of material, and this time went right down to the ankles. Girls could safely feel they had all the trappings of a fairy-tale princess to wear. A golden age seemed to have come again."[15] Dresses and skirts with yards of fabric in long fullness were a delight; details of big bows, turned-back cuffs, wide collars, deep pleats, and similar varieties of excess were a welcome change to the prohibitions of L-85 utility styles. In addition, the New Look was more than just a reconfiguring of the feminine silhouette, it was a total look lavishly accessorized from head to toe. (Figure 8.9.) After the deprivations of the Great Depression and the rationing during the war, women were eager to splurge. Stores suddenly were filled with leather shoes and a complete accoutrement of matching accessories, costume jewelry in colorful multipiece sets, gloves in new types of fabric, sheer nylon hose in tints and textures, and hats that made a fashion statement.

Accessories, Dior wrote in 1954, "are so important to the well-dressed woman . . . With one frock and different accessories you can always be well turned out." In buying accessories, he advised, "It is a question of care and taste. Don't buy much but make sure that what you buy is good . . . You must choose a color that will match many clothes in your wardrobe."[16] Much to Dior's chagrin, though, consumer-driven American women of the postwar era were:

> in the habit of spending enormous sums of money in order to achieve so little real luxury. America . . . represents the triumph of the quantitative over the qualitative. Men and women both prefer buying a multitude of mediocre things to acquiring a few carefully chosen articles. The American woman, faithful to the ideal of optimism which the United States seems to have made their rule of life, seems to spend money entirely in order to gratify the collective need to buy. She prefers three new dresses to one beautiful one. She never hangs back from making a choice, knowing perfectly well that her fancy will be of short duration and the dress she is in the process of buying will be jettisoned very soon.[17]

Figure 8.9 Dior's vision of the New Look was a total feminine fashion statement from head to toe with a complete complement of accessories. Shirtwaist dress by Jerry Gilden, fully accoutered with hat, gloves, jewelry, self-belt, and matching handbag and shoes, 1957.

Yet, as Dior conceded, despite Europeans' perception of the American woman as cavalier and profligate about her wardrobe, she could at least count on being "marvelously protected against errors of taste" by the excellence of the shops that "offer them the complete run of the creations of every country."[18] Dior also neglected to mention the excellence of America's fashion press, from trade journals like *Women's Wear Daily* that advised shop owners and department store buyers to mass-circulation fashion magazines for consumers such as *Harper's Bazaar, Charm, Mademoiselle, Seventeen,* and *Vogue.* Too, fashion advertising and catalogs from retailers and ready-to-wear makers further provided American women with news of the latest trends and served as style guides for accessorizing, hairstyles, and makeup.

Most American women of the baby boom years usually wore hats except for the most casual occasions. As Dior advised women, a hat "is really the completion of your outfit and in another way, it is very often the best way to show your personality. It is easier to express yourself sometimes with your hat than it is with your clothes . . . A hat is the quintessence of femininity with all the frivolity this word contains."[19] During the 1950s, two contingencies of hat wearers were noted by the fashion press: those who opted for the "more-hat hat" and those preferring the "less-hat hat."[20] (Figure 8.10.) The more-hat hats of the era were sometimes enormous geometric shapes resembling Alexander Calder sculptures. Others mostly covered the hair somewhat like inverted baskets, bowls, or bells while some more-hat hats were piled with trimmings. From the mid-fifties through the mid-sixties, more-hat hats adorned with colorful masses of seasonal silk flowers or floral fabric were popular year-round. The less-hat hats were small pads or geometric shapes pinned to the hair, often at the back of the head, such as the pillbox made famous by Jackie Kennedy. Other less-hat hats were fabric crescents, circlets, or partial hemispheres with a veil or jutting feather attached. By the mid-1960s, hats began a rapid decline as an important accessory. Not only did the emerging youthquake generation associate hats with their mothers, but also the bouffant hairstyles of the time made hats difficult to wear.

Not every woman wore hats, but they all wore shoes. Dior hated "fancy shoes of any description," and only endured colored shoes for certain evening wear. Otherwise, his recommendation was the plain "court" high heel, known in America as the opera pump, in black, brown, or navy.[21] The mid-calf hemlines of New Look skirts required a high heel. Most important was the four-inch "stiletto" (Italian for dagger) with its slender, tapered heel, introduced from Italy in 1950. Increasingly, Italy became the fashion leader in women's footwear throughout the 1950s. Other heel varieties included the low spool heel of 1952, shaped like a wooden spool for thread, and the short, spiked heel of 1956 with its two-inch pencil-point heel and sharply pointed toe. In 1951, Salvatore Ferragamo started a trend for strappy styles with his day-into-evening "bareback" mules. Later strappy variations from shoe makers were called illusion shoes because of

More-hat hats from Montgomery Ward, 1958.

Figure 8.10 (this page and facing page) Most women of the postwar years wore hats. In the 1950s, some women preferred the more-hat hat, which mostly covered the hair and could be enormous sculptural shapes. The less-hat hat was small, sometimes hardly more than a cap or hairband with a net.

WOMEN'S FASHIONS OF THE BABY BOOM ERA

Bateau more-hat hat, 1951.

Straw basket more-hat hat, 1956.

Bell more-hat hat by Nelly Don, 1956.

"Éclair" less-hat hat by Gage, 1952.

Skull cap less-hat hat from Bonwit Teller, 1954.

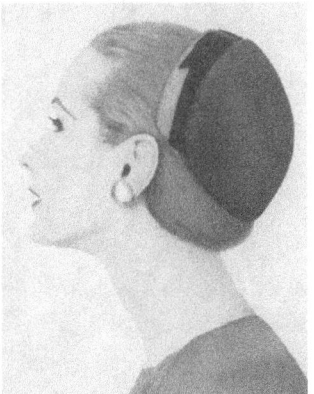

Skull cap less-hat hat by Gage, 1955.

the large cutaways and thin, barely-there straps. Another form of illusion shoes, called Cinderella pumps, were made with clear Lucite high heels and clear vinyl vamps. Among the short-lived experiments from footwear designers was a high-heel shoe with a metal track under the sole into which various heels could attach, and a novelty "no-heel" style with a cantilevered metal sole that was too tricky to walk in without the support of a heel. In the early 1960s, youthquake teens and young women largely abandoned the high heel in favor of flats and, especially, boots. In 1964, André Courrèges created a global fad for white go-go boots when he presented them with his Space Age Collection. Throughout the late 1960s and into the 1970s, boots of all materials and heights remained hugely popular.

The other key accessories to the total look were handbags, jewelry, and gloves. Leather handbags, like leather shoes, of the postwar years were again plentiful and relished by women after the many cotton, rayon, basket, and fake leather versions during the war. Ideally, the color and finish of a handbag should match the shoes (and belt and other small leather items). But most women preferred a functional black leather pouch or tote style that worked with everything. For special occasions, the small box bag was popularized by several Paris designers in 1950. (Figure 8.11.) Box bags were mostly rectilinear but also included other geometric shapes from trapezoid, to octagonal, to round, and for evening, made of clear Lucite with brass or silver grillwork and edges. Matching leather accessory sets often included wallets, coin purses, key caddies, cigarette cases, leather-clad lighters, and eyeglasses cases.

Like leather, the use of base metals was restricted during the war, forcing jewelry makers to use more expensive silver or cheap forms of plastic like Catalin or Bakelite. In the postwar years, costume jewelry makers made up for lost time with prolific collections of matching pieces, especially gold-tone metals. Paris designer and manufacturer Francis Winter created as many as 2,500 models each year. Major American manufacturers such as Trifari, Monet, and Napier

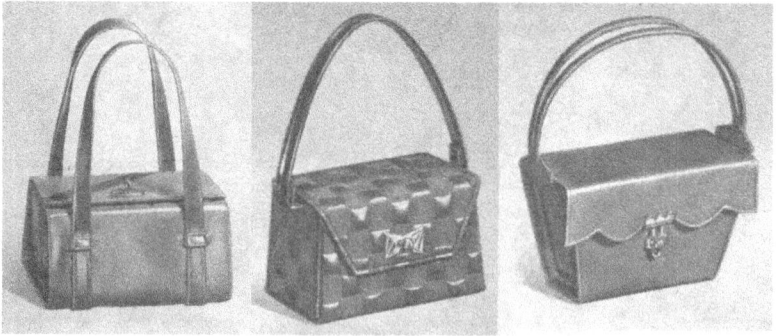

Figure 8.11 The small box bag was one of the innovative accessories of the 1950s. Because it was barely large enough for a handkerchief and compact, it was primarily for special occasions and evening events. Box bags from Spiegel, 1951.

likewise produced extensive assortments of matching multipiece collections and provided department stores with special showcases and display fixtures to present them. Among the most popular revival items of the era for girls and women was the charm bracelet. Amber topaz, both real and fake, was the era's iconic jewel, even inspiring a line of beauty and fragrance products from Avon called Topaze.

Day gloves were also an important accessory for most women until the mid-1960s—leather for fall and winter and cotton or one of the new lightweight synthetics for spring and summer. Middle- and upper-income women always wore gloves in town shopping, to luncheons with friends, and at women's club meetings. For evening wear, long gloves extending high on the upper arms were a dress requirement. Even working-class women had at least one pair of pristine white gloves for church and special social events. In the early 1960s, the fashion trend of three-quarter sleeves prompted glovers to offer gauntlet styles embellished with eyelet lace, machine embroidery, brass buttons, and other trimmings.

In addition to the critical necessaries of hats, shoes, handbags, and gloves, many women went further with their total look. With the end of wartime fabric restrictions, scarves were a revival favorite for an easy, eye-catching accent for a basic dress. Another revival was hosiery ornamented with knit-in clocking at the ankles, some studded with rhinestones for evening wear. Seamless hosiery was not new in the 1950s but gradually made back-seamed styles seem old-fashioned. And even the newly engineered slim umbrellas were carried, rain or shine, as an added accessory, somewhat like the pre-World War I walking sticks of affluent women.

Decade of "miracle fabrics"

By 1947, most US textile and apparel manufacturers had completed their retooling and conversion from wartime to peacetime production. That year, more than 8,000 textile mills were in operation, employing 1.2 million workers.[22] Through the baby boom years, textile mills and chemical companies continually developed new synthetic yarns and fabric treatment processes for all varieties of apparel. The 1950s, especially, was the age of "miracle fabrics."

The first true synthetic fiber was introduced by chemical giant DuPont in 1939—its petroleum-based thermoplastic fiber called nylon. The durable, easily dyed filament made from nylon was especially used in making sheer knits for hosiery, the first examples of which were presented at the New York World's Fair that year. Within the following year, more than 64 million pairs of nylon stockings were sold.[23] But during the Second World War, nylon became a vital defense material and its commercial use was severely restricted. In the postwar years, though, DuPont expanded the use of nylon to make carpets, toothbrushes, ropes, nets, and even cording in tires. It was combined with other plastics to make containers, combs, food packaging, and auto parts. In woven textiles, nylon was commonly blended with cotton, wool, and other synthetics such as polyester to produce fabrics that were cool, breathable, and elastic. Branded nylon blends of the 1950s included Nyfoyle and Helanca. In knit hosiery, a porous nylon georgette with a creped surface was launched in 1952, followed a year later with a nylon pinpoint mesh and a nylon sheer lace patterned knit.

In 1948, DuPont developed an acrylic fiber that was branded Orlon when it was commercially launched two years later (discontinued in 1990). The fiber was made by extruding a polymer in a solvent through a sieve-like spinneret, where the solvent evaporated from the filament. Orlon was a soft, lightweight fiber that took dyes well and remained colorfast. It was blended with more costly natural fibers to produce less expensive textiles. Orlon was used especially in knit garments such as sweaters, scarves, gloves, and hats, and in deep-pile fake furs. Because it was resistant to sunlight, it was also used for outdoor furniture upholstery, patio umbrellas, and awnings.

In 1949, Union Carbide improved its early versions of vinyl fibers with the development of Dynel. It is mostly known as a filament used in wigs and fake furs because of its stability, quick-drying properties, and flame resistance. Dynel was also used for knits, especially fleece garments with napped surfaces. In the 1960s, Pierre Cardin made Dynel famous with his collection of heat-molded dresses made of the synthetic.

In 1952, DuPont introduced Dacron, a synthetic polyester fiber unrelated to nylon or Orlon. Fabrics made of Dacron blends were easily laundered, quick-drying, and wrinkle and shrink-resistant, making them ideal for men's shirts and women's daywear. Dacron ushered in the era of wash-and-wear clothing, a marketing promise often featured in ads of the time, such as the one shown in Figure 8.12.

In addition to chemically produced synthetics, some plant-based fibers such as rayon remained in common use for postwar fabrics. Popular variations of cellulose fibers included Arnel, the branded name for cellulose acetate introduced in 1954 by Celanese (discontinued in 1986). It was a wash-and-wear colorfast fabric that held creases and pleats better than natural fibers.

Lurex is the trademarked name of a synthetic yarn which is coated with a metallic finish and also the name of the fabric made from the metalized yarn. Developed in 1946, Lurex was used largely in fabric for evening wear and millinery, and for embroidery on pageantry garments.

The decade of miracle fabrics concluded with the launch of newly developed synthetic stretch fibers to replace rubberized yarns. Even though elasticized fabrics had been continually improved since their introduction in the 1820s, they were limited in use, usually as insets for ankle boots, gloves, and corsets. In the 1930s, a leap forward was made with Lastex, a two-way

Figure 8.12 The 1950s was the age of "miracle fabrics" during which chemical companies and textile mills introduced new synthetic fibers, improved existing synthetics such as rayon and nylon, and developed fabric treatments for wash-and-wear and permanent-press clothing. Dacron ad, 1958; Lurex ad, 1957.

stretch knit used primarily for women's and men's swimwear and underwear. But over time, with exposure to saltwater, perspiration, heat, sun, and use, the rubber in elasticized textiles would lose elasticity and deteriorate. In 1958, DuPont solved those problems with the introduction of its synthetic stretch fiber branded Lycra. Used in stretch fabrics generically called "spandex" (an anagram of "expands"), elastomeric synthetic fibers like Lycra could stretch more than 500 percent and recover their shape. Spandex textiles had greater tensile strength and were more lightweight and durable than rubberized yarns. In 1960, *Vogue* emphasized the lightness of undergarments made with Lycra by piling nine girdles and bras into a grocer's scale that showed a total weight of 1 3/4 pounds.[24] Similarly, the DuPont ad shown in Figure 8.13 of the same year promoted the "molding, holding power" of Lycra spandex as well as a longer life span against "all the old girdle saboteurs—heat, detergents, body oils, perspiration."[25] In addition, Lycra fibers could be combined easily with other synthetics such as nylon and acetate for a wide range of fabric textures and surfaces. And of special importance to the American ready-to-wear market, spandex had broader applications in clothing production than rubberized textiles, including skiwear, bodysuits, activewear, sportswear, sleepwear, sweaters, T-shirts, hosiery, socks, and gloves.

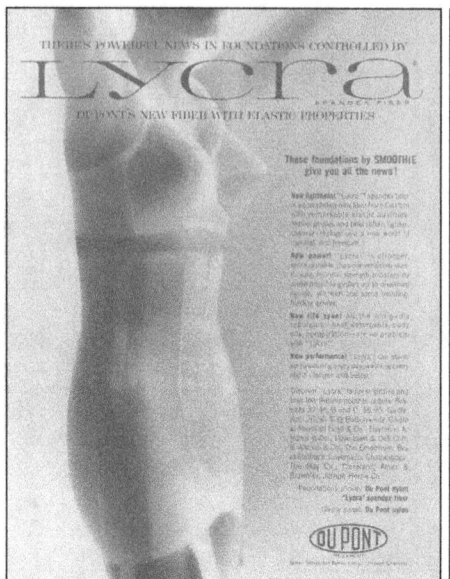

Figure 8.13 In 1958, DuPont introduced a stretch synthetic fiber named Lycra. Unlike rubberized yarns that deteriorated over time, Lycra retained its elasticity and was resistant to the effects of sun, perspiration, and wear. Left, Lycra Smoothies Foundations ad, 1960; right, Lycra sportswear ad, 1964.

Conclusion

In 1947, Paris couturier Christian Dior launched his debut collection of women's fashions that came to be known as the New Look. The ultrafeminine silhouettes of dresses with full, sweeping skirts and hemlines to the ankles were a marked contrast to the narrow, knee-length utility styles of the war years. Fitted, curvaceous suits replaced the boxy, masculine styles of the 1940s, and body-molding sheaths were revived from the 1930s. Through the baby boom years, American fashion followed the dictates of Paris. The hemlines gradually rose again, inching up to just below the knees by the end of the 1950s. In the second half of the 1950s, alternatives to cinched-waist styles were introduced, such as loose-fitting chemises, sack dresses, balloon-back designs, A-line cuts, and the trapeze. In the early 1960s, new trends influenced by the mod styles from Swinging London began to influence American fashions. The miniskirt was introduced, at first as a hemline just slightly above the knee, but in the late 1960s it became the thigh-high iconic look of the decade. Also in the 1960s, many accessories that had been all-important for the total look of the 1950s were abandoned, such as hats, gloves, and matching ensembles of jewelry and small leathers. The baby boom era concluded with a transition of women's dress from the New Look to a youthful, personalized dress identity of the youthquake generation.

9
BABY BOOM CHILDREN

An era of children

The population of children in America during the 1950s was enormous. More than 29 million children born during the late Depression and the Second World War years were in school in the 1950s, and more than 70 million baby boomers were added to the population between 1946 and 1964.[1] It was an era in which American society focused on children in a way it never had before. In pre-industrial days, children were a necessary labor resource for the survival of predominantly farm families and began to assume work duties by the age of five or six. Education was often sporadic and minimal; health and safety were too often disregarded by parents. With the urbanization and industrialization of America in the second half of the nineteenth century, children of poor families in cities became wage-earners, working long, miserable hours in dangerous factories, mines, and service sectors to contribute to family needs. Child labor laws in the United States only began to be considered in the early twentieth century but were widely resisted well into the 1930s. Only during the Depression, when high adult unemployment lingered, were children excluded from the labor force, and laws and governmental policies regulating child labor could be put into effect. As Helen and Robert Lynn observed in their 1937 Middletown study, "Children in this culture are increasingly mouths and decreasingly 'hands.'"[2]

These realities for American children growing up during the 1930s and 1940s had a profound impact on them as adults in the postwar years. Their approach to parenting was more than simply a grown-up's responsibility to feed, clothe, and provide a roof for their offspring. The corporate man in the gray flannel suit pushed himself hard as the family provider to ensure his children had a safer, more secure life than he had as a child. The suburbanite mother devoted herself to her children, forgoing higher education and a career to be home for her children. Baby boom parents were much more interested in their children's development, health, and security than most of their parents had been a generation earlier. Moms and dads of the 1950s sought the advice of childcare experts in *Parents' Magazine* and *P.T.A. Magazine,* and in books such as Dr. Spock's *Common Sense Book of Baby and Child Care* and the *Gesell Institute's Child Behavior* by Drs. Frances Ilg and Louise B. Ames. Being a parent was not just a responsibility, it was a "privilege," asserted Ilg and Ames. "The more you know about the normal changes which ordinarily take place in behavior as a child grows, the more successful you can be in guiding your child along the complicated path which leads to maturity."[3] Mothers of school-age children checked homework, joined PTAs, and attended school recitals. Fathers likewise made time for their children, for play, to listen, and to mentor. "Enjoy him as he is—that's how he'll grow up best," advised Dr. Spock.[4]

Of course, these privileged children were of white middle- and upper-class families. In the postwar years, millions of African American, Latino, Asian, American Indian, and other ethnic children endured Jim Crow discrimination and poverty across the nation far removed from suburbia's comfortable ranch houses and modern schools. Often, both parents of these lower socioeconomic families had to work to make ends meet, and they seldom had the time to study child care books, let alone indulge in music lessons, vacations to Disneyland, or Scouting retreats.

Gender role socialization

In the postwar years a regressive conservativism dominated American culture. In a backlash to the social disruptions of the Depression and the Second World War, government propaganda, social science, and popular culture urged a return to normalcy as defined by conformity to traditionalism. Marriages spiked after years of decline during the Depression, and the baby boom lasted for 18 years from 1946 to 1964. The successful American male was the corporate man in the gray flannel suit, the family breadwinner who commuted six days a week from his suburban ranch house into a nearby city; the successful American woman was a suburbanite wife and mother dressed in her cinched, ultrafeminine New Look clothes. Young married couples were urged and expected to have at least two children, ideally a boy first and a girl second.

Parenting meant that children would be trained within specific sociocultural lanes for each sex. All boys and girls would have certain normative objectives and goals to ensure their proper masculinity or femininity as they matured. (Figure 9.1.) The focus on gender role socialization in American society of the 1950s especially centered on boys more than on girls. As social critic Paul Goodman wrote in 1956, a boy must learn "how to be useful and make something of oneself," but "a girl does not *have* to, she is not expected to 'make something' of herself. Her career does not have to be self-justifying, for she will have children, which is absolutely self-justifying."[5]

This emphasis on the gender role socialization of boys had a legacy in American culture dating to the late nineteenth century when the nation underwent a rapid urbanization and industrialization. The farmers and village craftsmen increasingly worked away from the home in urban factories, offices, and service sectors twelve hours a day, six days a week. This meant boys were left in the care of women—mothers, teachers, elder sisters, aunts, and other female caregivers—for extended periods. As a result, medical professionals, social critics, military leaders, and journalists sounded the alarm about the threat of a feminization of boys.

Among the countermeasures to this perceived threat that were developed in the late nineteenth century were competitive sports. Team athletics of the time that were invented and organized into national leagues included baseball (1871), intercollegiate football (1873), basketball (1891), and volleyball (1895). Sports were viewed as an effective way for boys to develop the masculine qualities expected of them in manhood: physical strength, health, ruggedness, perseverance, self-discipline, and stoicism.

In addition to sports, another way for boys to secure their masculinity as they matured was to learn self-sufficiency and self-confidence through rustic adventures away from women and their feminizing influences. In the late nineteenth and early twentieth centuries, male educators, church leaders, and social reformers organized boys' clubs such as the Woodcraft Indians, Sons of Daniel Boone, and the Boy Scouts. These groups took day excursions and overnight camping trips into the wilderness where the boys would get plenty of exercise hiking, swimming, canoeing, and other healthful activities. They would also learn how to use tools to make useful things. Further, they would learn to compete in masculine environments against peers in strength, agility, endurance, and achievement. These Darwinian lessons also taught them many "don'ts" of masculinity: don't show weakness, don't be a coward, don't be emotional—in other words, don't be feminized, don't be a sister—that is, a sissy.

These lessons became standards of American culture for boys, generation after generation. To mature into proper masculine men, American boys needed the warrior training of sports competitions; they needed to have the self-confidence of wielding tools and making or repairing things; and they needed the health and vitality that outdoor activities provided. The fathers of the baby boom era boys had learned these tenets of masculine identity in their boyhood during the 1930s from their fathers, who had been the first generation of basketball players and Boy Scouts.

Yet, even with the traditions of these models of masculinity as a guide for the gender role socialization of baby boom boys, the risk of the feminization of boys was as worrisome in the postwar years as it had been in the nineteenth

Figure 9.1 In the baby boom era, parents, teachers, government propaganda, and popular culture relentlessly trained children with norms of specific masculine and feminine identities. These efforts of gender role socialization taught children gendered behavior and dress to which they were expected to adhere as adults.

century. Coming out of the Second World War straight into the Cold War and the Korean War, the need for a strong male population was acutely felt throughout the baby boom years, and the masculine preparation of boys for manhood was a particular focus of government policies, schools, religious institutions, and popular culture. "The modern middle-class boy . . . is forced to compete with others, to achieve—which demands a certain degree of independence, firmness of purpose, aggressiveness, self-assertion," wrote Betty Friedan in 1963.[6] As noted in Chapter 7, a particularly persistent argument was that the development of boys was under threat of feminization from overbearing or indulgent mothers. Childcare authors Ferdinand Lundberg and Marynia Farnham devoted a great deal of their postwar research to how different types of mothers could foster an assortment of neuroses in their sons, resulting in boys who, at best, ended up as juvenile delinquents and criminals, or at worst, "sissies," as in "passive-feminine or passive-homosexual males."[7] Fathers, coaches, teachers, and other male role models were continually urged to be on their guard against these types of mothers, and to take an active role in guiding boys into manhood. For example, Dr. Spock advised fathers of many do's and don'ts in their efforts to help their sons "grow up to be manly." "The thing that makes [a boy] feel and act like a man is being able to copy, to pattern himself after, men and older boys."[8] Similarly, Frances Ilg and Louis Ames of the Giselle Institute observed "the grave concern to parents, particularly to fathers," of a son becoming feminized—the boy who "shuns anything rough and tumble" but instead "favors such activities as painting, singing, play-acting." The Giselle handbook recommended that a father should "permit the artistic, creative activities which the child enjoys, but also try to encourage him to play with boys."[9] Dr. Spock likewise made note of the son who, by age five, "is avoiding boys, or is regularly preferring to take the part of a mother or girl in house play." That could mean "the mother is being too protective and enveloping," and the boy "needs a friendlier relationship with his father." (But if the "feminine boy" does not outgrow such behavior by about age eleven, Giselle's suggested psychiatric treatment,[10] and Spock similarly recommended the boy "needs child-guidance help.")[11]

In a 1961 episode of *Leave It to Beaver,* the Beaver has acquired a coaster cart needing a set of wheels. A girl classmate offers him the wheels of an old doll's carriage, which the Beaver collects and proceeds to push home. Two women stop in their tracks upon seeing the Beaver with the carriage and turn in astonishment to watch him continue down the sidewalk. He then passes a pair of middle-aged men on the street who look disapprovingly at the boy and refer to Beaver as a "sissy." In the next block, two little girls giggle and sneeringly ask Beaver if he has his dolly in the carriage. Meanwhile, at home, Beaver's teenage brother Wally hears about the doll carriage and rushes to intercept Beaver, telling their mother that "some wise guy is liable to clobber him." Mrs. Cleaver asks why Wally would think that. "Gee, Mom, guys always pick on someone who's different," Wally replies. Besides protecting his little brother, Wally is also concerned that "a thing like this could put a curse on the whole family." Mrs. Cleaver then asks her husband what he would have done as a youngster if he had seen a boy pushing a doll's carriage down the street. "I'd clobber him, of course," shrugged Beaver's dad. The scenario may have been intended as a comedy in 1961, but the episode "Beaver's Doll Buggy" (June 17, 1961) demonstrated the rigid expectations of boys by all of Cold War American society, and the consequences for any boy who strayed from that inflexible gender role could range from ridicule to actual physical danger.

The gender role socialization of girls, on the other hand, received less emphasis through most of the baby boom era. Whereas boys were supposed to resist any feminizing influences from mothers, elder sisters, teachers, or other authority females in their lives, girls were in effect apprentices of their mothers and most other female role models. "The girl in struggling to become an adult woman must rely upon some pattern or model from which she can derive a design for femininity," wrote Lundberg and Farnham. "She is provided with one in her mother and she will have to believe for a long time that her mother's nature, temperament and attitudes are ideals toward which she must strive as a woman."[12] From their earliest stage at which they recognized a difference between the sexes, girls began to emulate their mothers in play and gradually became mother's helper. They developed skills in the kitchen and learned how to use household appliances. They also studied Mom's beauty regimen, fashion sense, and clothing choices. (Figure 9.2.) The girl depicted on the front cover of this book is represented as the era's ideal little girl, excelling in her femininity with her neatly pressed pink dress, carefully arranged hair, and coordinating accessories. She hesitatingly stands back from her brothers who aggressively clamor over their dad in their casual playwear. Such girls were not especially encouraged to excel in school, where curricula were often tailored to a girl's future as wife and mother with classes in home economics and gender-segregated "health" classes. For middle- and upper-income families who sent their daughters to college, the goal was often to find a better grade of husband, rather than to complete a degree that might lead to a career.

Where parents were somewhat encouraging of a daughter, suggests Wini Breines in her study of "growing up female in the fifties," was in a girl's pursuit of beauty and popularity.

> Because girls could not plan their futures as boys could—since their future and self-definition depended on the men they would marry—there was a lack of reality evident in the girls' imaginations of their future . . . Marriage, the only sanctioned goal for girls in the 1950s, does not lend itself to rational planning, as does a career. Girls were explicitly discouraged from planning; their activity revolved around their gender identity, particularly their appearance.

Figure 9.2 Whereas boys were taught to resist the feminizing influences of mothers, girls were encouraged to be apprentices of their mothers to prepare them for their future roles as wives and mothers. Ad, 1959.

Parents, movies and television programming, women's magazines, advertising, and most aspects of popular culture coached and cajoled American girls toward courtship and marriage through an emphasis on appearance, and hence, desirability. The multi-million-dollar cosmetic, beauty, and fashion industries promoted the ideal American girl as white with straight hair and straight teeth, hygienically scrubbed and well groomed, and dressed in the current clothing styles, whether she was seven or seventeen. Those girls with such advantages, in turn, were accredited with a wholesomeness, a good-girl halo.

> Although image and being seen have always been central to feminine identity, white, middle-class girls in the 1950s learned to construct and imagine themselves almost exclusively through consumer goods and images in the media . . . Dreams of (white) princes rescuing their beautiful selves on white horses occupied much psychic space as girls 'prepared' for adulthood . . .

From this perspective, the entire culture colluded in keeping girls passively focused on appearances, daydreaming of movie stars and romance, longing to be seen and chosen, waiting to become wives and mothers.[13]

Of course, for girls without the prerequisite standards of beauty and suburban affluence—girls of color, girls of ethnic immigrant heritage, girls of lower-income families—this barrage of cultural messaging often left them feeling inferior, less desirable, and unprepared for the ultimate competition in the adult arena of husband hunting.

Betty Friedan called out this double standard of society's emphasis on the development of boys and minimal interest in that of girls. She wrote,

> Many saw the tragic waste of American sons who were made incapable of achievement, individual values, independent action; but they did not see as tragic the waste of the daughters . . . Educators and sociologists applauded when the personality of the middle-class girl was consistently absorbed from childhood through adulthood by her "role as woman" . . . The waste of human self was not considered a phenomenon to be studied in women.

Friedan concluded, "By permitting girls to evade tests of reality, and real commitments, in school and the world, by the promise of magical fulfillment through marriage, the feminine mystique arrests their development at an infantile level, short of personal identity, with an inevitably weak core of self."[14]

As cautionary as childcare specialists were about boys and the influence of their mothers, few experts had much to say about girls and their fathers. Almost as an afterthought, Spock reminds dads that "a girl needs a friendly father, too." He does not provide the "pattern" for her development as he does for a son, but rather "by learning to enjoy the qualities in her father that are particularly masculine, a girl is getting ready for her adult life in a world that is half made up of men." When she is older, her dating choices, and especially "the kind of married life she makes, are all influenced strongly by the kind of relationship she has had with her father throughout her childhood."[15] In the Giselle's guide, much of the chapter on father-child relationships is generic with little indication of specific gender role socialization. Before the child is age ten, the handbook suggests, father is primarily the disciplinarian. A child's rebelliousness against eating, getting dressed, or going to bed "can be turned to relatively docile obedience by a word from Father." By age ten, though, the emphasis from Giselle's is the importance of the role model relationship of father and son, for which "boys and their fathers may group together against feminine interference."[16]

Gender role socialization began at birth, even though children did not become aware of sex distinctions until around the age of three. Parents of the baby boom era carefully selected the gender-appropriate color for their child's clothing and environment: blue for boys and pink for girls. Textile historian Jo B. Paoletti details in her book *Pink and Blue, Telling the Boys from the Girls in America* the emergence of the gender identity colors of blue for boys and pink for girls. "Pink and blue symbolism is so firmly embedded in American popular culture that it's hard to believe that their gender associations are relatively new."[17] Some indications of gender color coding had emerged in the late nineteenth century, but the evolution was a gradual sociocultural process that only began to be standardized by the American ready-to-wear industry between the world wars. Until the 1940s, pink and blue were largely considered applicable to children's clothing of either sex. By the 1950s, though, "the gendering of pink and blue . . . was driven by the twin engines of young children's desire for sharper distinctions and an increasing inclination, by the grown-up children who were their parents, to satisfy that desire."[18] Pink, especially, became associated with femininity, a favorite color frequently worn by First Lady Mamie Eisenhower, and boys were steered to blue as the masculine identity color.[19]

Toys were another way for parents to reinforce gender role socialization.[20] Boys were given train sets, model airplanes, trucks, cars, cap pistols, plastic soldiers, Lincoln Logs and other construction sets, tool kits, and sports equipment. They could dress up in diminutive costumes as Davy Crockett or the Lone Ranger based on the TV heroes. Girls were given baby dolls, Barbies, doll wardrobes, doll houses, doll carriages and bassinettes, tea sets, miniature kitchen and home appliances, cookware, play beauty kits, and starter sewing sets. Girl's costumes provided them with plastic high heels and jewelry, simulated cosmetics, aprons, and similar feminine accoutrement that allowed them to pretend to be housewives, nurses, fashion models, or princesses.

For boys, any plaything that might threaten him with feminization to any degree was strictly prohibited. Dolls especially were taboo for boys. Dr. Spock noted, "A father may be upset if his son at 2 likes to play occasionally with dolls and doll carriages. This is too early to start worrying." But such a predilection could become worrying if, by age 3 or 4, the boy does not "show a preference for conventional activities of [his] own sex."[21] Even many unisex toys of the baby boom era could be a threat to the gender role socialization of boys. Plush animals had to be color-appropriate for boys—nothing pink, frilly, or flowery, no animals in dresses or bonnets. Boots for roller and ice skates were black for boys and white for girls. Boy's bicycles had a distinctive top bar between the seat and handlebars, but girls' models were without a top frame bar, supposedly so she could step off without lifting a leg up and over, possibly flipping up her skirt. A boy risked being ridiculed by peers if seen riding a girl's bike or playing with anything designated specifically for girls, especially if pink in color. Girls, however, were allowed to play with boy's toys without any concern from parents that their femininity would be undermined, particularly if she hero-worshiped an older brother. The "tomboy" who liked baseball, toy fire engines, and cap pistols was fully expected to outgrow this phase by her teen years without impeding her gender-as-destiny roles of wife and mother.

Popular culture was also a significant reinforcement of children's gender role socialization in the baby boom era. Children's books, movies, and television programs provided representations and depictions of behavioral norms for white, middle-class boys and girls. "Both the film and television representations of family life tend toward producing and maintaining sex stereotyping," writes media historian Nina Leibman. "On the whole, this means adhering to a strict oppositional construct in which men and boys are ideally associated with strength, intelligence, logic, consistency, and humor, while women and girls are rendered intuitive, dependent, flighty, sentimental, and self-sacrificing . . . The dialogue commands that women and girls marry and that men and boys take responsibility for their actions."[22] Television family programs especially presented distinct, visual messages of children's gender-appropriate clothing, grooming, environments, and activities to the masses week after week. In effect, TV characters were supplemental role models for American children and teens. Popular family programs of the baby boom era featuring children characters included: *Adventures of Ozzie and Harriet* (1952–1966), two boys; *Donna Reed Show* (1958–1966), one boy, one girl; *Father Knows Best* (1954–1960), one boy, two girls; *Make Room for Daddy* (1953–1964), one boy, one girl; *I Love Lucy* (1951–1957), one boy. Some TV programs featured children as the principals: *Lassie* (1954–1973), one boy; *Leave It to Beaver* (1957–1963), two boys; *Dennis the Menace* (1959–1963), one boy; *My Three Sons* (1960–1972), three boys and later, an adopted son and a stepdaughter. Sports themes and scenarios of mischievousness were common for TV boys, and domestic activities such as helping Mom with housekeeping or cooking were prevalent for TV girls. For example, a 1955 story of a boy's responsibility was presented in *Father Knows Best* when son Bud was not allowed to play in a baseball game because he had neglected his chores (episode March 27, 1955). Along the same line for girls was a 1962 episode of *Donna Reed* in which teen daughter Mary discovered housework was not as easy as she thought when she tries to make a cake but it turns into a disaster (episode August 23, 1962). In addition to these gender lessons in life demonstrated by TV children characters, they, in turn, often interacted with peers in gender-appropriate circumstances that further reinforced children's normative behavior and dress for the American audience.

A new consumer demographic

In the period between 1946 and 1964, America's population included almost 100 million children—nearly 30 million born in the late Depression and World War II years, and over 70 million baby boomers. (The US population at the end of the baby boom in 1964 was 191 million.)[23] In the postwar era of mass marketing, mass consumption, and mass communication through television, American children, especially teenagers, became a marketing demographic unlike any children's groups before. (Figure 9.3.) Where previously children may have made their wish lists for Santa or birthdays from looking through mail-order catalogs sent to their parents, or from window shopping when occasionally downtown, or even from observing the possessions of neighborhood peers, a world of consumer goods for postwar children was alluringly presented to them every time they watched television.

Figure 9.3 In the affluent 1950s, the 90 million children and teenagers became a new consumer demographic directly targeted with advertising, TV commercials, and marketing efforts by makers of soft drinks, snack foods, comic books, teenpics, and rock and roll producers. By the end of the decade, the youth market contributed almost $10 billion to the American economy. Ad, 1953.

Most middle-class school-age children and teenagers received a weekly allowance, usually as an incentive to perform chores such as tidying up their rooms or taking out the garbage. In 1953, *Boy's Life* reported that Ozzie and Harriet Nelson provided their sons with weekly allowances: 17-year-old Dave received $10, from which he had to pay for school lunches and supplies as well as any maintenance for his 1941 Ford (gas was charged to the family account), while 13-year-old Ricky received $1.50.[24] These were the discretionary dollars that makers of snack foods, sodas, toys and games, rock and roll music, teen magazines, comic books, movies, and clothing aggressively targeted through slick advertising in print and especially on television. For marketers, TV commercials and program sponsorships bypassed parents and appealed directly to the youth market with children's shows like *Captain Kangaroo* (1955–1984), *The Mickey Mouse Club* (1955–1959), *Lassie* (1954–1973), *Howdy Doody* (1947–1960), and for teens, *American Bandstand* (1952–1989). "The children's show was a candy store populated by dream parents who pandered forbidden products," notes Lynn Spigel in her assessment of "seducing the innocent" by early television programming. "Even more important, these programs taught children the art of persuasion, advising them how to tell their parents about the wondrous items advertised on the show." Children learned "how to influence their parent's product choices, and in the process the child's narrative pleasure is inextricably intertwined with the pleasure of consumption."[25]

Equally important to the consumption-driven market of the 1950s was the role television advertising played in lining up the next generation of consumers. In 1957, social critic Vance Packard examined the "psycho-seduction of children" in his analysis of American marketing. In addition to enticing children to spend their allowances and pocket change now, advertisers also banked on these children as future adult consumers. "The potency of television in conditioning youngsters to be loyal enthusiasts of a product, whether they are old enough to consume it or not, became indisputable early in the fifties . . . Merchandisers sought to groom children not only as future consumers but as shills who would lead or 'club' their parents into the salesroom."[26] Marketing researchers were delighted to report to beer, cigarette, and auto manufacturers that their catchy ad jingles were commonly sung at home and school by children long after the television had been turned off, thereby perpetuating brand and product awareness in young minds.

The extravagant spending and consumption of this growing economic demographic, though, became an issue of criticism for many social scientists and journalists of the era, whose editorial essays and books questioned such indulgent permissiveness of parents and its effect on children. In his look at the "suburban myth" in the 1960s, Scott Donaldson asserted that the postwar "social organization is not only not that of traditional patriarchy; it is not that of matriarchy either. The system is one of filiarchy; the children are in control.

Youngsters in the suburbs are hopelessly pampered and coddled and coaxed along. They are overprotected, and learn nothing of the trials and difficulties of life from their permissive parents."[27] A *Harper's* magazine report on suburbia had made a similar assessment in 1953. "Nothing's too good for the kids! . . . On visiting these communities, one cannot fail to be impressed, nonetheless, by the parents' devotion to and sacrifices for their children." As one suburban toy store owner noted, "If the kid sees it and wants it, [the parents] buy it; that's it."[28] Richard Gordon called these baby boomers the "gimme kids" in his study of suburbia. American suburbs are full of "spoiled, lazy, materialistic children," he complained in *The Split-Level Trap*. "No one has cracked down on them. They take what they want because their parents have not insisted that they earn it . . . Life has been given to them on a silver platter, and they expect the handout to continue."[29] American manufacturers of consumer goods and services counted on this to be true and were rewarded by the end of the decade when the purchasing power of America's youngsters had grown to nearly $10 billion.[30]

Social critics of the era also took note of this powerful economic demographic and its influence on culture and society. One of the most potent challenges to the ultraconservative social norms of the 1950s was the popularization of rock and roll music. The term "rock and roll" originated in 1951 from a Cleveland radio station show called "Moondog's Rock 'n' Roll House Party," hosted by deejay Alan Freed.[31] Rock and roll music, with its "hard-driving beat; the sexual innuendos in the song lyrics; its roots in African-American rhythm and blues," was initially viewed as "race music," which greatly alarmed white suburban parents, teachers, religious leaders, and other traditionalists.[32] "Rock was sexy, audacious, defiant, unfettered, all the things that country and western, at one extreme, and pop, at the other were not—all the things, in short, that Americans as a whole were not supposed to be."[33] Coupled with the sexually suggestive new forms of dancing, exemplified by Elvis "the Pelvis" Presley, this immoral, lewd "Devil's music" must be a plot by the communists, many conservatives thought, to destroy the American way of life by encouraging race mixing.[34] But teenagers expressed their enthusiastic endorsement of rock and roll not only by buying newly released records week after week but also by going to rock concerts by Black as well as white performers, by listening to rock music on their radios, and by watching TV programs that featured rock bands and singers. Between 1955 and 1959, US record sales nearly tripled to $600 million.[35] Hollywood likewise tapped into the rock and roll phenomenon by starring Elvis and his music in 31 movies beginning in 1955 and attracting teenage box office dollars with film titles such as *Rock Around the Clock* (Bill Haley and His Comets, 1956); *Shake, Rattle, and Rock* (Fats Domino, 1956); *Rock All Night* (The Platters, 1957); and *Let's Rock* (The Tyrones, 1958).

In addition to movies featuring rock and roll music, Hollywood targeted teenagers with "teenpics," low-budget films with themes and content performed by young actors that appealed to American teenagers. To offset declining attendance at theaters, due largely to the ever-increasing number of households with television sets, movie studios began experimenting with new iterations of what were called "exploitation films" to attract teenagers. Exploitation films had been around since the establishment of Hollywood, and dealt with "forbidden" topics, including "sex and sex hygiene, prostitution and vice, drug use, nudity, and any other subjects considered to be in bad taste."[36] They were usually made by small, independent operations with low production values ranging from cheap sets to poor camerawork, sound, and editing. In the 1950s, these filmmakers expanded the exploitation genre to include representations of dangerous youth and juvenile delinquents, hot-rod racing, space horror, and rock and roll. "Few teenpics of the late 1950s relied on only one exploitation hook," observed film historian Thomas Doherty. "Combining the double-bill strategy into one picture, they mixed two or more exploitation items—rock 'n' roll, drag racing, high school vice—in inventive hybrids. The result was a bizarre cross-pollination of gimmicks, a kind of exploitation overload."[37] These movies attracted two types of teenagers: those who wanted to see something they knew about—rock and roll bands, the latest dances, hot rods—and those who were simply curious about some aspect of teen popular culture with which they were unfamiliar.

Yet, most American teenagers who went to see these movies did not identify with the characters or their behavior. Conservatism prevailed throughout postwar American society, and teenagers of the 1950s were far more conformist than the protagonists in teensploitation movies. One of the biggest hits with teens of the time was *Rebel Without a Cause* (1955). Although the movie included some "cross-pollination of gimmicks," such as a "chicken-run" car race and a switchblade knife fight, the movie was more about "youth trying to discover themselves and declare their identity within the prosperous torments of the postwar world."[38] Boys were more likely to copy James Dean's look and don a red cotton jacket and jeans than a leather biker's jacket from *The Wild One* (1953), and most girls likely preferred Natalie Wood's circle skirt and cashmere sweater to anything worn by girls in *Young and Dangerous* (1957) or *Juvenile Jungle* (1958). Similarly, most white, middle-class teenagers of the time identified best with the clean-cut, all-American characters in the Gidget series or the surfer and beach party movies that began at the end of the 1950s and proliferated in the early 1960s.

As concerned as many baby boom era parents were about rock and roll music and teenpics, one youth product that incited a national furor was comic books. By the early 1950s, more than 600 comic book titles generated $90 million in revenue for publishers.[39] Crime and horror comic books in particular became exceedingly lurid with stories in vivid color featuring gore, violence, lust, and vice. The sociocultural panic about comic books was exacerbated by the 1954 book *Seduction of the Innocent* from psychiatrist Fredric Wertham, who avowed that comic books were harmful to children, leading them to juvenile delinquency and ultimately to drugs, violence, and crime. Although it was later found that Wertham's book "manipulated, overstated, compromised, and fabricated evidence,"[40] at the time of publication, his conclusions added fuel to the fire. Religious groups and other moral crusaders organized campaigns against comic books, communities instigated bonfires to burn comic books, cities banned or restricted the sale of certain titles, the New York City police raided the offices of one publisher, and even Congress held hearings in 1954 to investigate the relation of comic books to juvenile delinquency. Both Dr. Spock's and Giselle's childcare books included segments about comics. Dr. Spock advised, "Conscientious parents often read the comic strips and comic books, thinking that they ruin their children's taste for good reading, fill their minds with morbid ideas, keep them indoors, interfere with homework, and waste good money . . . Certainly you have the right and the duty to forbid comics that are morally objectionable." Dr. Spock's recommendation was to allow children to read comic books, but in moderation, perhaps by setting limits on the number allowed per week. As to the question of comic books contributing to juvenile delinquency, he told parents they do not (since "delinquency is a manifestation of a fundamental defect in a child's character.")[41] Giselle's similarly advised that most children were not "highly fragile objects, supersensitive to every aspect of the environment and likely to be permanently scarred by any and every event in life . . . Time and again, they show a capacity to bounce back after a difficult real-life situation, let alone after reading a comic book."[42] Even so, comic book publishers responded to the threat of legislative censorship and regulations by establishing a self-policing Comics Code Authority (CCA) in 1954 that provided industry guidelines for comic book content. Suddenly prohibited were depictions of vampires, werewolves, and zombies; excessive gore and bloodshed; torture, sexual assault, sexual perversion, sadism, and masochism; and nudity or exaggerated female anatomy.[43] Comic books that complied with the code were permitted to display a seal of approval by the CCA as a guide to retailers, parents, and consumers.

For the new consumer group of postwar youngsters, comic books, teenpics, and rock and roll music were more than moments of diversion and entertainment, they formed a cache of youth identity that was independent of, and often counter to, adult role models and established norms. These media sources were guides to modernity from which children and teenagers saw how their more knowledgeable and sophisticated peers behaved and dressed. Consequently, those youngsters who were in the know could talk to their friends about the latest rock idols and their music or a new comic book super hero in an exclusive language their parents and teachers could not understand. All the while, American marketers, publishers, apparel manufacturers, and especially movie, television, and music producers continually refined and intensified their focus on the youth market to great success.

Children's dress

Children's clothing of the mid-twentieth century was primarily miniature versions of adult styles, as they had been for centuries. One distinctive form of boys' dress was the knicker suit, a style adopted from men's casual country styles in the 1880s to become the standard dress for school-age boys until the Second World War. (Figure 9.4.) A rite of passage for boys during this 50-year span was his social transition from boyhood to young manhood with his first pair of long trousers at about age 13. The gendered boys' dress of voluminous knickers was discontinued abruptly in 1942 with the implementation of the wartime L-85 restrictions on the use of fabric in making apparel. Even with the lifting of clothing production limitations after the war, boy's knickers were not revived.

The postwar Ivy League suit was adopted from men's styles in scaled-down versions for boys with the same boxy, straight-hanging jacket and wide-legged, cuffed pants. As with men's suit jackets, the expanse of the rolled lapels was wide and gradually narrowed through the 1950s. One variation of suits exclusively for

Figure 9.4 For more than 50 years prior to World War II, the standard dress of schoolboys was the knicker suit. But with the implementation of fabric restrictions on clothing production in 1942, the style was abandoned and not revived afterward. Boy's knicker suits from Spiegel, 1941.

Figure 9.5 The leisure suit for boys was a casual alternative to the Ivy League suit. Jackets were made with sleeves, collars, and lapels of a contrasting fabric to the body and trousers. The leisure suit was not adapted to men's wear until the 1970s. Boys' leisure suit from Spiegel, 1951.

boys in the early 1950s was the two-tone "leisure suit," made with sleeves, collar, and lapels in a contrasting fabric, usually a vividly hued plaid. (Figure 9.5.) Small boy's versions sometimes featured the reverse, with a plaid torso but solid sleeves and collar to match the pants. By the second half of the 1950s, boys' suits reflected the new cut of men's Continental styles. Jackets were shaped with a slightly tapered waist and sleeves and lapels were noticeably narrowed, as were trouser legs.

One of the new design elements for boys' casual pants in the mid-1950s was the addition of an adjustable buckle strap at the center back just below the waistband. (Figure 9.6.) Called the Ivy League trouser, the style was actually trimmer than Ivy suit trousers, and featured a plain, unpleated front.

Increasingly important for boys and especially teenagers was the popularization of jeans in the baby boom years. Often called "dungarees" in advertising and catalogs, jeans of the early postwar years were largely viewed as durable work pants, as they had been since their invention in the 1870s, worn primarily by farmers, ranchers, cowboys, miners, lumberjacks, and laborers. From the 1920s through the 1940s, Easterners brought jeans home with them from vacations at Western dude ranches, but primarily wore them for weekend yard work or house maintenance chores. Even at the end of the 1950s, catalogs referred to jeans as "Westerns," "saddle pants," and "pioneer jeans,"[44] and often photographed models wearing cowboy boots, hats, and yoke-front shirts or holding props like spurs, lariats, or farm implements. Jeans were commonly shown in movies, television programs, and in ads and catalogs with the cuff turned up several inches or rolled up. (Figure 9.7.) Marlon Brando and his

Figure 9.6 One of the new dress fads for boys in the 1950s was the Ivy trouser, made with an adjustable buckle strap sewn to the back just below the waistband. Buckle-back strap pants from Sears, 1957.

biker crew all wore their jeans turned up in the movie *The Wild One* (1953), as did James Dean and his high school classmates in *Rebel Without a Cause* (1955) (although some promotional photos of Dean show the cuffs down). Because jeans were associated with work clothes, and often as the dress of juvenile delinquents due in part to Hollywood, most school dress codes prohibited the style to be worn on campus until well into the 1970s. The sexualization of jeans for teenage boys and young men emerged in the late 1950s as an influence of the trim cut of Continental suits. By the beginning of the 1960s, teenagers and young men preferred jeans with a snug fit. Levi's introduced "Thirteens" with narrow legs that tapered to just 13 inches at the cuff,[45] and slim white Levi's especially became a trend with high-school teens and collegians through the decade.

Sportswear for boys largely followed men's casual styles. Comfortable, striped knit shirts such as those worn by the two boys in the front cover illustration (and the author on the title page) were ubiquitous. Common for both men's and boys' woven sport shirts were screen prints in vibrant colors of Hawaiian tropical

Figure 9.7 During the 1950s, jeans (called dungarees) gradually evolved from work clothes for farmers, ranchers, and cowboys into casual wear for children and especially teenagers. Through the decade, jeans were bought with a long pant leg that could be turned up at the cuff. Boy's jeans from Montgomery Ward, 1958.

scenes, sports or hunting equipment, sailboats, cars and trucks, and geometric abstractions. Gender-specific screen prints for preteen school-age boys included licensed images of TV masculine heroes like Roy Rogers, the Lone Ranger, and Superman. Ready-to-wear makers targeted teens with styles designed just for them such as the "Rock 'n' Roll" shirts shown in Figure 9.8, which featured flexible stays in the collars that could be turned up like Elvis, Fabian, and Ricky Nelson wore theirs on stage.

For baby boom era girls, the American ready-to-wear market had it both ways—adaptations of ultrafeminine New Look styles and, at the same time,

Figure 9.8 American ready-to-wear makers began to target the youth market with clothes made specifically for them, rather than simply scaled-down versions of adult styles. The "rock 'n' roll" shirts shown here were constructed with stays inserted into the collar that could be turned up like Elvis and other performers sometimes wore theirs. Boys' "rock 'n' roll" shirts from Spiegel, 1956.

appropriations of boys' wear. The wartime utility clothes of narrow skirts, simple jackets, and plain blouses for girls had lingered for a few seasons after the war, but by 1948, dresses were made with full skirts, puff sleeves, and big collars, embellished with an abundance of pleats, ruffles, bows, and other trimmings. Hemlines for school-age girls remained just below the knees, but for teenagers, the long skirts of the New Look women's styles prevailed, gradually inching up through the 1950s to the knees again by the end of the decade. One of the iconic looks for girls, especially teenagers, of the 1950s was the circle skirt. (Figure 9.9.) Sometimes called a poodle skirt, the style was variously adorned with three-dimensional appliques of fluffy yarn poodles or cats, hearts, flowers, butterflies, music notes, and even actual vinyl records or Christmas ornaments. As New Look silhouettes shifted, girls' dresses followed women's trends, including Dior's A-Line and H-Line. (Figure 9.10.)

Figure 9.9 One of the iconic youth styles for girls of the 1950s was the circle skirt. Versions were often embellished with a variety of appliques including yarn poodles or cats and even objects such as vinyl records and Christmas ornaments. Circle skirt from Sears, 1952.

Despite the regressive conservatism of the postwar era, slacks for women and girls grew in popularity and variety. During the war, women wearing pants to work in defense plants and service sectors had been a common sight on city streets and in public buildings. In the postwar years, though, slacks for women were regarded as inappropriate for in town, restaurants, and most other public spaces. The exception was parks, golf courses, resorts, and similar recreational sites. Workplace and school dress codes strictly prohibited feminine slacks well into the 1970s. Lengths of women's and girls' pants ranged from ankle-length capri pants, mid-shin pedal pushers, and above-knee Bermuda shorts.

Jeans for young girls were after-school and weekend playwear. A favorite style was lined with colorful striped or plaid cotton flannel that added flair at the turned-up cuffs. For teen girls, jeans became a casual look often worn with scuffed saddle oxfords or penny loafers. The cuffs were usually rolled to mid-calf or even to just below the knees. (Figure 9.11.) In the early 1950s, the fit was loose and baggy, but by the end of the decade, jeans became more formfitting. "In the bobby-socks and poodle-skirt vernacular of the era, blue jeans spoke of sex and danger," particularly as the dress and identity of bad-girl characters in

Figure 9.10 Throughout the 1950s, girls' dresses often followed the New Look trends of women's styles, including the H-Line silhouette. Girls' dresses from Montgomery Ward, 1956.

some teenpics.[46] In 1959, Wrangler launched tailored denim jackets and pants (worn without a cuff) for girls and teens in pale yellow, baby blue, and dusty rose, elevating dungarees to fashion status. By the mid-1960s, jeans became the dress identity of the youthquake generation, worn with a painted-on fit, hiphugger waistband, and bell-bottom cuffs.

In 1958, the skort was introduced by the mass merchandiser Montgomery Ward as playwear for girls. "Latest fashion rage for active play, pleated skirt plus attached panty, that's a skort!" declared the retailer in their spring 1958 catalog.[47] (Figure 9.12.) Ready-to-wear makers quickly adapted versions to women's sportswear for tennis, golf, and similar activities.

Most accessories for children and teens were adaptations of adult styles, with the exception of footwear. Saddle oxfords had been introduced in the 1930s and remained a favorite look for both boys and girls through the 1950s. Variations of girls' styles included white rubber soles, "Scottie" plaid saddles, and buckle-back straps. (Figure 9.13.) Girls began their training for high heels at about age ten with party shoes made with 1-inch Louis heels. Boots had not been a feminine fashion for girls and women since the ankle boot disappeared in the early 1920s. But when André Courrèges featured low, shiny white boots with his Space Age Collection in 1964, the go-go look became a global sensation for girls of all ages well into the 1970s.

BABY BOOM CHILDREN

Figure 9.11 In the 1950s, jeans gradually transitioned from work clothes to casual wear for children and especially teenagers. Girls wore jeans with the cuff rolled to mid-calf of just below the knees. Jeans for girls from Sears, 1952.

American shoe makers offered men and boys an astonishing variety of footwear in the 1950s. Shoes with Velcro tabs that closed over the vamp were introduced in 1958. Another new construction for masculine shoes was the Shu-lok fastener, a mechanical slide device that flipped the tongue forward, allowing the foot to easily step in, and then flipped closed with a locking mechanism. In 1955, teenage boys discovered a new walking experience with the launch of the Ripple Sole, which featured rubber cleats angled toward the back, making each step springy and forward propelling. Boots became a fashion trend for boys in the mid-1950s with the Australian bush boot. These short ankle boots with elastic insets at the sides were inspired by walkabout boots tourists brought home from the 1956 Melbourne Summer Olympics. A similar fashion style for teen boys of about the same time was the crepe-soled, soft suede chukka boot copied from the desert military equipment of British South Africa. In the early 1960s, boots were again a fashion trend with American teenage boys when they saw the Beatles wearing the razor-toed, Cuban-heel Chelsea boot.

Standardization of children's sizes and textile regulations

One of the important developments in the manufacturing of children's wear in the postwar years was a standardization of sizes. Previously, children's ready-

Figure 9.12 The skort was a short skirt with a bloomer type panty attached to the waist seam underneath. The style was introduced as girls' playwear in 1958 and was quickly adapted to women's sportswear for tennis, golf, and similar active sports. Girls' skorts from Montgomery Ward, 1958.

to-wear clothing sizes were largely based on age by retailers and mail-order catalogs. In 1946, the Division of Trade Standards from the US Department of Commerce established children's standard size designations and body measurements for "the guidance of those engaged in producing, or preparing specifications for, ready-to-wear garments and patterns."[48] Mail-order catalog retailers, especially, emphasized the importance of ordering by size, not age, and commonly provided illustrated instructions and tables for ensuring a correct fit for the child. (Figure 9.14.) Not only did this standardization of sizes enhance customer satisfaction, but also retailers were spared the costs and hassles of returns, refunds, or exchanges, and could better manage inventory. "Be sure to order by size—not by age," reminded the header of the measurements page of Spiegel catalogs in the 1950s.[49]

Flammability of fabrics and apparel was a concern for parents in choosing clothing for their young children. After the war, highly flammable synthetics such as rayon and acetate were commonly used in producing children's wear, as were cotton textiles with a fuzzy napped finish that could catch fire easily and burn quickly. Nylon also was increasingly used in children's clothing, and although it did not ignite easily, when afire it melted, causing serious flesh burns.

BABY BOOM CHILDREN

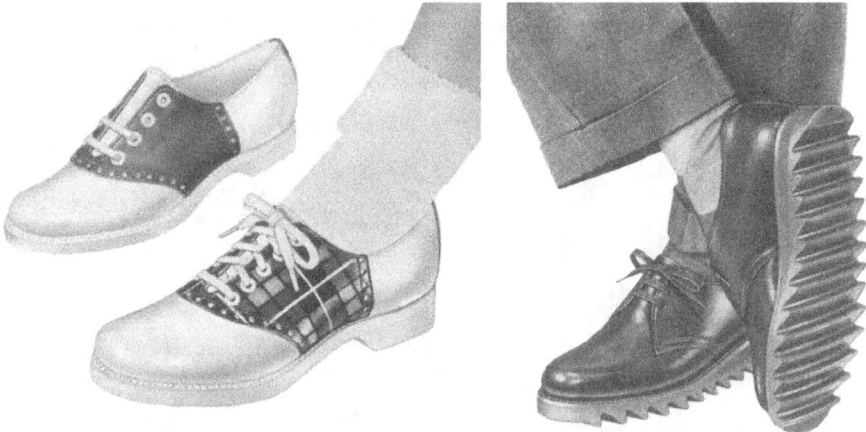

Figure 9.13 Among the types of footwear specifically for baby boom era children and teens was the saddle oxford, a style first introduced in the 1930s but popularized anew in the 1950s. Girls' versions included "Scottie" plaid saddles and white rubber soles. Footwear just for boys and teens included chukka boots and ripple sole shoes with rubber cleats. Girls' saddle oxfords from Spiegel, 1956; boys' ripple soles from Montgomery Ward, 1958.

In 1953, the US Congress passed the Flammable Fabrics Act, authorizing the Commerce Department to "establish test methods, procedures, and standards for determining the rapid and intense burning of wearing apparel and fabrics." Anyone producing clothing that failed these tests faced confiscation of the products and fines or even prison.[50] To comply with the new regulations, textile mills and ready-to-wear manufacturers began treating fabrics with a variety of chemical flame retardants, which, in themselves, caused new health and safety concerns.

Children's body modifications

In the baby boom years, children's body modifications often were a class or ethnic identity. Orthodontic braces were costly and uncomfortable for children, but the "railroad tracks" a child wore indicated the family's affluence. In an era of television commercials for toothpaste, often depicting children with perfect teeth, a teen whose family could not afford expensive dental work often felt self-conscious or even inferior with a visibly broken, overlapping, or missing tooth.

Body piercings were limited to girls' ear lobes and, prior to the 1950s, were primarily practiced by some African Americans, Hispanics, and certain immigrant groups. Although Queen Elizabeth had her ears pierced in 1947 in order to wear

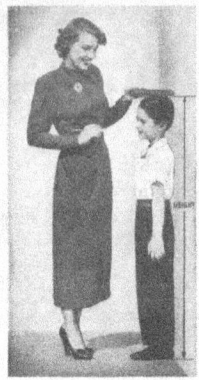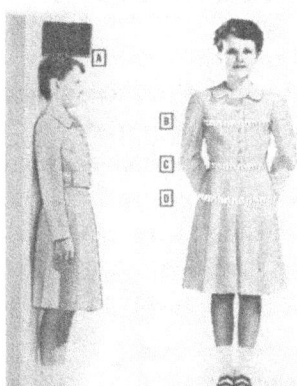

Figure 9.14 In the postwar years, the US government and ready-to-wear makers developed standardized sizes for children's wear. Previously, mail-order catalogs and retailers used age as a guide for children's sizes. Instructions in a 1951 Spiegel catalog for ensuring the correct size for boys' and girls' clothing.

a set of diamond earrings she had received as a wedding gift, the look was not considered respectable among the white middle classes in America. In the late 1950s, though, some college girls held piercing parties during which participants would numb their ear lobes with an ice cube and a companion would pierce the ear with a sterilized sewing needle, into which a metal post would be inserted until healed. The trend for women's pierced ears became more prevalent in the late 1960s as part of a counterculture identity for some young women who wanted to rebel against the conventions of their parents.[51]

For baby boom boys, a newborn's circumcision was a common body modification in America, with about 90 percent of male infants undergoing the procedure.[52] The additional cost was a factor for poor parents, and home births in remote rural areas precluded the option, thus making the practice one of class distinction. Dr. Spock advised in 1957, "If circumcision is performed in early infancy, there will be no risk of psychological harm from having to do it later. I think circumcision is a good idea, especially if most of the boys in the neighborhood are circumcised—then a boy feels 'regular.'"[53] Many uncircumcised baby boomers felt the social stigma growing up and opted for the procedure as young adults, especially cost-free while in the military.

Conclusion

The American baby boom era is defined by the post-World War II surge in the birthrate that added more than 70 million babies to the population between 1946 and 1964. These children grew up in a society that was affluent, consumption-driven, and socially conservative. Parents, teachers, and social scientists focused on the gender role socialization of children, with an emphasis on normative objectives to ensure their proper masculinity or femininity as they matured. Boys were more rigorously guided and guarded in their development than were girls.

In the sociocultural anxiety of the Cold War years, Americans worried that the baby boom generation of boys too easily could be feminized by doting mothers, women teachers, and other authority females in their lives, thus weakening the nation under threat from communists and nuclear annihilation. To counter this risk, boys were subjected to a rigorous gender role socialization by parents and teachers, religious institutions, government propaganda, and popular culture. Boys were urged to compete in sports for the development of their strength and vitality, and as warrior training. They were encouraged to learn about tools, machinery, and repairing things to develop self-reliance and self-confidence. Toys had to be strictly masculine, providing preparatory lessons for manhood. Cap guns, plastic soldiers, and other mock implements of war developed aggression, dominance, and courage. Electric trains and toy cars, trucks, and fire engines taught boys how machinery worked. Lincoln logs and construction sets prepared boys for future home ownership, maintenance, and improvement. But playing with dolls, riding a girl's bicycle, or taking on any girl's roles while playing house was forbidden.

Baby boom girls, however, were allowed greater flexibility in their gender role development. Parents were largely unconcerned with tomboy daughters who played backyard ball games with their brothers and neighborhood boys. Girls were as likely to receive a toy fire truck as a Barbie among their birthday gifts. Blue clothing was common for girls, but pink anything was largely avoided by boys beyond toddler age. Moreover, school, ready-to-wear makers, television programming, and popular culture in general reinforced the gender-as-destiny identities for girls as future wives and mothers. In school, girls were taught gender-segregated classes in home economics, health, and physical education. They studied the same math and social studies as boys, but girls' academic performance and grades were perhaps a point of pride for parents, but held less significance than those of sons since a girl's "book-learning" was viewed as little use to the suburban housewife. Television dramas and commercials showed white, middle-class girls how to behave and dress. Girls' toys were mostly miniaturized housewares, kitchen and cleaning appliances, tea sets, and furniture that helped train them to become Mom's little helpers. Feminine costumes with plastic high heels and jewelry, play cosmetics kits, and dolls were tools for training the ideal wife and mother.

Children's dress likewise was subject to the same gendered constraints as with toys, popular culture consumption, and behavioral training. As with boys of previous generations, baby boom boys wore scaled-down versions of adult clothing. The boxy Ivy League suit with its straight-hanging jacket and wide-legged trousers prepared boys for the gray flannel uniform like their dads wore in the corporate world. As with men's casual clothes, boys' sportswear offered some degree of personal style, but within narrow limits. A pink shirt was a brief fad in the late 1950s, but for the most part, dress for boys rigorously avoided anything that might suggest feminization. At the end of the 1950s, the new trim, fitted silhouette of men's suits called the Continental style—an influence from Italy—also translated into slimmer cuts of boys' wear. For teen boys, especially, the slim cut of trousers and jeans began the trend of sexualization of masculine dress in the early 1960s that expanded into the Peacock Revolution.

Girls' fashions of the baby boom years followed the tenets of Dior's New Look. In sharp contrast to the narrow, plain utility styles of the Second World War, dresses were made with full skirts, puff sleeves, and an abundance of detailing and trimmings. The silhouettes that marked the evolving trends from Paris, such as the A-Line and H-Line, were quickly adapted to girls' fashions by American ready-to-wear makers. Among the iconic looks of the 1950s were teen girls' circle skirts, often adorned with appliques of poodles, music notes, flowers, butterflies, and the like, worn with saddle oxfords. But unlike with boys' guarded ban of anything feminine, baby boom girls were at ease appropriating masculine clothes, especially slacks and jeans. Girls usually rolled their jeans to just below the knees and might don their older brother's (or boyfriend's) varsity sweater, sweatshirt, or oversized knit top. By the early 1960s, as with adult versions, girls' jeans, slacks, and shorts became snug and contouring.

Through the baby boom era, American culture assigned children gendered roles at birth and vigorously inculcated them with standards of behavior and dress through parent and teacher guidance, government propaganda, and popular culture reinforcement. They were trained by parents and teachers to be conformists with expectations of growing up as a family breadwinner husband and a stay-at-home wife and mother. Their identities were defined by their gendered clothes, toys, games, academics, and school activities. As the baby boom concluded in 1964, though, a youthquake of baby boom teenagers and young adults began to explore radically new identities that rejected the traditions and conventions of their parents, opening new paths of individuality and personal expression in their dress, politics, and life goals.

NOTES

Preface

1. U.S. Bureau of the Census, *Historical Statistics of the United States: Colonial Times to 1970,* Part 1 (Washington, DC: U.S. Department of Commerce, 1975), 49.
2. Casey Nelson Blake, et al., *At the Center: American Thought and Culture in the Mid-Twentieth Century* (Lanham, MD: Rowman and Littlefield, 2020), 92.
3. Betty Friedan, *The Feminine Mystique* (New York: Laurel, 1982), 186.
4. "Woman problem": Friedan, 19, 38; "Suburban syndrome": Robert Coughlan, "Changing Roles in Modern Marriage," *Life,* December 24, 1956, 111, 116.
5. Richard Gordon, et al., *The Split-Level Trap* (New York: Dell, 1960), 25, 30.
6. William L. O'Neill, *American High, The Years of Confidence, 1945-1960* (New York: Free Press, 1986), 41.

Chapter 1

1. Robert and Helen Lynd, *Middletown in Transition: A Study in Cultural Conflicts* (New York: Harcourt, Brace and Company, 1937), 7, 176.
2. Lynd, 178.
3. Vincent Sullivan, ed., *Action Comics #1* (New York: Detective Comics, June 1938), 1.
4. Lynd, 291–292.
5. E. Anthony Rotundo, *American Manhood* (New York: Basic Books, 1993), 241.
6. Lynd, 405.
7. Lynd, 404, 425.
8. Frank Crowninshield, ed., "For the Well-Dressed Man," *Vanity Fair,* November 1928, 143.
9. Crowninshield, October 1928, 131.
10. John Murdocke, "The Riviera Presents Many New Ideas for the Men's Wear Trade," *Men's Wear,* October 9, 1935, 21.
11. Coopers Jockey ad: *Esquire,* September 1936, 188.
12. Sullivan, 13.

13 Robert Anderson, ed., *Physical Standards in World War II* (Washington, DC: Office of the Surgeon General, Department of the Army, 1967), 15.
14 Tom Brokaw, *The Greatest Generation* (New York: Random House, 2004), xxvii.
15 Christina S. Jarvis, *The Male Body at War: American Masculinity during World War II* (DeKalb, IL: Northern Illinois University Press, 2010), 185–186.
16 Henry Luce, ed., "Heroes, A Time of Gallantry," *Time*, October 19, 1942, 15.
17 Anderson, 11.
18 Anderson, 40, 65.
19 Anderson, 16.
20 Anderson, 37.
21 Tiffany Leigh Smith, *4-F: The Forgotten Unfit of the American Military during World War II* (Denton, TX: Texas Woman's University Graduate School, 2013), 9.
22 Anderson, 40.
23 Audie Murphy, *To Hell and Back* (New York: Gosset and Dunlap, 1949), 94.
24 Camel Cigarettes ad: *Life,* September 3, 1945, back cover.
25 Superintendent of Documents: Bulletin 789, *Cost of Clothing for Moderate-Income Families 1935–1944* (Washington, DC: US Department of Labor, Bureau of Labor Statistics, 1944), 16.
26 W. D. Williams, ed., "Defense Fashions," *Men's Wear,* February 25, 1942, 18.
27 O.E. Schoeffler, "Fit to Wear Longer," *Esquire,* September 1942, 87.
28 Anon., "Men's and Boy's Lightweight Clothing Simplified in Move to Save Rayon, Cotton," *Victory: Official Weekly Bulletin of the Office of War Information,* Vol. 3, No. 44, November 3, 1942, 29.

Chapter 2

1 Robert Anderson, ed., *Physical Standards in World War II* (Washington, DC: Office of the Surgeon General, Department of the Army, 1967), 118.
2 Frederick Robin, Lt., "When Your Soldier Comes Home," *Ladies Home Journal,* October 1945, 183, 204.
3 Robin, 183, 204.
4 Ad "prepared by the War Advertising Council, Inc., in cooperation with the Office of War Information and the Retraining and Reemployment Administration," *McCall's,* September 1945, 140.
5 Abraham Polonsky, " 'The Best Years of Our Lives': A Review," *Hollywood Quarterly,* April 1947, 258. The reviewer also criticizes the movie ending for falling into the Hollywood "trap" of a "demand for happy endings." For Polonsky, "The truth of the matter is veterans have been sold out en masse by society. The picture exposes the fraud of America's promise to its soldiers, the promises of businessmen and cheap publicists . . . Where the economics of life make naked the terror of a return to a bad old world, the southern California mist moves in and obscures the truth."

NOTES

6 U.S. Bureau of the Census, *Historical Statistics of the United States: Colonial Times to 1970,* Part 1 (Washington, DC: U.S. Department of Commerce, 1975), 126.

7 U.S. Bureau of the Census, *Historical Statistics,* Part 1, 126.

8 Raymond E. Freed, "The Reemployment Provisions of the Selective Service Act," *Washington and Lee Law Review,* Vol. 5, Spring 1948, 49.

9 Claudia Goldin, *Marriage Bars: Discrimination Against Married Women Workers 1920s to 1950s* (Cambridge, MA: National Bureau of Economic Research, 1988), 3–4.

10 Anon., "Cold War Veterans' Bill Passed by Senate," *CQ Almanac 1965*, 21st ed., 401–404.

11 Glenn C. Altschuler and Stuart M. Blumin, *The GI Bill: A New Deal for Veterans* (New York: Oxford University Press, 2009), 8.

12 U.S. Bureau of the Census, *Historical Statistics,* Part 1, 379–380.

13 U.S. Bureau of the Census, *Historical Statistics,* Part 1, 381.

14 Robert A. Israel, dir., *One Hundred Years of Marriage and Divorce Statistics, United States, 1867–1967,* Series 21, #24 (Rockville, MD: National Center of Health Statistics, Division of Vital Statistics, 1973), 22.

15 U.S. Bureau of the Census, *Historical Statistics,* Part 1, 19.

16 Walter Stokes, *Modern Pattern for Marriage: The Newer Understanding of Married Love* (New York: Rinehart, 1948), 12.

17 Jessica Weiss, *To Have and to Hold: Marriage, the Baby Boom, and Social Change* (Chicago, IL: University of Chicago Press, 2000), 4.

18 Karen S. Wampler, ed., *The Handbook of Systemic Family Therapy* (Hoboken, NJ: John Wiley and Sons, 2020), 534.

19 Karen Wilkinson, "The Broken Family and Juvenile Delinquency: Scientific Explanation or Ideology?" *Social Problems,* June 1974, 729–734.

20 Robert and Helen Lynd, *Middletown in Transition: A Study in Cultural Conflicts* (New York: Harcourt, Brace and Company, 1937), 161–162.

21 U.S. Bureau of the Census, *Historical Statistics,* Part 1, 64.

22 Clifford R. Adams, "Making Marriage Work," *Ladies Home Journal,* May 1951, 26.

23 Laura Oren, "No-Fault Divorce Reform in the 1950s: The Lost History of the 'Greatest Project' of the National Association of Women Lawyers," *Law and History Review,* November 2018, 876.

24 Kristin Celello, *Making Marriage Work* (Chapel Hill, NC: University of North Carolina Press, 2009), 73.

25 Milton Greenberg, *The GI Bill: The Law That Changed America* (New York: Lickle, 1997), 78.

26 Harry Henderson, "The Mass-Produced Suburbs: How People Live in America's Newest Towns," *Harper's,* November 1953, 25.

27 Henderson, November 1953, 26.

28 Talcott Parsons and Robert F. Bales, *Family, Socialization and Interaction* (Glencoe, IL: Free Press, 1955), 13.

29 Henderson, November 1953, 27.
30 Weiss, 5.
31 Adams, "Making Marriage Work," *Ladies Home Journal,* March 1951, 26.
32 Elaine Tyler May, *Homeward Bound: American Families in the Cold War Era* (New York: Basic Books, 2008), 158.
33 Henderson, November 1953, 27.
34 Harry Henderson, "Rugged American Collectivism: The Mass-Produced Suburbs, Part II," *Harper's,* December 1953, 80.
35 William H. Whyte, *The Organization Man* (New York: Simon and Schuster, 1956), 314.
36 John C. Keats, *The Crack in the Picture Window* (Boston: Houghton Mifflin, 1956), xxii.
37 Whyte, 306.
38 Whyte, 312.
39 Carly Osborn, "Sacrifice in 1950s Suburbia: The Tragedy of the 'The Crack in the Picture Window,' " *Australasian Journal of American Studies,* July 2018, 65, 69.
40 Keats, 193.
41 Henderson, December 1953, 80.
42 Keats, 87.
43 Keats, 170.
44 Osborn, 65, 69.
45 Henderson, November 1953, 30.
46 Henderson, December 1953, 85.
47 David Kushner, *Levittown: Two Families, One Tycoon, and the Fight for Civil Rights in America's Legendary Suburb* (New York: Walker, 2009), 43, 66.
48 Pamela Loos, *A Reader's Guide to Lorraine Hansberry's A Raisin in the Sun* (Berkeley Heights, NJ: Enslow, 2007), 21.
49 Louis Lee Woods, "Almost 'No Negro Veteran Could Get a Loan': African Americans, the GI Bill, and the NAACP Campaign Against Residential Segregation, 1917-1960," *Journal of African American History,* Summer 2013, 394.
50 Kevin Fox Gotham, *Race, Real Estate, and Uneven Development: The Kansas City Experience 1900-2010,* 2nd ed. (Albany, NY: SUNY Press, 2014), 49–50.
51 Richard Portan, "American Dreams, Suburban Nightmares," *Cineaste,* Vol. 20, No. 1, 1993, 12–13.
52 Henderson, December 1953, 83–84.
53 Whyte, 385.
54 Henderson, November 1953, 27.
55 U.S. Bureau of the Census, *Historical Statistics,* Part 1, 49.
56 May, 139.
57 Bret E. Carroll, ed., *American Masculinities: A Historical Encyclopedia* (Thousand Oaks, CA: Sage, 2003), 233.

NOTES

58 May, 130.
59 Benjamin Spock, *The Common Sense Book of Baby and Child Care* (New York: Duell, Sloan and Pearce, 1957), 27.
60 Spock, 27.
61 Frances L. Ilg and Louise Bates Ames, *The Gesell Institute's Child Behavior* (New York: Dell, 1955), 228–237.
62 Spock, 274.
63 Adams, "Making Marriage Work," *Ladies Home Journal,* May 1951, 26.
64 Spock, 356–358.
65 Spock, 362–363.
66 U.S. Bureau of the Census, *Historical Statistics,* Part 1, 796.
67 Nina C. Leibman, *Living Room Lectures: The Fifties Family in Film and Television* (Austin, TX: University of Texas Press, 1995), 29, 31.
68 Ralph LaRossa, "The Culture of Fatherhood in the Fifties: A Closer Look," *Journal of Family History,* January 2004, 63.
69 Richard S. Tedlow, "Intellect on Television: The Quiz Show Scandals of the 1950s," *American Quarterly,* Autumn 1976, 483–495. In 1959, a blackmail scheme by a former television quiz show contestant led to a New York grand jury investigation, and ultimately a public Congressional hearing, about TV game shows being rigged. It was discovered that certain contestants were provided answers in advance of broadcasting. Caught perpetrating fraud on the public were the sponsors of the shows, represented by the marketing executives and the ad agencies of companies that dictated just about every aspect of production. "Advertising agencies and their clients, with profit always uppermost in mind, forced absurd restrictions on what could be broadcast" (Tedlow, 493). The result was the cancellation of some quiz shows by networks, but more important, the old sponsorship structure of programming was ended and replaced with a formula for paid commercials from multiple sponsors.
70 Leibman, 112.
71 Jon Lewis, *Hollywood v. Hard Core: How the Struggle over Censorship Saved the Modern Film Industry* (New York: New York University Press, 2002), 102–104.
72 Henderson, November 1953, 28.
73 Leibman, 136–140.
74 Michael Kimmel, *The Gendered Society* (New York: Oxford University Press, 2000), 131.
75 Michael Kimmel, *Angry White Men: American Masculinity at the End of an Era* (New York: Nation Books, 2013), 147.

Chapter 3

1 Bret E. Carroll, ed. *American Masculinities: A Historical Encyclopedia* (Thousand Oaks, CA: Sage, 2003), 292.
2 Arthur Schlesinger, "The Crisis of American Masculinity," *Esquire,* November 1958, 63.

3 Henry R. Luce, ed., "The New American Domesticated Male," *Life,* January 4, 1954, 42–45.

4 Philip Wylie, "The Abdicating Male, And How the Gray Flannel Mind Exploits Him through His Women," *Playboy,* November 1956, 23-24, 50, 79; and "The Womanization of America, An Embattled Male Takes a Look at What Was Once a Man's World," *Playboy,* September 1958, 52, 77.

5 Richard Gordon, et al., *The Split-Level Trap* (New York: Dell, 1960) 34.

6 Schlesinger, 65.

7 William H. Whyte, *The Organization Man* (New York: Simon and Schuster, 1956), 3.

8 Whyte, 13, 18.

9 Schlesinger, 65.

10 David Riesman, *The Lonely Crowd: A Study of the Changing American Character* (New Haven, CT: Yale University Press, 1961), 7–8, 15, 17.

11 Elaine Tyler May, *Homeward Bound: American Families in the Cold War Era* (New York: Basic Books, 2008), 15–16, 26.

12 Carroll, 100.

13 Gordon, 72.

14 Carroll, 351.

15 Robert and Helen Lynd, *Middletown in Transition: A Study in Cultural Conflicts* (New York: Harcourt, Brace and Company, 1937), 234, 406.

16 Gordon, 73.

17 Whyte, 308.

18 David M. Potter, *People of Plenty: Economic Abundance and the American Character* (Chicago, IL: University of Chicago Press, 1954), 48.

19 Hans Selye, *The Stress of Life* (New York: McGraw-Hill, 1956), 211.

20 Robert M. Lindner, *Must You Conform?* (New York: Rinehart, 1956), 89, 138–139, 168–170.

21 Sharin N. Elkholy, ed., *The Philosophy of the Beats* (Lexington, KY: University Press of Kentucky, 2012), 3.

22 Stephen Petrus, "Rumblings of Discontent: American Popular Culture and Its Response to the Beat Generation, 1957-1960," *Studies in Popular Culture,* October 1997, 3.

23 John Clellon Holmes, "The Philosophy of the Beat Generation," *Esquire,* February 1958, 36.

24 Petrus, 10.

25 Diane M. Huddleston, *The Beat Generation: They Were Hipsters Not Beatniks* (Monmouth, OR: Western Oregon University, 2012), 11.

26 Brock Yates, *Outlaw Machine: Harley-Davidson and the Search for the American Soul* (New York: Broadway Books, 1999), 7, 15.

27 William E. Thompson, *Hogs, Blogs, Leathers and Lattes* (Jefferson, NC: McFarland, 2012), 5.

28 Luce, "Cyclist's Holiday: He and Friends Terrorize a Town," *Life,* July 21, 1947, 31.
29 Howard P. Chudacoff, *The Age of the Bachelor: Creating an American Subculture* (Princeton, NJ: Princeton University Press, 1999), 3–4.
30 Clifford R. Adams, "Making Marriage Work," *Ladies Home Journal,* January 1951, 26.
31 Hugh Hefner, "Volume 1, Number 1" Editorial, *Playboy*, December 1953, 3.
32 Elizabeth Fraterrigo, *Playboy and the Making of the Good Life in Modern America* (Oxford: Oxford University Press, 2009), 1, 4.
33 Fraterrigo, 5.
34 Hefner, 3.
35 Hefner, 3.
36 R. Marie Griffith, "The Religious Encounters of Alfred C. Kinsey," *The Journal of American History,* September 2008, 349.
37 Lynd, 169, 410.
38 Paul Krassner, ed., *Playboy* press release cited in *The Realist*, 1958, 3.
39 Hugh Hefner, ed., "Mike Wallace Interviews Playboy," *Playboy*, December 1957, 83.
40 Frank Alexander Larsen, *From Fatherhood to Bachelorhood: An Analysis of Masculinities in the 1950s U.S. through Forbidden Planet, Invasion of the Body Snatchers, and Playboy* (Oslo: University of Oslo, 2012), 74.
41 David K. Johnson, *The Lavender Scare: The Cold War Persecution of Gays and Lesbians in the Federal Government* (Chicago, IL: University of Chicago Press, 2004), 216.
42 Naoko Wake, "The Military, Psychiatry, and 'Unfit' Soldiers, 1939-1942," *Journal of the History of Medicine and Allied Sciences,* October 2007, 482, 485.
43 Lindner, 32, 41–42, 75.
44 Clyde R. Hoey, Committee Chairman, *Employment of Homosexuals and Other Sex Perverts in Government* (Washington, DC: Committee on Expenditures in the Executive Departments, Investigation Subcommittee, December 15, 1950), 3–4, 5, 19.
45 Hoey, 4.
46 Robert P. Odenwald, *The Disappearing Sexes* (New York: Random House, 1965), 139, 148.
47 In the 1960s, US Representative John Dowdy (D Texas), led a crusade with Congressional hearings against those who are "banned under the laws of God, the laws of nature, and are in violation of the laws of man." His 1964 revisions to a nonprofit donations act targeted the license of the Mattachine Society, a gay rights advocacy group. In the late 1970s, former beauty pageant contestant Anita Bryant led the "Save Our Children" campaign against the newly emerging gay rights ordinances in progressive cities, declaring that such laws were "the legal right to propose to our children that theirs is an acceptable alternate way of life." In the 1980s, Jerry Falwell, founder of a Christian school in Virginia, led an evangelical group called the Moral Majority against immorality in America, suggesting that AIDS was "God's punishment for the society that tolerates homosexuals." In the 1990s, U.S. Representative Bob Barr (R Georgia) campaigned against same-sex marriage

and authored the Defense of Marriage Act in 1994, which enshrined into federal law the words "moral disapproval of homosexuality." (Ruled unconstitutional by the US Supreme Court in 2013 and repealed by the Respect for Marriage Act in 2022.) In the early 2000s, Senator Rick Santorum (R Pennsylvania) vehemently advocated for laws against same-sex sex, same-sex marriage, and gays in the military from the floor of Congress and the podiums of conservative events. During the 2020s, state legislatures and governors such as Greg Abbott of Texas (R) and Ron DeSantis (R) of Florida revived antigay animus through anti-transgender laws and directives, and "don't say gay" legislation banning the discussion of homosexuality in schools.

48   Donald Webster Cory (Edward Sagarin), *The Homosexual in America: A Subjective Approach* (New York: Greenberg, 1951), xiv, 6, 77, 90–91, 200–221.
49   Harry Hay, *Radically Gay: Gay Liberation in the Words of Its Founder* (Boston: Beacon Press, 1996), 112–113.
50   John Loughery, *The Other Side of Silence: Men's Lives and Gay Identities, A Twentieth-Century History* (New York: John MacRae/Owl Books, 1999), 228, 232.
51   Joyce Murdock and Deb Price, "ONE Standard of Justice," in *Courting Justice: Gay Men and Lesbians v. the Supreme Court* (New York: Basic Books, 2001), 48.
52   Schlesinger, 65.

Chapter 4

1   David Smart, ed., "Mr. T Esquire's New Trim Look Takes Over," *Esquire,* November 1950, 88.
2   Henry R. Luce, ed., "The Ivy Look Heads Across U.S.," *Life,* November 22, 1954, 68–72.
3   Walter H.T. Raymond, ed., "75 Years of Fashion," *Men's Wear,* June 15, 1965, 163.
4   Smart, "Colors to a T," March 1951, 65, 68.
5   Everett Mattlin, ed., "Off the Cuff," *Gentleman's Quarterly,* May 1962, 6.
6   Farid Chenoune, *A History of Men's Fashion* (Paris: Flammarion, 1993), 245.
7   Mattlin, 6.
8   Oscar E. Schoeffler, ed., "The Slim-Line Suit," *Esquire,* January 1958, 72; Mattlin, "The Shaped Suit," *Gentleman's Quarterly,* October 1958, 100–101; Artcraft Edge Suits catalog, Spring and Summer 1956, 14.
9   Mattlin, "The Three-Button and the Double-Breasted Continental," September 1959, 70.
10   Oscar E. Schoeffler and William Gale, *Esquire's Encyclopedia of Twentieth-Century Men's Fashions* (New York: McGraw-Hill, 1973), 29; copy from a Brookfield men's wear ad: "Traditional Ivy for lads who play it straight; Jivey one-button and two-button Continentals," *Men's Wear,* May 11, 1962, 120.
11   Andrew Pallack suit ad: *Gentleman's Quarterly,* December 1959, 36–37.
12   Schoeffler, "It's the Bold Look for You for Fall 1948," September 1948, 58, 62.
13   Whitney Shirts ad: *Esquire,* July 1948, 105.

14. Schoeffler, "The Bold Look for Summer," July 1948, 64–5.
15. Schoeffler, "Coordinate to a T," March 1951, 62.
16. Ernest F. Hubbard, "Hat Life: The Teen Becomes a Hatted Man," *Men's Wear*, June 19, 1962, 69.
17. William Galvin, "Hats Are All Over the Store," *Men's Wear*, May 22, 1964, 82.
18. Hubbard, "Hat Life," March 29, 1963, 120–122.
19. International Silk Association ad: *Gentleman's Quarterly*, December 1958, 23.
20. Raymond, "The Teen Touch in Slacks," May 11, 1962, 169.
21. Bill Ullmann, "Bill Ullmann Reports: One-button Suit," *Men's Wear*, June 15, 1962, 54.
22. Jack Haber, "There's Sources Aplenty: So Give Your Teen Man What He Wants," *Men's Wear*, May 10, 1963, 113.
23. Al Morch and Jack Hyde, "In San Francisco: It Was Love at First Sound; But in Los Angeles: It's the Surfer Look," *Men's Wear*, March 15, 1963, 190–191.
24. Truval Shirts ad: *Men's Wear*, May 11, 1962, 28.
25. Hubbard, "Hat Life," May 22, 1964, 112.
26. J.R. Osherenko, ed., "Pants Go to All Lengths," *California Men's and Boy's Stylist*, January 1956, 57.
27. Luce, "Men Try Shorts for Town," *Life*, August 3, 1953, 61–2.
28. Andrew Pallack suit ad: *Gentleman's Quarterly*, December 1959, 36–37.
29. Mattlin, "The Hidden Fly," September 1959, 118.
30. Paxton slacks shown in a Macy's Men's Store ad: *Gentleman's Quarterly*, December 1958, 60; Jaymar slacks ad: *Gentleman's Quarterly*, December 1958, 51.
31. Smart, "Mr. T the Traveler's Aide," February 1951, 48.
32. Schoeffler, "Mr. T Esquire's New Trim Look Takes Over," *Esquire*, November 1950, 88.
33. Belmont Clothes ad: *Esquire*, November 1950, 121.
34. Worsted-Tex ad: *Esquire*, March 1951, 18B.
35. Schoeffler and Gale, 420–428; Daniel Delis Hill, *History of Men's Underwear and Swimwear*, 2nd ed. (San Antonio: GeminiDragon, 2020), 77–110.
36. Arnold Gingrich, ed., "White Trunks Emphasize the Torso's Tan," *Esquire*, January 1935, 138.
37. Christopher Fremantle, ed., "Ocean Beach . . . Pool Side," *Gentry*, Summer, 1955, 74.
38. Schoeffler, "In Brief . . . The Bikini," *Esquire*, June 1960, 141; Mattlin, "Bikinis on the Rocks," *Gentleman's Quarterly*, June 1960, 94.
39. Cooper's ad: *Esquire*, September 1936, 188.
40. Jockey Skants ad: *Esquire*, December 1959, 64.
41. Mattlin, "1 Button," September 1961, 94.
42. Mattlin, "One-Button Countdown," March 1962, 94–95; "One-Button Individualists," September 1962, 121; "Highlight on Pattern," March 1963, 93.

43 Mattlin, "Missionary X and Checks," March 1964, 115.
44 Mattlin, "In the Best of Taste," February 1964, 70.
45 Schoeffler and Gale, 35.
46 Mattlin, "The London Line Advances into Fall," September 1961, 74.
47 Perkins H. Bailey, "Body Tracing," *Men's Wear,* March 29, 1963, 114–116.
48 Centers for Disease Control and Prevention (CDC) statistics, "Population by Age Groups, Race, and Sex, 1960–1997," 2.
49 Diana Vreeland, ed., "Youthquake," *Vogue,* January 1, 1965, 112.
50 Francis Goodman, "Alexander Plunket Greene," *Gentleman's Quarterly,* October 1961, 99.
51 Perkins H. Bailey, "Fashion Checking in London," *Men's Wear,* August 10, 1962, 36–39.
52 David Block, *Carnaby Street* (London: Lord Kitchener's, 1970), 8.
53 Tom Salter, *Carnaby Street* (Walton-on-Thames, Surrey: Margaret and Jack Hobbs, 1970), 50.

Chapter 5

1 Malcolm X, *The Autobiography of Malcolm X* (New York: Ballantine, 1999), 116, 148.
2 Leslie V. Tischauser, *Jim Crow Laws* (Santa Barbara, CA: Greenwood, 2012), ix. In 1896, the US Supreme Court ruled in *Plessy v. Ferguson* that "separate but equal" regimes were constitutional, thereby upholding Jim Crow state laws and sanctioning racial segregation for the following 60 years.
3 Robert and Helen Lynd, *Middletown in Transition: A Study in Cultural Conflicts* (New York: Harcourt, Brace and Company, 1937), 463.
4 Brian Purnell, ed., *The Strange Careers of the Jim Crow North: Segregation and Struggle Outside of the South* (New York: New York University Press, 2019), 5.
5 Kathy Peiss, *Zoot Suit: The Enigmatic Career of an Extreme Style* (Philadelphia: University of Pennsylvania Press, 2011), 27–32; Luis Alverez, *The Power of the Zoot: Youth Culture and Resistance during World War II* (University of California Press, 2008), 83–86.
6 Neil Gale, "Everything You Wanted to Know about the 'Zoot Suit' Created in Chicago by Harold C. Fox, and the National Zoot Suit Riots," *Digital Research Library of Illinois History Journal,* drloihjournal.blogspot.com, February 13, 2017.
7 Alvarez, 99.
8 Malcolm X, 74, 87, 116.
9 Malcolm X, 60.
10 Malcolm X, 66.
11 Alvarez, 99.

NOTES

12. Spiegel catalog #152, Spring and Summer 1941: worsted wool single- and double-breasted suits, 12.95–16.95 (p. 276); broadcloth dress shirts, 1.00 (p. 240); leather oxfords, 1.89–2.98 (pp. 204–206); silk ties, 98¢ (p. 230); wool felt fedoras, 1.39–1.98 (p. 233).
13. Catherine S. Ramirez, "Crimes of Fashion: The Pachuca and Chicana Style Politics," *Meridians,* Vol. 2, No. 2, 2002, 6.
14. Peiss, 62.
15. Malcolm X, 58–62.
16. Alvarez, 80.
17. Alvarez, 80.
18. Peiss 86.
19. John Franceschina, *Duke Ellington's Music for the Theatre* (Jefferson, NC: McFarland, 2001), 31.
20. Anon., "Zoot Gets Boot," *Victory: Official Weekly Bulletin of the Office of War Information,* Vol. 3, No. 36, September 8, 1942, 8.
21. Henry Luce, ed., "Zoot Suits: WPB Order Ending Jive-Garb Production Outrages Nation's Teenage Jitterbugs," *Life,* September 21, 1942, 44–45.
22. Luce, 44–45.
23. Alvarez, 94.
24. Alvarez, 160–161.
25. Eduardo Obregón Pagán, "Los Angeles Geopolitics and the Zoot Suit Riot, 1943," *Social Science History,* Spring 2000, 239.
26. Pagán, 246.
27. Luce, *Life,* June 21, 1943, 30.
28. Peiss, 119.
29. Peiss, 113.
30. Peiss, 112.
31. Roger Bruns, *Zoot Suit Riots* (Santa Barbara, CA: Greenwood, 2014), xv.
32. Douglas Henry Daniels, "Los Angeles Zoot: Race Riot, the Pachico, and Black Music Culture," *Journal of African American History,* Vol. 87, Winter 2002, 100.
33. Alvarez, 155–199; Daniels, 98–118; Pagán, 223–256; Peiss, 106–130.
34. Alvarex, 181–182.
35. Jennifer R. Scanlon, ed., *The Gender and Consumer Culture Reader* (New York: New York University Press, 2000), 171.
36. From *Ebony,* August 1966: Nadinola Bleaching Cream ad, 8; Artra Skin Tone Cream ad, 23; Ultra Sheen Permanent Creme Relaxer, 47, 71; Long-Aid K7 for Hair and Scalp, 53; Lustrasilk hair straightener, 55; Raveen Bleaching Creme, 66; Dr. Fred Palmer's Skin Whitener, 88; Epic hair relaxer, 89; Perma-Strate Cream Hair Straightener, 100; Johnson's Ultra Wave Hair Culture for Men, 107; Black and White Bleaching Cream, 122; Hair Strate, 131; Bleach and Glow Cream, 132; Palmer's Skin Success Cream, 143.
37. John H. Johnson, ed., "Integration Comes to the Beauty Business," *Ebony,* August 1966, 140, 142.

38 Charles V. Hamilton, "How Black Is Black?" *Ebony,* August 1969, 46–47.
39 Tanisha C. Ford, *Liberated Threads: Black Women, Style, and the Global Politics of Soul* (Chapel Hill: University of North Carolina Press, 2015), 7.

Chapter 6

1   Robert and Helen Lynd, *Middletown in Transition: A Study in Cultural Conflicts* (New York: Harcourt, Brace and Company, 1937), 176.
2   *Ladies' Home Journal* ad: *Saturday Evening Post,* June 21, 1930, 142.
3   Laura Hapke, *Daughters of the Great Depression: Work, Women, and Fiction in the American 1930s* (Athens, GA: University of Georgia Press, 1995), xv–xvi.
4   Hapke, 4.
5   U.S. Bureau of the Census, *Historical Statistics of the United States: Colonial Times to 1970,* Part 1 (Washington, DC: U.S. Department of Commerce, 1975), 128.
6   Henry R. Luce, ed., "Life Looks at Summer Sports Clothes," *Life,* May 9, 1938, 20.
7   U.S. Bureau of the Census, *Historical Statistics,* Part 1, 126.
8   Mildred A. Joiner and Clarence M. Weiner, "Employment of Women in War Production," *Social Security Bulletin,* July 1942, 4–15.
9   Joiner and Weiner, 7.
10 Anon., *When You Hire Women.* Special Bulletin #14 (Washington, DC: Women's Bureau, U.S. Department of Labor, 1944), ii–iv.
11 Anon., *When You Hire Women,* 1, 3.
12 U.S. Bureau of the Census, *Historical Statistics,* Part 1, 131.
13 Henry Luce, ed., "Women, Women Everywhere," *Time,* October 19, 1942, 20.
14 Mary Anderson, Women's Bureau Director, *Safety Clothing for Women in Industry,* Special Bulletin #3 (Washington, DC: Women's Bureau, U.S. Department of Labor, 1941), 1.
15 Anderson, 10.
16 J.S. Knowlson, Director of Industry Operations, Press Release for General Limitation Order #L-85, April 8, 1942, 3–8.
17 Stanley Marcus, *Minding the Store* (Denton, TX: University of North Texas Press, 1997), 116–117.
18 Jessica Daves, ed., "Vogue's-Eye View of Law-abiding Clothes," *Vogue,* May 1, 1942, 41.
19 Ernest O. Hauser, "Those Wonderful G.I. Janes," *Saturday Evening Post,* September 9, 1944, 26–27.
20 Adjutant General's Department, *G.I. Jane Writes Home from Overseas* (Washington, DC: Women's Army Corps, 1944), 18.
21 Adjutant General's Department, *65 Questions and Answers about WACS in the Army Air Forces* (Washington, DC: Women's Army Corps, 1944), 10.

NOTES

22 Katherine Vincent, "The Waves' Uniforms: Womanly, Workmanlike," *New York Herald,* August 29, 1942, 1, 6.
23 Fashion Frocks ad: *Ladies' Home Journal,* September 1944, 115.
24 Tangee ad: *Silver Screen,* September 1943, 65.
25 Page Doughtery Delano, "Making Up for War: Sexuality and Citizenship in Wartime Culture," *Feminist Studies,* Spring 2000, 42–43.
26 Leisa D. Meyer, *Creating GI Jane: Sexuality and Power in the Women's Army Corps during World War II* (New York: Columbia University Press, 1996), 3.
27 Kathryn S. Dobie and Eleanor Lang, eds., *Her War: American Women in World War II* (Lincoln, NE: iUniverse, 2003), 69.
28 Yashila Permeswaran, "The Women's Army Auxiliary Corps: A Compromise to Overcome the Conflict of Women Serving in the Army," *The History Teacher,* November 2008, 97.
29 Beth Bailey, et al., *Managing Sex in the U.S. Military: Gender, Identity, and Behavior* (Lincoln, NE: University of Nebraska Press, 2022), 73.
30 Luce, "Catholics v. WAACs," *Time,* June 15, 1942, 39.
31 Marynia F. Farnham and Ferdinand Lundberg, "Men Have Lost Their Women," *Ladies' Home Journal,* November 1944, 23.
32 Bailey, 72, 81–84.
33 Tangee ad: *Ladies' Home Journal,* September 1944, 122.
34 Bettie J. Morden, *The Women's Army Corps 1945–1978* (Washington, DC: Center for Military History, 2011), 42, 44.

Chapter 7

1 Mona Gardner, "Has Your Husband Come Home to the Right Woman?" *Ladies' Home Journal,* December 1945, 41, 72.
2 Gardner, 72.
3 Claudia Dale Goldin, *Marriage Bars: Discrimination Against Married Women Workers 1920s to 1950s* (Cambridge, MA: National Bureau of Economic Research, 1988), 4.
4 Elizabeth Janeway, "Meet a Demobilized Housewife," *Ladies' Home Journal,* November 1945, 157–160, 170.
5 Robert A. Israel, dir., *One Hundred Years of Marriage and Divorce Statistics, United States, 1867–1967,* Series 21, #24 (Rockville, MD: National Center of Health Statistics, Division of Vital Statistics, 1973), 22.
6 U.S. Bureau of the Census, *Historical Statistics of the United States: Colonial Times to 1970,* Part 1 (Washington, DC: U.S. Department of Commerce, 1975), 19.
7 Jessica Weiss, *To Have and to Hold: Marriage, the Baby Boom, and Social Change* (Chicago, IL: University of Chicago Press, 2000), 25.
8 Clifford R. Adams, "Making Marriage Work," *Ladies Home Journal,* June 1951, 28.

9. Elaine Tyler May, *Homeward Bound: American Families in the Cold War Era* (New York: Basic Books, 2008), 192.
10. Weiss, 41.
11. Inez Robb, "How to Stay Married," *Vogue,* March 1, 1959, 151.
12. Nina C. Leibman, *Living Room Lectures: The Fifties Family in Film and Television* (Austin, TX: University of Texas Press, 1995), 118–136.
13. U.S. Bureau of the Census, *Historical Statistics,* Part 1, 385.
14. Mabel Newcomer, *A Century of Higher Education for Women* (New York: Harper Brothers, 1959), 210.
15. Phyllis Richman, "Answering Harvard's Question About My Personal Life, 52 Years Later," *washingtonpost.com/opinions,* June 6, 2013.
16. Patsy Parker, "The Historical Role of Women in Higher Education," *Administrative Issues Journal: Connecting Education, Practice, and Research,* Spring 2015, 9.
17. Lee Norman, *The Grand Creation: Other Worlds, Other Universes* (Bloomington, IN: AuthorHouse, 2011), 133.
18. John H. Johnson, ed., "Lonely Wives of Medical Students," *Ebony,* March 1960, 77.
19. Nancy Reeves, *Womankind Beyond the Stereotypes,* 2nd ed. (New York: Aldine, 1982), 34.
20. Kathleen Miller, *Fair Share Divorce for Women: The Definitive Guide to Creating a Winning Solution,* 2nd ed. (New York: St. Martin's Griffin, 2007), 54.
21. Gardner, 74.
22. U.S. Bureau of the Census, *Historical Statistics,* Part 1, 64.
23. Ferdinand Lundberg and Marynia Farnham, *Modern Woman: The Lost Sex* (New York: Grosset and Dunlap, 1947), 37, 387.
24. Robert Coughlan, "Changing Roles in Modern Marriage," *Life,* December 24, 1956, 109–110, 116.
25. U.S. Bureau of the Census, *Historical Statistics,* Part 1, 134.
26. Adams, 28.
27. Juliette Louise Despert, *Children of Divorce* (New York: Double Day, 1953); violence, 137; runaways, 136–137; permanent scars, ix, 94; suicide, 98. Despite these forewarnings, though, in the end, Despert advises, "A marriage can be saved at too great a cost, especially to the children. It is the children who pay the heaviest price" (ix). "Little good can be done by forcing a man and woman to remain married when they have tried and are yet unable to make the necessary adjustment. Some divorces are, like surgery, the only cure" (5).
28. Laura Oren, "No-Fault Divorce Reform in the 1950s: The Lost History of the 'Greatest Project' of the National Association of Women Lawyers," *Law and History Review,* November 2018, 875–876.
29. J. Herbie DiFonzo, "Coercive Conciliation: Judge Paul W. Alexander and the Movement for Therapeutic Divorce," *University of Toledo Law Review,* Vol. 25, No. 3 (1994), 538, 556–557.
30. Oren, 876–877.
31. Elaine Tyler May, 193.

NOTES

32 Betty Friedan, *The Feminine Mystique* (New York: Laurel, 1982), 15–16.

33 William H. Whyte, *The Organization Man* (New York: Simon and Schuster, 1956), 301–302.

34 J. John Palen, *The Suburbs* (New York: McGraw-Hill, 1995), 44.

35 Harry Henderson, "The Mass-Produced Suburbs: How People Live in America's Newest Towns," *Harper's,* November 1953, 26.

36 Robert F. McPartlin, *Redlining, Discrimination in Residential Mortgage Loans: A Report to the Illinois General Assembly* (Springfield, IL: Illinois General Assembly, 1975), 2.

37 Gordon Nelson, *Some Perspectives on Redlining* (Washington, DC: Federal National Mortgage Association, 1976), 6, 11.

38 Lizabeth Cohen, *A Consumers' Republic: The Politics of Mass Consumption in Postwar America* (New York: Vintage, 2004), 278.

39 Vance Packard, *The Hidden Persuaders* (New York: David McKay, 1957), 169.

40 Interview with Nicholas Graham, president of Joe Boxer Inc., featured in "Unmentionables, A Brief History," Weller/Grossman Productions, *A&E TV,* January 17, 1999.

41 Examples of men's wear ads in *Vogue*: Lebow suits, February 15, 1951, 2; Countess Mara ties, September 15, 1954, 61; Izod sportswear, May 15, 1954, 12; Rabhor robes, December 1956, 24; Lee hats, February 1, 1956, 85.

42 Richard Gordon, et al., *The Split-Level Trap* (New York: Dell, 1960), 19.

43 Packard, 123.

44 Gordon, 33.

45 Mary Ellen Chase, "She Misses Some Goals," *Life,* December 24, 1956, 25–26.

46 Friedan, 15.

47 Coughlan, 111, 116.

48 Robert and Helen Lynd, *Middletown in Transition: A Study in Cultural Conflicts* (New York: Harcourt, Brace and Company, 1937), 164, 176, 410.

49 U.S. Bureau of the Census, *Historical Statistics,* Part 1, 49.

50 Benjamin Spock, *The Common Sense Book of Baby and Child Care* (New York: Duell, Sloan and Pearce, 1957), 14–15.

51 Spock, 354.

52 Lundberg and Farnham, 303–315.

53 Philip Wylie, *Generation of Vipers*, revised ed. (New York: Rinehart 1955), 194. In a 1954 interview, Wylie explained that the notion of "momism" was intended as a "gag" meant to be "hilariously funny." Rebecca Jo Plant, *Mom: The Transformation of Motherhood in Modern America* (Chicago, IL: University of Chicago Press, 2010), 21.

54 Friedan, 203.

55 Edward Strecker, *Their Mothers' Sons: The Psychiatrist Examines an American Problem* (Philadelphia: J.B. Lippincott, 1946, 1951), 13, 30, 32, 37, 54, 161–163.

56 David K. Johnson, *The Lavender Scare: The Cold War Persecution of Gays and Lesbians in the Federal Government* (Chicago, IL: University of Chicago Press, 2004), 34–35; Coughlan, 112.

57 In 1948, Alfred Kinsey published *Sexual Behavior in the Human Male* in which he asserted that about 10 percent of the male population was exclusively homosexual, and as much as 37 percent had homosexual experiences. Alfred C. Kinsey, *Sexual Behavior in the Human Male* (Bloomington, IN: Indiana University Press, 1948), 621–636.
58 Coughlan, 114.
59 Lundberg and Farnham, 349.
60 Spock, 274.
61 Strecker, 131.
62 Friedan, 275.
63 Ashley Marie Aidenbaum, "Mother-Blaming and the Rise of the Expert," *Michigan Journal of History,* September 2006, 20.
64 Nancy Patton Mills, *Portraits Through the Lens of Historicity: The American Family as Portrayed in Ladies' Home Journal 1950–1959* (Pittsburgh, PA: Duquesne University, 2006), 14.
65 Strecker, 24.
66 Cary O'Dell, *June Cleaver Was a Feminist! Reconsidering the Female Characters of Early Television* (Jefferson, NC: McFarland, 2013), 24.
67 Vince Waldron, *The Official Dick Van Dyke Show Book* (New York: Applause Theatre, 2001), 127–128.
68 O'Dell, 26.
69 U.S. Bureau of the Census, *Historical Statistics,* Part 1, 131.
70 William Henry Chafe, *The American Woman: Her Changing Social, Economic and Political Roles, 1920–1970* (New York: Oxford University Press, 1972), 211.
71 Chafe, 210–215.
72 Henry R. Luce, ed., "American Woman's Dilemma," *Life,* June 16, 1947, 101.
73 U.S. Bureau of the Census, *Historical Statistics,* Part 1, 132.
74 Elizabeth Longford, *All in the Family: Parenting the 1950s Way* (Stroud, UK: History Press, 1954, 2008), 199.
75 Coughlan, 116.
76 Lundberg and Farnham, 234–235.
77 Howard A. Meyerhoff, ed., "National Manpower Council," *Science,* June 5, 1953, 617.
78 Susan M. Harman, "Women's Employment and the Domestic Ideal," in *Not June Cleaver: Women and Gender in Postwar America, 1945–1960* (Philadelphia: Temple University Press, 1994), 90.
79 James P. Mitchell, National Manpower Council, "Coming Problems in the Labor Force," in *Work in the Lives of Married Women: Proceedings of a Conference on Womanpower* (New York: Columbia University Press, 1958), 15.
80 Henry David, National Manpower Council, "Conference Findings," in *Work in the Lives of Married Women: Proceedings of a Conference on Womanpower* (New York: Columbia University Press, 1958), 201.

NOTES

81 U.S. Bureau of the Census, *Historical Statistics,* Part 1, 132.

82 Cornelia Otis Skinner, "Women Are Misguided," *Life,* December 24, 1956, 73; Coughlan, 110, 118.

83 Marynia F. Farnham and Ferdinand Lundberg, "Men Have Lost Their Women," *Ladies' Home Journal,* November 1944, 23, 139.

84 Kate Weigand, *Red Feminism: American Communism and the Making of Women's Liberation* (Baltimore, MD: Johns Hopkins University Press, 2001), 4.

85 Leila J. Rupp, "Eleanor Flexner's 'Century of Struggle': Women's History and the Women's Movement," *NWSA Journal,* Summer 1992, 160–161.

86 Chafe, 227.

87 Imelda Whelehan, *Modern Feminist Thought from the Second Wave to Post-Feminism* (New York: New York University Press, 1995), 9; Jane Gerard, *Desiring Revolution: Second-Wave Feminism and the Rewriting of American Sexual Thought 1920 to 1982* (New York: Columbia University Press, 2001), 88; Elizabeth Whitaker, *An Analysis of Betty Friedan's The Feminine Mystique* (London: Macat, 2017), 70; Chafe, 227.

88 Friedan, 282, 305, 307.

Chapter 8

1 Edna Woolman Chase, ed., "Paris Collections, Autumn 1945," *Vogue,* October 15, 1945, 99.

2 Christian Dior, *Dior by Dior* (London: Weidenfeld & Nicolson, 1957), 22–23.

3 Jeanne Perkins, "Dior," *Life,* March 1, 1948, 86–87.

4 In 1947, some women objected to the longer hemlines and formed "A Little Below the Knee Club" with branches nationwide. Photos of the time show women in the Chicago club picketing a department store with placards reading, "Mr. Dior, We abhor, Dresses to the floor." Similarly, in 1947, the Tacoma, Washington club went before a Congressional Joint Committee on Housing, and in an opening statement declared, "I know that there is some amusement in the name of our group, and perhaps it seems peculiar that the women's group in Tacoma is against being dictated to in styles and that they should be interested in housing . . .," etc. Ralph A. Gamble, Chairman, *Statement of Mrs. V.M. Ellison, Representing Tacoma Little-Below-the-Knee Club* (Washington, DC: Eightieth Congress, U.S. Government Printing Office, 1948), 4558. In Dallas, Texas, a government bulletin reported that "1500 women formed 'The Little Below the Knee Club' and paraded with a band through downtown traffic carrying placards." Anon., *Department of State Air Bulletin* (September 12, 1947), 12. In March 1948, *Life* magazine announced, "About a month ago the Little Below the Knee Club, a nationwide organization of some 300,000 embattled women, succumbed to the overwhelming pressure of events and admitted that its valiant fight to preserve America from the New Look had ended in defeat." Jeanne Perkins, "Dior," *Life,* March 1, 1948, 85.

5 Perkins, 87.

6   Alexandra Palmer, *Couture and Commerce* (Vancouver, Canada: University of British Columbia Press, 2001), 134.
7   Palmer, 174.
8   Chase, "1950 Body Line," January 1950, 114.
9   Jessica Daves, ed., "Measure of Change," *Vogue,* January 1, 1958, 65.
10 Daves, "A New Look in American Fashion Based on the Legs," February 1, 1958, 107.
11 Daves, "Changes 1960," *Vogue,* January 1, 1960, 91, 105–107.
12 Daves, "Fashion Naturals U.S.A.," *Vogue,* January 1, 1960, 139.
13 Daves, "Vogue's Eye View of a Look," *Vogue,* August 1, 1961, 55.
14 Jenny Lister, *Mary Quant* (London: V&A, 2019), 124.
15 Dior, 34.
16 Christian Dior, *Christian Dior's Little Dictionary of Fashion* (London: Cassell, 1954), 6.
17 Dior, *Dior by Dior,* 52.
18 Dior, *Dior by Dior,* 52.
19 Dior, *Christian Dior's Little Dictionary of Fashion*, 39.
20 Daves, "Change in the Hat: Changing 1956 Fashion," January 1, 1956, 93, 95; Daves, "Great Comeback for Black: Here with Brown," September 1, 1956, 240.
21 Dior, *Christian Dior's Little Dictionary of Fashion*, 75.
22 U.S. Bureau of the Census, *Historical Statistics of the United States: Colonial Times to 1970,* Part 2, (Washington, DC: U.S. Department of Commerce, 1975), 670–671.
23 Pap A. Ndiaye, *Nylon and Bombs*, trans. Elborg Forster (Baltimore, MD: Johns Hopkins University Press, 2007), 182.
24 Daves, "Weightlessness on the Rise," March 15, 1960, 139.
25 Lycra ad: *Vogue*, March 15, 1960, 39.

Chapter 9

1   Births during the Depression and World War II years 1935-1945, and baby boom years 1946-1964. U.S. Bureau of the Census, *Historical Statistics of the United States: Colonial Times to 1970,* Part 1 (Washington, DC: U.S. Department of Commerce, 1975), 49.
2   Robert and Helen Lynd, *Middletown in Transition: A Study in Cultural Conflicts* (New York: Harcourt, Brace and Company, 1937), 164.
3   Frances L. Ilg and Louise Bates Ames, *The Gesell Institute's Child Behavior* (New York: Dell, 1955), 13.
4   Benjamin Spock, *The Common Sense Book of Baby and Child Care* (New York: Duell, Sloan and Pearce, 1957), 48.
5   Paul Goodman, *Growing Up Absurd: Problems of Youth in the Organized Society* (New York: New York Review Books, 1956, 2012), 21.

NOTES

6   Betty Friedan, *The Feminine Mystique* (New York: Laurel, 1982), 202.
7   Ferdinand Lundberg and Marynia Farnham, *Modern Woman: The Lost Sex* (New York: Grosset and Dunlap, 1947), 304–305.
8   Spock, 274.
9   Ilg and Ames, 75.
10 Ilg and Ames, 74–75.
11 Spock, 272.
12 Lundberg and Farnham, 228.
13 Wini Breines, *Young, White, and Miserable* (Boston: Beacon Press, 1992), 106–108.
14 Friedan, 202–203, 290.
15 Spock, 274–275.
16 Ilg and Ames, 233, 236.
17 Jo B. Paoletti, *Pink and Blue* (Bloomington, IN: Indiana University Press, 2012), 16. The gendered colors of blue for boys and pink for girls ceased to be so prevalent in American popular culture from the late 1960s through the 1970s due to sociocultural shifts such as the Second Wave Feminism, which regarded pink as a color representing traditional female roles and ideas of femininity (Paoletti, 86), as well as the Peacock Revolution in men's wear that embraced vivid colors including gender-bending sherbet pastels (Daniel Delis Hill, *Peacock Revolution: American Masculine Identity and Dress in the Sixties and Seventies* (London: Bloomsbury, 2018), 113–114. But in the 1980s, gender-specific colors, particularly pink for girls, rebounded and "reached the level of moral imperative" for children aged three to seven (Paoletti, 86). Since 2000, though, "the resistant uses of pink have appeared on the scene for both boys and girls. This uneasy, protracted transition traces the underlying shape of changing and conflicted attitudes toward sexuality as it applied to infants and toddlers, in addition to uncertainty and anxiety about those parts of American culture identified as 'feminine.' " (Paoletti, 86).
18 Paoletti, 93.
19 A popular exception for a masculine use of pink in clothing occurred around 1958 when the Italian-inspired Continental suit became a trend in America for young men. As a counter to the staid Ivy League styles of men's wear, pink dress shirts were a statement of nonconformity and modernity that men in certain businesses such as the arts, entertainment, and advertising could assert. Some boys' ready-to-wear makers likewise offered pink dress shirts.
20 Although the overwhelming majority of American toy makers, retailers, and advertisers targeted the white, middle classes, a number of toys were created specifically for ethnic markets. Numerous varieties of Black dolls in particular were commonly manufactured dating back to the late nineteenth century. Many toys that represented African Americans, such as Aunt Jemima, "Mammy," or "Uncle Mose" figurines, were caricatures that perpetuated stereotypes for decades in print cartoons, advertising, and minstrel shows. Similarly, toys, games, and mechanical banks manufactured with depictions of African Americans, Mexicans, Asians, and Native Americans were primarily for white consumption, and too often stereotyped ethnicities by clichéd costumes and exaggerated facial features.
21 Spock, 272.

22 Nina C. Leibman, *Living Room Lectures: The Fifties Family in Film and Television* (Austin: University of Texas Press, 1995), 174.

23 U.S. Bureau of the Census, *Historical Statistics,* Part 1, 8.

24 Tom MacPherson, "Those Nelson Boys," *Boy's Life,* December 1953, 79. In a 1955 episode of *Ozzie and Harriett,* Ricky asks for his allowance and is given $2.00.

25 Lynn Spigel, *Welcome to the Dreamhouse, Popular Media and Postwar Suburbs* (Durham, NC: Duke University Press, 2001), 204–205.

26 Vance Packard, *The Hidden Persuaders* (New York: David McKay, 1957), 159.

27 Scott Donaldson, The *Suburban Myth* (New York: Columbia University Press, 1969), 15.

28 Harry Henderson, "Rugged American Collectivism: The Mass-Produced Suburbs, Part II," *Harper's,* December 1953, 84.

29 Richard Gordon, et al., *The Split-Level Trap* (New York: Dell, 1960), 126–128.

30 Henry R. Luce, ed., "A Young $10-Billion Power: The U.S. Teenager Has Become a Major Factor in the Nation's Economy," *Life,* August 31, 1959, 78.

31 Richard Aquila, *Let's Rock! How 1950s America Created Elvis and the Rock & Roll Craze* (Lanham, MD: Rowman and Littlefield, 2017), 44, 48. Alan Freed also made appearances in a number of 1950s teenpics centered on rock and roll.

32 Lisa Jo Sagolla, *Rock and Roll* (Santa Barbara, CA: Greenwood, 2011), xiii.

33 William L. O'Neill, *American High: The Years of Confidence, 1945–1960* (New York: Free Press, 1986), 269.

34 Glenn C. Altschuler, *All Shook Up: How Rock 'n' Roll Changed America* (Oxford: Oxford University Press, 2003), 7–8; Roy Shuker, *Understanding Popular Music Culture,* 4th ed. (New York: Routledge, 2013), 205.

35 Mitchell K. Hall, *The Emergence of Rock and Roll: Music and the Rise of American Youth Culture* (New York: Routledge, 2014), 27.

36 Eric Schaefer, *Bold! Daring! Shocking! True! A History of Exploitation Films, 1919–1959* (Durham, NC: Duke University Press, 1999), 5.

37 Thomas Doherty, *Teenagers and Teenpics* (Philadelphia: Temple University Press, 2002), 93.

38 Timothy Shary, *Teen Movies: American Youth on Screen* (London: Wallflower, 2005), 21.

39 Jess Nevins, *The Evolution of the Costumed Avenger: The 4,000-Year History of the Superhero* (Santa Barbara, CA: Praeger, 2017), 242.

40 Carol L. Tilley, "Seducing the Innocent: Fredric Wertham and the Falsifications that Helped Condemn Comics," *Information and Culture: A Journal of History,* Vol. 47, No. 4, 2012, 386.

41 Spock, 338–340.

42 Ilg and Ames, 268–269.

43 Amy Kiste Nyberg, *Seal of Approval: The History of the Comics Code* (Jackson, MS: University Press of Mississippi, 1998), 166–168.

44 Montgomery Ward Catalog, Spring and Summer 1958, 325.

NOTES

45   Levi's "Thirteens" ad: *Men's Wear,* May 4, 1962, 84.
46   Alice Harris, *The Blue Jean* (New York: Powerhouse, 2002), 39.
47   Montgomery Ward Catalog, Spring and Summer 1958, 248.
48   Henrietta Mary Thompson, *Clothing for Children* (New York: John Wiley and Sons, 1949), 238–239, 310.
49   Spiegel Catalog, Spring and Summer 1951, 192.
50   Charles Wolverton, chairman, Flammable Fabrics Act (Washington, DC: Committee on Interstate and Foreign Commerce, U.S. House of Representatives, April 1953), 6–8.
51   Don Rauf, *The Culture of Body Piercing* (New York: Rosen, 2019), 17–18; Valerie Steele, ed., *The Berg Companion to Fashion* (Oxford: Berg, 2010), 235.
52   Harvey B. Simon, *The Harvard Medical School Guide to Men's Health* (New York: Simon and Schuster, 2002), 253. In the baby boom years, one of the key decisions parents had to make for their newborn boy was circumcision. Dating back to the ancient Egyptians more than five thousand years ago, the practice was both hygienic and cultural. In America, circumcision of newborns became increasingly prevalent for the middle and upper classes in the late nineteenth century. In 1891, physician Peter C. Romandino analyzed and documented the medical reasons for infant circumcision in his study *History of Circumcision from the Earliest Times to the Present: Moral and Physical Reasons for Its Performance.* Victorian medical science determined that there were higher health risks for uncircumcised males than circumcised men that ranged from simple genital infections to penile cancer. In the late 1960s, though, anti-circumcision advocates viewed the procedure as a potential detriment to the psychological health and sexual sensation of the adult. As a result, in 1971 the American Academy of Pediatrics (AAP) recommended against circumcision. Through the 1980s, further studies found that uncircumcised infants were at greater risk for urinary tract infections, and uncircumcised adults were three to seven times more likely to get infected by HIV after heterosexual exposure than were circumcised men. Ed Schoen, *Ed Schoen, MD, on Circumcision* (Berkeley, CA: RDR Books, 2005), 6. From the conclusions of these studies, the AAP reversed its position against circumcision in 1989, asserting the preventive health benefits of the procedure. By the 2000s, pediatric experts viewed circumcision as "analogous to infant immunizations because it is a pediatric health measure, which prevents future disease . . . extending over a lifetime." Schoen, 8.
53   Spock, 155.

BIBLIOGRAPHY

Albrecht, Donald, and Phyllis Magidson, eds. *Mod New York, Fashion Takes a Trip*. New York: Monacelli, 2017.

Altschuler, Glenn C. *All Shook Up, How Rock 'n' Roll Changed America*. Oxford: Oxford University Press, 2003.

Altschuler, Glenn C., and Stuart M. Blumin. *The GI Bill: A New Deal for Veterans*. New York: Oxford University Press, 2009.

Alvarez, Luis. *The Power of the Zoot: Youth Culture and Resistance during World War II*. Berkeley, CA: University of California Press, 2008.

Amies, Hardy. *An ABC of Men's Fashion*. London: Newnes, 1964.

Anderson, Kent. *Television Fraud: The History and Implications of the Quiz Show Scandals*. Westport, CT: Greenwood, 1978.

Anderson, Mary, Women's Bureau Director. *Safety Clothing for Women in Industry*. Special Bulletin #3. Women's Bureau of the U.S. Department of Labor, Washington, DC, 1941.

Anderson, Mary, Women's Bureau Director. *When You Hire Women*. Special Bulletin #14. Women's Bureau of the U.S. Department of Labor, Washington, DC, 1944.

Anderson, Robert, ed. *Physical Standards in World War II*. Washington, DC: Office of the Surgeon General, Department of the Army, 1967.

Aquila, Richard. *Let's Rock! How 1950s America Created Elvis and the Rock & Roll Craze*. Lanham, MD: Rowman and Littlefield, 2017.

Bailey, Beth, et al. *Managing Sex in the U.S. Military: Gender, Identity, and Behavior*. Lincoln, NE: University of Nebraska Press, 2022.

Bellafaire, Judith L. *The Women's Army Corps, A Commemoration of World War II Service*. Washington, DC: U.S. Army Center of Military History, Government Publication US D 114.2:W84, 1993.

Bennett, Michael J. *When Dreams Come True: The GI Bill and the Making of Modern America*. Sterling, VA: Potomac Books, 1996.

Blake, Casey Nelson, et al. *At the Center: American Thought and Culture in the Mid-Twentieth Century*. Lanham, MD: Rowman and Littlefield, 2020.

Block, David. *Carnaby Street*. London: Lord Kitchener's, 1970.

Bonaparte, Margaret. *Reexamining the 1950s American Housewife: How the Editors and Writers of Ladies' Home Journal Challenged Domestic Expectations During the Postwar Period*. Claremont, CA: Scripps College, 2014.

Brandow-Faller, Megan, ed. *Childhood by Design: Toys and the Material Culture of Childhood, 1700–Present*. New York: Bloomsbury Visual Arts, 2018.

Breines, Wini. *Young, White, and Miserable: Growing Up Female in the Fifties*. Boston: Beacon Press, 1992.

BIBLIOGRAPHY

Brock, Julia, et al., eds. *Beyond Rosie: A Documentary History of Women and World War II*. Fayetteville, AK: University of Arkansas Press, 2015.
Brokaw, Tom. *The Greatest Generation*. New York: Random House, 1998.
Bruns, Roger. *Zoot Suit Riots*. Santa Barbara, CA: Greenwood, 2014.
Carroll, Bret E., ed. *American Masculinities: A Historical Encyclopedia*. Thousand Oaks, CA: Sage, 2003.
Catt, Courtney. *Trapped in the Kitchen: How Advertising Defined Women's Roles in 1950s America*. Waco, TX: Baylor University, 2014.
Chafe, William Henry. *The American Woman: Her Changing Social, Economic and Political Roles, 1920–1970*. New York: Oxford University Press, 1972.
Chenoune, Farid. *A History of Men's Fashion*. Paris: Flammarion, 1993.
Chudacoff, Howard P. *The Age of the Bachelor: Creating an American Subculture*. Princeton, NJ: Princeton University Press, 1999.
Cohen, Lizabeth. *A Consumers' Republic: The Politics of Mass Consumption in Postwar America*. New York: Vintage Books, 2003.
Cory, Donald Webster. *The Homosexual in America: A Subjective Approach*. New York: Greenberg, 1951.
Cuordileone, Kyle. *Manhood and American Political Culture in the Cold War*. New York: Routledge, 2004.
De Casanova, Erynn Masi. *Buttoned Up: Clothing, Conformity, and White Collar Masculinity*. Ithaca, NY: Cornell University Press, 2015.
De Vries, Peter. *Comfort Me with Apples*. Boston: Little, Brown, 1956.
Despert, Juliette Louise. *Children of Divorce*. New York: Double Day, 1953.
De Vries, Peter. *Comfort Me with Apples*. Boston: Little, Brown, 1956.
Dior, Christian. *Christian Dior's Little Dictionary of Fashion*. London: Cassell, 1954.
Dior, Christian. *Dior by Dior*. London: Weidenfeld & Nicolson, 1957.
Doherty, Thomas. *Teenagers and Teenpics: The Juvenilization of American Movies in the 1950s*. Philadelphia, PA: Temple University Press, 2002.
Donaldson, Scott. *The Suburban Myth*. New York: Columbia University Press, 1969.
Douglas, William. *Television Families, Is Something Wrong in Suburbia?* Mahwah, NJ: Lawrence Erlbaum, 2003.
Dumas, Alexander G., and Grace Graham Keen. *A Psychiatric Primer for the Veteran's Family and Friends*. Minneapolis, MN: University of Minnesota Press, 1945.
Ehrenreich, Barbara. *The Hearts of Men: American Dreams and the Flight from Commitment*. Garden City, NY: Anchor Press, 1983.
Elder, Glen H. *Children of the Great Depression: Social Change in Life Experience*. Boulder, CO: Westview Press, 1999.
Elkholy, Sharin N., ed. *The Philosophy of the Beats*. Lexington, KY: University Press of Kentucky, 2012.
Ford, Tanisha C. *Liberated Threads: Black Women, Style, and the Global Politics of Soul*. Chapel Hill: University of North Carolina Press, 2015.
Franceschina, John. *Duke Ellington's Music for the Theatre*. Jefferson, NC: McFarland, 2001.
Fraterrigo, Elizabeth. *Playboy and the Making of the Good Life in Modern America*. Oxford: Oxford University Press, 2009.
Friedan, Betty. *The Feminine Mystique*. New York: Laurel, 1982.
Gambone, Michael D. *The Greatest Generation Comes Home: The Veteran in American Society*. College Station, TX: Texas A&M University Press, 2005.
Gans, Herbert J. *Levittowners: Ways of Life and Politics in a New Suburban Community*. New York: Columbia University Press, 2017.

Gerard, Jane. *Desiring Revolution: Second-Wave Feminism and the Rewriting of American Sexual Thought 1920 to 1982*. New York: Columbia University Press, 2001.

Gilbert, James. *Men in the Middle: Searching for Masculinity in the 1950s*. Chicago, IL: University of Chicago Press, 2005.

Goldin, Claudia. *Marriage Bars: Discrimination Against Married Women Workers 1920s to 1950s*. Cambridge, MA: National Bureau of Economic Research, 1988.

Goodman, Paul. *Growing Up Absurd: Problems of Youth in the Organized Society*. New York: New York Review Books, 1956, 2012.

Gordon, Richard, et al. *The Split-Level Trap*. New York: Dell, 1960.

Gotham, Kevin Fox. *Race, Real Estate, and Uneven Development: The Kansas City Experience 1900–2010*, 2nd ed. Albany, NY: SUNY Press, 2014.

Greenberg, Milton. *The GI Bill: The Law That Changed America*. New York: Lickle, 1997.

Hains, Rebecca C., and Nancy A. Jennings, eds. *The Marketing of Children's Toys: Critical Perspectives on Children's Consumer Culture*. Cham, Switzerland: Palgrave Macmillan, 2021.

Hall, Mitchell K. *The Emergence of Rock and Roll: Music and the Rise of American Youth Culture*. New York: Routledge, 2014.

Hapke, Laura. *Daughters of the Great Depression: Work, Women, and Fiction in the American 1930s*. Athens, GA: University of Georgia Press, 1995.

Harris, Alice. *The Blue Jean*. New York: Powerhouse, 2002.

Harris, Dianne. *Second Suburb: Levittown, Pennsylvania*. Pittsburgh, PA: University of Pittsburgh Press, 2010.

Hay, Harry. *Radically Gay: Gay Liberation in the Words of Its Founder*. Boston: Beacon Press, 1996.

Henry, David, et al., National Manpower Council. *Work in the Lives of Married Women: Proceedings of a Conference on Womanpower*. New York: Columbia University Press, 1958.

Hill, Daniel Delis. *American Menswear from the Civil War to the Twenty-first Century*. Lubbock, TX: Texas Tech University Press, 2011.

Hill, Daniel Delis. *Fashion from Victoria to the New Millennium*. New York: Pearson, 2012.

Hill, Daniel Delis. *History of Men's Underwear and Swimwear*, 2nd ed. San Antonio, TX: GeminiDragon, 2021.

Hill, Daniel Delis. *Necessaries: Two Hundred Years of Fashion Accessories*. San Antonio, TX: GeminiDragon, 2015.

Hill, Daniel Delis. *Peacock Revolution, American Masculine Identity and Dress in the Sixties and Seventies*. London: Bloomsbury, 2018.

Huddleston, Diane M. *The Beat Generation: They Were Hipsters Not Beatniks*. Monmouth, OR: Western Oregon University, 2012.

Humphreys, Kristi R. *Housework and Gender in American Television: Coming Clean*. Lanham, MD: Lexington Books, 2016.

Ilg, Frances L., and Louise Bates Ames. *Child Behavior from Birth to Ten*. New York: Harper and Row, 1955.

Ilg, Frances L., and Louise Bates Ames. *The Gesell Institute's Child Behavior*. New York: Dell, 1955.

Jackson, Kenneth T. *Crabgrass Frontier: The Suburbanization of the United States*. Oxford: Oxford University Press, 1985.

Jarvis, Christina S. *The Male Body at War: American Masculinity during World War II*. DeKalb, IL: Northern Illinois University Press, 2010.

Jensen, Margit. *Dreaming of Suburbia: Postwar Idealization of the Golden Era Traditional Family*. Copenhagen: University of Copenhagen, 2011.
Johnson, David K. *The Lavender Scare: The Cold War Persecution of Gays and Lesbians in the Federal Government*. Chicago, IL: University of Chicago Press, 2004.
Kahn, Suzanne. *Divorce, American Style: Fighting for Women's Economic Citizenship in the Neoliberal Era*. Philadelphia, PA: University of Pennsylvania Press, 2021.
Keats, John. *The Crack in the Picture Window*. Boston: Houghton Mifflin, 1956.
Kimmel, Michael. *Angry White Men: American Masculinity at the End of an Era*. New York: Nation Books, 2013.
Kimmel, Michael. *The Gendered Society*. New York: Oxford University Press, 2000.
Kinsey, Alfred C. *Sexual Behavior in the Human Male*. Bloomington, IN: Indiana University Press, 1948.
Knowlson, J.S., Director of Industry Operations. Press Release for General Limitation Order #L-85, April 8, 1942.
Kushner, David. *Levittown: Two Families, One Tycoon, and the Fight for Civil Rights in America's Legendary Suburb*. New York: Walker, 2009.
Kuznick, Peter J., and James Gilbert, eds. *Rethinking the Cold War Culture*. Washington, DC: Smithsonian Books, 2001.
Larsen, Frank Alexander. *From Fatherhood to Bachelorhood: An Analysis of Masculinities in the 1950s U.S. through Forbidden Planet, Invasion of the Body Snatchers, and Playboy*. Oslo, Norway: University of Oslo, 2012.
Leibman, Nina C. *Living Room Lectures: The Fifties Family in Film and Television*. Austin, TX: University of Texas Press, 1995.
Lewis, Jon. *Hollywood v. Hard Core: How the Struggle over Censorship Saved the Modern Film Industry*. New York: New York University Press, 2002.
Lindner, Robert. *Must You Conform?* New York: Rinehart, 1956.
Lister, Jenny. *Mary Quant*. London: V&A, 2019.
Longford, Elizabeth. *All in the Family: Parenting the 1950s Way*. Stroud, UK: History Press, 1954, 2008.
Loos, Pamela. *A Reader's Guide to Lorraine Hansberry's A Raisin in the Sun*. Berkeley Heights, NJ: Enslow, 2007.
Loughery, John. *The Other Side of Silence: Men's Lives and Gay Identities, A Twentieth-Century History*. New York: John MacRae/Owl Books, 1999.
Lundberg, Ferdinand, and Marynia Farnham. *Modern Woman: The Lost Sex*. New York: Grosset and Dunlap, 1947.
Lynd, Robert S., and Hellen Merrell Lynd. *Middletown: A Study in Contemporary American Culture*. New York: Harcourt, Brace, 1929.
Lynd, Robert S., and Hellen Merrell Lynd. *Middletown in Transition: A Study of Cultural Conflicts*. New York: Harcourt, Brace, 1937.
Malcolm X. *The Autobiography of Malcolm X*. New York: Ballantine, 1964.
Marcus, Stanley. *Minding the Store*. Denton, TX: University of North Texas Press, 1997.
May, Elaine Tyler. *Homeward Bound: American Families in the Cold War Era*. New York: Basic Books, 2008.
Mazón, Mauricio. *The Zoot-Suit Riots: The Psychology of Symbolic Annihilation*. Austin, TX: University of Texas Press, 1984.
McPartlin, Robert F. *Redlining, Discrimination in Residential Mortgage Loans: A Report to the Illinois General Assembly*. Springfield, IL: Illinois General Assembly, 1975.

Meyer, Leisa D. *Creating GI Jane: Sexuality and Power in the Women's Army Corps during World War II*. New York: Columbia University Press, 1996.
Meyerowitz, Joanne, ed. *Not June Cleaver: Women and Gender in Postwar America, 1945–1960*. Philadelphia, PA: Temple University Press, 1994.
Miller, Donald C. *Coming of Age in Popular Culture: Teenagers, Adolescence, and the Art of Growing Up*. Santa Barbara, CA: Greenwood, 2018.
Miller, Kathleen. *Fair Share Divorce for Women: The Definitive Guide to Creating a Winning Solution*, 2nd ed. New York: St. Martin's Griffin, 2007.
Mills, Nancy Patton. *Portraits Through the Lens of Historicity: The American Family as Portrayed in Ladies' Home Journal 1950–1959*. Pittsburgh, PA: Duquesne University, 2006.
Minta, Steven. *Domestic Revolutions, A Social History of American Family Life*. New York: Free Press, 1988.
Mitchell, James P., et al., National Manpower Council. *Work in the Lives of Married Women: Proceedings of a Conference on Womanpower*. New York: Columbia University Press, 1958.
Mitchell, Taylor Joy. *Cold War Playboys: Models of Masculinity in the Literature of Playboy*. Tampa, FL: University of South Florida, 2011.
Monhollon, Rusty, ed. *Baby Boom: People and Perspectives*. Santa Barbara, CA: ABC-Clio, 2010.
Morden, Bettie J. *The Women's Army Corps 1945–1978*. Washington, DC: Center for Military History, 2011.
Murdock, Joyce, and Deb Price. *Courting Justice: Gay Men and Lesbians v. the Supreme Court*. New York: Basic Books, 2001.
Murphy, Audie. *To Hell and Back*. New York: Henry Holt, 1949.
Nelson, Gordon. *Some Perspectives on Redlining*. Washington, DC: Federal National Mortgage Association, 1976.
Nevins, Jess. *The Evolution of the Costumed Avenger: The 4,000-Year History of the Superhero*. Santa Barbara, CA: Praeger, 2017.
Newcomer, Mabel. *A Century of Higher Education for Women*. New York: Harper Brothers, 1959.
Norman, Lee. *The Grand Creation: Other Worlds, Other Universes*. Bloomington, IN: Author House, 2011.
Nyberg, Amy Kiste. *Seal of Approval: The History of the Comics Code*. Jackson, MS: University Press of Mississippi, 1998.
O'Dell, Cary. *June Cleaver Was a Feminist! Reconsidering the Female Characters of Early Television*. Jefferson, NC: McFarland, 2013.
Odenwald, Robert P. *The Disappearing Sexes*. New York: Random House, 1965.
Ogata, Amy F. *Designing the Creative Child: Playthings and Places in Midcentury America*. Minneapolis, MN: University of Minnesota Press, 2013.
O'Neill, William L. *American High, The Years of Confidence, 1945–1960*. New York: Free Press, 1986.
Packard, Vance. *The Hidden Persuaders*. New York: David McKay, 1957.
Packard, Vance. *The Status Seekers*. New York: David McKay, 1959.
Palen, J. John. *The Suburbs*. New York: McGraw-Hill, 1995.
Palmer, Alexandra. *Couture and Commerce: The Transatlantic Fashion Trade in the 1950s*. Vancouver, Canada: University of British Columbia Press, 2001.
Paoletti, Jo B. *Pink and Blue, Telling the Boys from the Girls in America*. Bloomington, IN: Indiana University Press, 2012.

Parsons, Talcott, and Robert F. Bales. *Family, Socialization and Interaction Process*. Glencoe, IL: Free Press, 1955.
Peiss, Kathy. *Zoot Suit: The Enigmatic Career of an Extreme Style*. Philadelphia, PA: University of Pennsylvania Press, 2011.
Plant, Rebecca Jo. *Mom: The Transformation of Motherhood in Modern America*. Chicago, IL: University of Chicago Press, 2010.
Potter, David M. *People of Plenty: Economic Abundance and the American Character*. Chicago, IL: University of Chicago Press, 1954.
Purnell, Brian, et al., eds. *The Strange Careers of the Jim Crow North, Segregation and Struggle Outside of the South*. New York: New York University Press, 2019.
Rauf, Don. *The Culture of Body Piercing*. New York: Rosen, 2019.
Reeves, Nancy. *Womankind Beyond the Stereotypes*, 2nd ed. New York: Aldine, 1982.
Riesman, David. *The Lonely Crowd: A Study of the Changing American Character*. New Haven, CT: Yale University Press, 1961.
Sagolla, Lisa Jo. *Rock and Roll Dances of the 1950s*. Santa Barbara, CA: Greeenwood, 2011.
Salter, Tom. *Carnaby Street*. Walton-on-Thames, Surrey, UK: Margaret and Jack Hobbs, 1970.
Satin, Joseph, ed. *The 1950s, America's Placid Decade*. Boston: Houghton Mifflin, 1960.
Scanlon, Jennifer R., ed. *The Gender and Consumer Culture Reader*. New York: New York University Press, 2000.
Schaefer, Eric. *Bold! Daring! Shocking! True! A History of Exploitation Films, 1919-1959*. Durham, NC: Duke University Press, 1999.
Schoeffler, O.E., and William Gale. *Esquire's Encyclopedia of Twentieth-Century Men's Fashions*. New York: McGraw-Hill, 1973.
Schoen, Ed. *Ed Schoen, MD, on Circumcision*. Berkely, CA: RDR Books, 2005.
Selye, Hans. *The Stress of Life*. New York: McGraw-Hill, 1956.
Shary, Timothy. *Teen Movies: American Youth on Screen*. London: Wallflower, 2005.
Shuker, Roy. *Understanding Popular Music Culture*, 4th ed. New York: Routledge, 2013.
Simon, Harvey B. *The Harvard Medical School Guide to Men's Health*. New York: Simon and Schuster, 2002.
Smith, Tiffany Leigh. *4-F: The Forgotten Unfit of the American Military during World War II*. Denton, TX: Texas Woman's University Graduate School, 2013.
Spigel, Lynn. *Make Room for TV: Television and the Family Ideal in Postwar America*. Chicago, IL: University of Chicago Press, 1992.
Spigel, Lynn. *Welcome to the Dreamhouse, Popular Media and Postwar Suburbs*. Durham, NC: Duke University Press, 2001.
Spock, Benjamin. *The Common Sense Book of Baby and Child Care*, Revised ed. New York: Duell, Sloan and Pearce, 1957.
Stokes, Walter R. *Modern Pattern for Marriage: The Newer Understanding of Married Love*. New York: Rinehart, 1948.
Strecker, Edward. *Their Mothers' Sons: The Psychiatrist Examines an American Problem*. Philadelphia, PA: J.B. Lippincott, 1946, 1951.
Tate, Ken. *The Best Years of Our Lives: The Good Old Days*. Berne, IN: House of White Birches, 2005.
Thompson, Henrietta Mary. *Clothing for Children*. New York: John Wiley and Sons, 1949.

Thompson, William E. *Hogs, Blogs, Leathers and Lattes: The Sociology of Modern American Motorcyling*. Jefferson, NC: McFarland, 2012.
Tischauser, Leslie V. *Jim Crow Laws*. Santa Barbara, CA: Greenwood, 2012.
Van Ells, Mark D. *To Hear Only Thunder Again*. Landham, MD: Lexington Books, 2001.
Walton, Frank L. *Thread of Victory: The Conversion and Conservation of Textiles, Clothing and Leather for the World's Biggest War Program*. New York: Fairchild, 1945.
Wampler, Karen S., ed. *The Handbook of Systemic Family Therapy*. Hoboken, NJ: John Wiley and Sons, 2020.
Weigand, Kate. *Red Feminism: American Communism and the Making of Women's Liberation*. Baltimore, MD: Johns Hopkins University Press, 2001.
Weight, Richard. *Mod: From Bebop to Britpop, Britain's Biggest Youth Movement*. London: Vintage, 2015.
Weise, Andrew. *Places of Their Own: African American Suburbanization in the Twentieth Century*. Chicago, IL: University of Chicago Press, 2004.
Weiss, Jessica. *To Have and to Hold: Marriage, the Baby Boom, and Social Change*. Chicago, IL: University of Chicago Press, 2000.
Westbrook, Robert B. *Why We Fought: Forging American Obligations in World War II*. Washington, DC: Smithsonian Books, 2004.
Weyr, Thomas. *Reaching for Paradise: The Playboy Vision of America*. New York: Times Books, 1978.
Whelehan, Imelda. *Modern Feminist Thought from the Second Wave to Post-Feminism*. New York: New York University Press, 1995.
Whitaker, Elizabeth. *An Analysis of Betty Friedan's The Feminine Mystique*. London: Macat, 2017.
Whyte, William H. *The Organization Man*. New York: Simon and Schuster, 1956.
Wylie, Philip. *Generation of Vipers*, Revised ed. New York: Rinehart 1955.
Yates, Brock. *Outlaw Machine: Harley-Davidson and the Search for the American Soul*. New York: Broadway Books, 1999.
Yellin, Emily. *Our Mothers' War: American Women at Home and at the Front during World War II*. New York: Free Press, 2010.
Young, William H., and Nancy K. Young. *World War II and the Postwar Years in America: A Historical and Cultural Encyclopedia*. Santa Barbara, CA: ABC-Clio, 2010.

INDEX

Afro hairstyles, 106, 107, 170
Afrocentric fashions, 106–107
Arnel, 178

baby boom era defined, viii, 35, 96, 181, 190
baby boomers. *See* children, baby boom
Balenciaga, Cristóbal, 162, 164
Bazaar boutiques, London, 90
Beatles, 91, 92, 169
beatniks, 51, 55–57, 59
Beats, 51, 54–55, 57
Bendel, Henri, 157
Bermuda shorts
    men's, 81, 82
    women's, 201
bikers, 57–59
bikini swimsuit
    men's, 87–88
    women's, 87
bikini underwear, men's, 88
body modification
    circumcision, 207
    piercings, 205–207
"Bold Look" in men's fashions, 75–76
boys' wear, x, xi, 6, 196–200
bra alphabet cup sizes developed, 111
"British Invasion," 91–92
buckle-back slacks, xi, 197

Calloway, Cab, 96–97
Carmichael, Stokely, 106
Carnaby Street, 90–92, 168
Carnegie, Hattie, 157
Cassini, Oleg, 168
Celanese, 178
Chambre Syndicale de la Couture, 161, 162
Chanel, Coco, 158–159, 161
children, baby boom, 181–207. *See also* gender role socialization of children
circle skirt, xi, 200–201
city shorts (men's), 81–82
civil rights movement, 51, 95, 105, 169
"conk" hairstyles, 99
Continental suit, 73–75, 78–79, 83, 84, 88–90, 197
Copland, Jo, 164
Courrèges, André, 176, 202

Dacron, 88, 178, 179
dashiki, 106
Dean, James, 194, 198
denim. *See* jeans
Dior, Christian, 157–158, 162–164, 168, 171–173
divorce, 23–26, 43, 130–134
drape cut suit, 3–5, 13, 75, 86, 98
Duke Ellington, 102–103

dungarees. *See* jeans
Dynel, 178

feminism, 151–153, 169
flammable fabrics, 205
footwear
    children's, 202–203, 205
    men's, 77, 92, 95, 98–99, 102, 203
    women's, 173, 176, 202
Friedan, Betty, viii, 134–135, 140, 144, 145, 153, 188

gay
    Congressional Hoey Report, 64–66
    criminality, viii, 65
    gay marriage, 66
    gay rights movement, 169
    "lavender lads," 63–67
    as mental disorder, 3, 10, 36, 43, 48, 62–67, 144–145
gender role socialization of children, x, 1–3, 36, 39, 144–146, 182–190
    boys' identities, x, 2–3, 36, 39, 144–145, 182–183, 185–186, 189
    girls' identities, x, 36, 39, 146, 182–183, 186, 187, 189
gendering of pink for girls and blue for boys, 189
generation gap, 92, 169
Gesell Institute, 36, 143, 185, 188, 195
GI Bill of Rights, 20–23, 26, 27, 33, 127, 128, 135
girls' wear, x, xi, 199–204

handbags, 176, 177
hats
    men's, 78, 97, 98, 100, 102, 136
    women's, 173–175, 177

Hawaiian print sport shirts, 85, 198
Hefner, Hugh, 60, 62, 63
Hollywood influences, 19–20, 32–34, 41, 43, 44, 57–59, 96–97, 103, 171, 193–194, 197–198
homosexuality. *See* gay
housewife. *See* women's identity

Ivy League suit, ix, 57, 71–73, 75, 76, 78, 79, 83–84, 86, 88–89, 197

Jantzen swimwear, 87
jeans
    boys', 197–199
    girls', 201–203
    men's, 57, 79, 92, 194, 197
    women's, 147, 169, 201, 203
jewelry
    men's, 22, 78, 92
    women's, 92, 106, 114, 176–177
Jim Crow laws, viii, 10, 95, 103
    Jim Crow North, 96
Jivey Ivy suit, 74–75, 88
Jockey underwear, 6, 88

Kennedy, John F., influence on men's fashions, 75, 78
kente cloth, 106
Kinsey, Alfred C., 62, 63, 66

L-85 World War II restrictions on clothing, 11–14, 20, 73, 100, 103, 115–116, 157–159, 165, 171
Lastex, 86–87, 178
Lavender Scare, 62, 63, 66
leisure suit, 197
Levi's "13s", 79, 198
London Line suits, 90
Lurex, 178, 179
Lycra, 179, 180

McCardell, Claire, 157, 163
McCarthyism, viii, 6, 28, 36, 51, 62–63, 145, 148, 152
Mainbocher, 118
Malcolm X, 95, 99, 100, 102
Man in the Gray Flannel Suit, book by Sloan Wilson, 71
marriage bars, 21, 148
masculine identity. *See* men's identity
Mattachine Society, 67
men's identity
  breadwinner, ix, 1, 21, 22, 24, 47, 52–53, 125, 134
  father, ix, 1, 35–45, 47, 125, 128, 181–182, 188
  husband, ix, 1, 23–26, 125–126, 128
  man in the gray flannel suit, ix, xi, 22, 50, 71
  playboy, 25–26, 58–63, 134
  soldier, 7–9, 12, 17–22, 125–126
  suburbanite, ix, 24, 28–30, 47, 48, 50, 72–73
mod fashions, 91–92, 168–171
"momism," 144–145

neckties, 77–78, 98, 100, 102, 136
New Look fashions, ix, xi, 157–167, 171, 182, 200, 202
Norell, Norman, 157
nylon, 87, 88, 111, 157, 171, 177–179

Orlon, 88, 178

Peacock Revolution, 92, 169
"Ph.T degree" (putting husband through college), 129–130
Playboy magazine, 26, 50, 60, 62, 63, 134. *See also* men's identity, playboy

pompadour hairstyles
  men's, 98
  women's, 114
prêt-à-porter, 162

Quant, Mary, 90, 168–169

racism, xi, 28, 30–34, 65, 95–96, 135
  by home owners associations, 33–34
  redlining, 33, 96, 135–136
  white flight, 30
raffia, 106
rayon, 115, 157, 176
ripple sole shoes, xi, 203, 205
rock and roll music, 36, 56, 193, 195, 199, 200

saddle oxfords, 202, 205
St. Laurent, Yves, 163, 166, 167, 169–170
Savile Row, 3, 90
Scholte, Frederick, 3
Semper Pratus—Always Ready (SPARS, US Coast Guard), 118
shoes. *See* footwear
Simpson, Adele, 157, 163
skorts, 202
socks, 77–78
spandex, 87, 179
Spock, Benjamin, 38, 39, 142–143, 182, 185, 188, 189, 195, 207
sportswear
  children's, 196–202
  men's, 78–85
  women's, 114, 147, 162–163, 165, 169–170
Stephen, John, "Mr. Carnaby," 91
"suburban syndrome," 131, 141

suburbia, ix, xi, 26–35, 48, 50, 134, 146, 147, 193
swank suits, 100–101
swimwear
   men's, 86–87

teenagers, x, 6, 30, 36, 38, 103, 190–195
television, xi, 25, 30, 36, 39–45, 56, 128, 146–148
   TV dads, 39–45, 146
   TV moms, 128, 146–148, 187, 190, 191
Trigére, Pauline, 163

Velcro, 84–85

Women Accepted for Voluntary Emergency Service (WAVES), 118, 119
Women Airforce Service Pilots (WASPS), 118, 119
Women's Army Corps (WACs), 116, 118, 119, 122
women's identity
   housewife, ix, 21, 31, 134–141, 151, 153
   mother, ix, 21, 109, 141–146, 151, 153, 181–182, 186, 188
   suburbanite, x, 28–29, 31, 134–141, 146–147, 153, 182
   wife, ix, xi, 21, 23–24, 109, 125–141, 147
   "woman problem," x, 131, 149–150
   working women, ix, 21, 109–110, 112–120, 126, 131, 147–151

zoot suit, 95–106

www.ingramcontent.com/pod-product-compliance
Lightning Source LLC
Chambersburg PA
CBHW071824300426
44116CB00009B/1425